WORKING AND LIVING IN

SAUDI ARABIA

Grace Edwards

Grosvenor House
Publishing Limited

The right of Grace Edwards to be identified as the author of this
work has been asserted in accordance with Section 78
of the Copyright, Designs and Patents Act 1988

The book cover picture is copyright to Grace Edwards

This book is published by
Grosvenor House Publishing Ltd
Link House
140 The Broadway, Tolworth, Surrey, KT6 7HT.
www.grosvenorhousepublishing.co.uk

A CIP record for this book
is available from the British Library

ISBN 978-1-78623-834-4

TABLE OF CONTENTS

INTRODUCTION

As organisations continue to globalise, many are looking to expand in the Middle East in general and in Saudi Arabia in particular. Saudi Arabia is promoting the growth and diversification of business opportunities beyond oil, and is welcoming more business travellers than ever before, including significant numbers of businesswomen.

Although Westerners have been living and working in Saudi Arabia for decades, many potential expatriates have a skewed and often negative view of the Kingdom. These negative views are not helped by mass media, who often portray the Kingdom through stories of social or religious oppression, relieved only occasionally by an article about the oil business.

There are only a limited number of publications and other resources available about the country. Few of these go beyond someone's personal experience with Saudi Arabia that is of little practical use for business travellers. This is particularly true of many blogs written by expatriates who may spend little time in Saudi Arabia outside of the expat bubble of their compound, other than occasionally venturing to restaurants and shopping malls.

Others have researched information that is now out of date and no longer accurate. Yet others may have a specific political or social agenda.

This book is written to be a practical and cultural guide for all Western business travellers and expatriates, with an additional emphasis on issues important to businesswomen. In this regard, it is a departure from publications written only to assist women who are living in Saudi Arabia as dependents known in the expatriate world as trailing spouses.

It is also intended to dispel inaccurate information and to remove the fear factor that can be found in many other publications, especially blogs and 'sensationalist' biographical works.

In addition to practical information about living in the Kingdom, the book also addresses hard core business issues on a number of levels that will have a practical impact on doing business successfully throughout the region. Working and living in Saudi Arabia can be very different even for people who have experience working or living elsewhere in the Gulf countries.

It is also important to recognise that Saudi Arabia is going through a period of rapid change. This has come about for a number of reasons. They include the impact of a new Ruler after nearly ten years under the reformist leadership of the late King Abdullah, who died in January 2015. A young generation that is much more globally aware thanks to the internet, social media and other technological revolutions also has a profound impact on the future of the Kingdom. Finally, improved educational standards that are beginning to reach a wider population, especially Saudi women, is projected to have the potential to shape the future in ways that are not yet obvious.

There is no real way to openly and honestly describe some of the real challenges Westerners often find when working or living in Saudi Arabia without discussing issues that may be very sensitive or sometimes interpreted as negative or even insulting to some Saudis and perhaps some other people as well. It is not the intention of the author to cause offence. However, with a lot of consideration, the author has also taken the decision not to avoid sensitive topics, but to address them as objectively and as usefully as possible for a Western audience. Although no cultures are wholly comfortable with occasional criticism, difficult information is included. The priority is to inform, with the best of intentions, but understanding that to some, it comes at the possible cost of touching sensitive nerves. The author hopes that the audience understands this, and hopes that those who might feel negative accepts the wider purpose of educating, in spite of difficult subject matter.

The tone is easy-to-read, with a directness appreciated by a Western audience.

There is some repetition in this book. As the author recognises that many readers may read this book out of sequence, the repetition may be intentional so that readers do not miss important points.

NB: All Arabic words have been transliterated into English. It is important to note that transliteration between the two alphabets is an inexact exercise. It is common to find multiple spellings and pronunciations of the same words in both languages. The author has tried to use words and spellings most familiar to Westerners that are also considered correct by educated Arabic speakers.

SECTION 1

UNDERSTANDING CULTURE

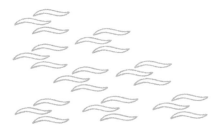

A BRIEF INTRODUCTION
TO CULTURE

Culture

Defining culture is not an easy task. We think we know what it is, but often find it difficult to articulate: it's 'how we do things around here'. For the purpose of this book, we will define culture as a set of typical beliefs, values and behaviour that defines one group of people from another. Culture includes traditions and eccentricities. People belong to many cultures throughout their life, including family, religion, nationality, and outside cultural influences such as the workplace.

It is important to recognise that any study of culture will almost certainly include judgments and opinions of the cultures being discussed. Cultural theorists point out that most people see another culture through a 'cultural lens' i. e. their own set of values and beliefs, often applying what they believe to be right and wrong to the new culture. Whilst it may be useful to try to understand another culture by comparing it to what a person already knows, it can also lead to misunderstandings.

By exploring the differences between stereotypes and generalisations, we set the stage for minimising these misunderstandings.

Stereotypes

Stereotypes are a fixed set of assumptions about a group of people. The person may believe that specific characteristics apply to all people within this group. Stereotypes are often verbalised by using phrases such as 'All xxxx are yyyy' or 'you know what xxxx are like'. It is a simplified and inaccurate view that is applied to an entire group of people without regard to individual variation.

Generalisations

Generalisations are a set of characteristics that often apply to many members of a group. However, it is not assumed that all members of the group will share the characteristics of the group. Generalisations are often verbalised by using phrases such as 'xxxx are often yyyy' or 'many xxxx might believe that yyyy'. It recognises the frequency of a characteristic without making the assumption than all individuals within that group share that characteristic.

As a Western business professional working with people from Saudi Arabia, it is important to keep these concepts in mind. You may find that your preconceived notion about someone or something in Saudi Arabia is far off the mark. You may also find that, at least once in a while, you encounter someone who is an exception to the particular characteristics shared by most of a group.

For example, many people in the West hold the stereotype that women in Saudi Arabia are uneducated, oppressed and forbidden to work outside the home. Whilst some Saudi women may come from families that expect her to behave in a certain manner, there are plenty of other Saudi women who are returning to the Kingdom with an honours degree from a university abroad, then establishing and running her own business. In fact, at the time of publication, Saudi women make up 60% of all university students. And although women currently make up only 16% of the labour market, these numbers have grown ten-fold since 2011 and are projected to continue to grow as the country continues to implement educational and employment reforms, especially for women.

It is suggested that the concepts of stereotypes and generalisations are considered throughout this book. Whilst every attempt has been made to portray an accurate and objective description of all topics raised, it is impossible to avoid presenting some points of view that may be disputed by some readers.

TRADITIONAL SAUDI CORE CULTURAL VALUES

Islam

Islam is much more than belief in a particular religion. It is a way of life. It is also a moral code that is expected to be adhered to by believers, especially in Saudi Arabia.

The interpretation of Islam's moral code in Saudi Arabia is much stricter than in other countries. This is due to the dominant belief system within a specific sect of Islam that became prominent in the 18th Century in what is now Saudi Arabia. This is described in greater detail in the *Salafis (Wahhabis)* Section on Islam found later in this book.

Of course, as in any group of people, some adherents are more committed than others to follow the rules in practice. However, in Saudi Arabia, the expectation is to live an exemplary life as per the beliefs, teachings and behaviours of the faith. This has been traditionally enforced by authority figures in the Kingdom, including by the *muttaween,* also known as the *muttawa,* or religious police.

Family

Family obligations are of the utmost importance to Muslims. Family is more important than work. Family obligations will often be the reason why someone doesn't meet you on time or cancels your appointment at the last minute.

Family includes members far beyond the Western definition of a nuclear family. It includes the entire extended family, including grandparents, uncles and aunts, cousins, and sometimes non-relatives who have earned a place as an honorary family member. Family can also mean a wider group of people in certain contexts, including tribes, people from the same ancestral village, or specific religious sects.

There is a well defined hierarchy within a Muslim family. Traditionally, men have more status than women. Men are expected to shoulder the responsibilities of the family in public; the woman is responsible for the well-being of the family and the family's private needs. In this regard, her powers are substantial.

Historically, these are no different than many family values found in most Western Christian communities, at least until very recently. However, this is changing in many parts of Saudi society, with women venturing out into the world of work and other public arenas in growing numbers. It's also why the Westerner can still observe separate treatment of women in public, both good and not so good. For example, women-only queues in places that vary from government buildings to a shopping mall food court are designed to treat women out in public with special respect.

Marital status is important, as is parenthood. Both genders are considered to have obtained a higher social status once they have married. It is expected that all Muslims will marry, regardless of personal or lifestyle preference.

Gay and lesbian Muslims are expected to marry and live an outwardly heterosexual lifestyle. In fact, many people in Saudi Arabia may ignore or even deny that there are any homosexuals amongst their family or their wider community. Homosexual practices are illegal in Saudi Arabia with potentially very serious punishments if discovered.

Young adults who are still single will almost always remain with their family until they wed. Cohabitation before marriage is unheard of in Saudi Arabia and is in fact also illegal, including for foreigners living in the Kingdom.

Parents have a higher status than childless couples. Sons are generally valued more than daughters. It is not unusual to see families with several older girls and one young boy.

Children born out of wedlock remain a strong taboo, in part because it complicates the family hierarchy. It would be highly unusual for a Westerner to be aware of this as it would be considered shameful for the family, and thus a topic to be avoided at all costs.

4

In addition, most Saudis struggle with the concept of adoption. This is in part because bloodlines are valued so strongly, but also because inheritance and other social laws do not always apply to adoptees in the same manner as for other children.

Age also has more status than youth. It is refreshing for older Westerners to receive a bit more respect simply due to their age. The author has also observed more than one Western man deciding to grow his greying beard when working in the region.

Do not be surprised if someone from Saudi Arabia occasionally asks you rather personal questions about your own family. From their perspective, it is not being rude. They are simply trying to work out where you fit in the hierarchy. They may also make some comments that would be considered judgmental in the West, although they are not meant to be harmful. Single people will often be pitied past a certain age if they are not married. Married but childless people past a certain age will be asked if they are going to have children soon. People with sons in particular will be praised for their good fortune.

For those Westerners who are not married or do not have children, or do not live a conventional lifestyle as would be expected by most Saudis, it is advised that you steer conversations toward other family members to show that you have strong family values. A nephew, sibling or an elderly grandparent are all safe options.

Honour

Personal and family reputation is very important. Throughout the Middle East, including Saudi Arabia, the action of an individual reflects not only on themselves but on their family. Men and women are expected to act in an honourable manner at all times, especially in public, to preserve the good reputation of their family.

There is a high motivation to avoid losing face, as it can sometimes lead to compromising one's honour. Try not to tease or embarrass anyone, even if it is only meant to be in the spirit of good humour. There is no doubt that many people in Saudi Arabia do have a good sense of humour. However, it's better to get to know someone first before using humour, especially sarcasm or irony.

Traditionally, your word and your handshake represent your honour. Many people in Saudi Arabia still subscribe to this practice with people they know well and trust, although written agreements are now common throughout the region as well. It remains prudent for the Western business professional to be very careful of what they say, even if it is only a casual or throwaway remark. Chances are good that your Saudi counterpart will remember your comment and expect you to honour it, even without a handshake, even after much time has passed.

Family honour is held to an even higher standard by the women of the family, and will be protected at all costs, sometimes even to an extreme degree. This is particularly relevant surrounding issues of sexuality.

Western business professionals should always keep this in mind whenever they are interacting with a Saudi or other Muslim woman. In today's business environment, many young Saudi women are the first female members of their family working outside the home. In general, Western business professionals, especially men, are safe by simply following the woman's lead, as she will not violate her own boundaries of honourable behaviour.

Western men in particular should avoid putting a Muslim woman in a situation where they are alone, even in an office environment. Try to ensure someone else is always nearby. Keep the office door open. Western women will find that very religious Muslim men will also avoid being alone with them.

The Western business professional should also be careful not to engage in any behaviour that could be interpreted as too familiar, including risqué or overly friendly remarks. This includes complimenting a woman's appearance or anything else that draws attention to her physicality. Off colour jokes or anything that could be interpreted as containing sexual content are completely out of bounds.

Loyalty

There is a code of loyalty amongst Saudis that exists in both social and business environments that will impact the Western business professional. In the business world, there is much more loyalty within and amongst organisations than is found in the West, including long tenure by employees and companies doing business with other companies simply because they have traded for many years.

This is particularly true in well established business relationships with Westerners, where trust has been earned and loyalty expected as a result. Your local business partner may expect you to provide them with information or business practices that could be seen as unfair advantages in the West. However, from the perspective of your Saudi colleague, the expectation is simply natural amongst loyal business partners.

As a Western business professional, you may still encounter a residual expectation of exclusivity in some partnership agreements. The demands of the modern business environment have moved on from exclusive relationships, but do not be surprised if your business partners expect you to remain loyal to them even if you are adding new partnerships in the region.

Courtesy

Courtesy is valued in Islam. There are formal greetings and replies that are repeated by Muslims whenever they meet, including Saudi Arabia, which reflect the nature of their relationship and their position within social hierarchies.

The Western business professional is not expected to know the intricacies of these greetings, although learning how to say hello and thank you in Arabic is appreciated. Westerners should always acknowledge their colleagues upon meeting them, even if they just saw them a few hours ago. Failure to greet each and every time is considered rude.

It is also important to remain courteous at all times, even if you become frustrated by circumstances. Confrontational behaviour, arguments and shouting are considered to be rude, and will cause someone to lose status and face, including Westerners. Therefore it is very important to control your reaction at all times, even if you would not do so in the West. Patience, patience, patience.

Respect

Islam values tolerance and respect for others. Attitudes and behaviour should be respectful at all times to both family (in its broadest sense) and others. However, there are many instances of behaviour that can be observed in Saudi Arabia where people appear to be anything but respectful to one another. This is particularly true when Saudis are interacting with someone who they may consider to be subordinate to them, especially expatriates from the non-Western world.

Hospitality and generosity

Hospitality is important throughout the Muslim world. It comes from the Bedouin tradition of offering shelter to any traveller making the difficult journey in desert conditions of the Arabian Peninsula. This hospitality also extends to food and drink. The guest's needs were always attended to first, even if it meant that the family went hungry.

Saudi hospitality remains legendary. As a Western business professional, you will be treated as an honoured guest whenever you visit the region. Your business contacts will ensure you are treated well. This will include anything from constant offerings of coffee or tea to elaborate dinners held in your honour, especially if you have completed a key stage of business.

Never refuse any gestures of hospitality or generosity. Even if you have already had twelve cups of coffee earlier in the day, accept one more. Try to drink the first cup; you can pretend to sip it if absolutely necessary. It's ok to politely refuse refills, which is done by gently tipping the cup from side to side or by placing your right hand over the top of the cup. Never make a gesture to pay the bill at a restaurant if you are not the host – it offends the sense of hospitality.

Insh'allah

Insh'allah means 'God's will' or 'if God wills it'. It is a reference to the fatalistic attitude of religious Muslims, who believe that worldly events are ultimately determined by Allah, the Arabic word for God.

It is one of the most common expressions heard throughout the Middle East, and one that most Western business professionals will quickly add to their own vocabulary. People who are finishing a meeting will often part with the comment 'we will meet again next week *insh'allah*' or 'tomorrow should be a lovely day *insh'allah*' or even 'our flight is scheduled to land at 10. 45 *insh'allah*'.

The Western business professional should not interpret the use of *insh'allah* as dishonest; quite the opposite. It's generally an indication that the speaker intends to do what they say – if nothing else gets in the way or becomes more important. If it does, then it happened because of God's will. The other party should not be offended, and can generally expect the situation to be rectified as soon as God wills it to happen.

Arabic language

The official language of Islam and of Saudi Arabia is Arabic. It is held in roughly the same regard as Hebrew in Judaism or Latin for many Christians.

Saudis and Arab speakers in general place a high value on being able to speak Arabic with sophistication and eloquence. If you speak Arabic fluently, you will be complimented on your linguistic ability. Otherwise, if your Arabic is anything other than fluent, it is strongly recommended that you avoid attempting to speak it, especially in a business environment, other than to use the basic courtesies. Not only are you diminishing the language from an Arab perspective, but you may also be implicitly insulting your Saudi host's ability to speak English.

On the other hand, in everyday public life, it is useful to learn 'survival Arabic' as you may encounter situations in Saudi where someone does not speak English. This can range widely, from a vendor, driver, other service employee or Saudi national who is older, rural, or less well educated.

SECTION 2
UNDERSTANDING SAUDI ARABIA

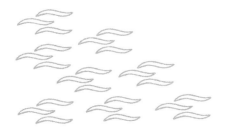

INTRODUCTION TO THE KINGDOM OF SAUDI ARABIA

Introduction

The following information is the briefest of overviews written for a business audience with a presumed passing level of interest in context of impacting their visits to Saudi Arabia. It is also written with the intention of providing commonly accepted information as viewed from a Western perspective. It is not the author's intention to highlight negative information about the ruling family or the Kingdom but to provide information that is generally deemed useful for Western business people working in or with Saudi Arabia. Nor do any of the following comments necessarily reflect the author's personal opinions.

For readers who are interested in an in depth history of the House of Saud, the author recommends that they find an independent source of information that focuses on this topic.

The Royal Family

The al Saud family has been the only ruling family since the creation of the modern Kingdom of Saudi Arabia. The House of Saud have been leaders during three separate points in history. Their origins are in Diriyah, located in Najd in central Saudi Arabia. In very modern times, Diriyah has become a de facto suburb of Riyadh.

The First Saudi State was ruled by the House of Saud from 1744 – 1818. It came about as the result of a power sharing agreement between Muhammed ibn Saud, its first ruler, and Muhammed ibn Abdul Wahhab. The latter believed in practicing Islam in its purest form, emulating the life of the Prophet Muhammed and the principles of the faith as understood by the first three generations of Muslims. It is where the terms Wahhabi and Wahhabism are derived, although adherents prefer to use the terms Salafist, a branch of the Hanbali school of Sunni Islam.

This agreement has endured from this time, nearly 300 years ago, and remains in place to the present time. The first intermarriage between the two families took place between a son of Muhammed ibn Saud to a daughter of Muhammed ibn Abdul Wahhab.

The First Saudi State encompassed much of the Arabian Peninsula. It met its demise after the first leader's son attacked the Shi'a city of Kerbala, now in modern day Iraq. His successors were eventually overpowered by the Egyptians and Ottoman Turks, who were dominant in the region at the time.

The Second Saudi State was ruled by the House of Saud from 1824 – 1891. It encompassed much less of the Arabian Peninsula other than the Najd and was plagued by infighting amongst family members. Most leaders of the Second Saudi State met a violent end. Other significant family members fled, including the family of Abdul Aziz ibn Saud, to what is now Kuwait.

The Third Saudi State became modern Saudi Arabia under the leadership of Abdul Aziz ibn Saud. At an early age, he captured the Masmak Fort in Riyadh, re-establishing power over this geography. Over much of his life, he gained or regained control over the Arabian Peninsula lands that are now a part of modern Saudi Arabia, doing so by overpowering, intermarrying and brokering agreements with other important families in the region, especially from the Hejaz region surrounding modern day Jeddah and the north. Additionally, ibn Saud became aligned with the British against the Ottomans in the last days of the Ottoman Empire. Abdul Aziz ibn Saud declared himself King of Saudi Arabia in 1932.

Brief History

1932 – 1953 King Abdul Aziz ibn Saud was the first King of Saudi Arabia, having consolidated distinctly diverse regions of the Kingdom as stated above.

Oil was discovered in the new Kingdom in 1938. The new King formed strong associations with American oil companies. Neutral during World War II, Saudi Arabia strengthened its bonds with then

President Franklin D Roosevelt. Under the rule of ibn Saud, Saudi Arabia also declared war against the State of Israel upon its independence in 1948.

King Abdul Aziz, often known as ibn Saud, ruled the Kingdom from its birth in 1932 until his death in 1953.

Line of Succession - Agnatic Seniority

Ibn Saud is believed to have had an estimated 45 sons by more than 20 wives and concubines. The documentation of the number and precise marital status of these women vary even amongst reliable sources.

The most important wife of ibn Saud is considered to be Hessa bint Ahmed al Sudairi. Her sons are known as the Sudairi Seven and have wielded significant power. They have included two kings, crown prices and other senior government officials. It appears that this line of descendants may further profit as the current King, King Salman is one of the Sudairi Seven. The current Crown Prince and Deputy Crown Prince are also both grandsons of Sudairi Seven fathers.

In an agreement reached during the lifetime of ibn Saud, the position of King is determined through the male line of the family. The sons and grandsons of ibn Saud would first determine which son would become the next king until no more eligible sons were left. Then, the same process would be used to choose amongst the grandsons. It is believed that the future beyond grandsons was not specified. However, with the naming of the current Crown Prince and Deputy Crown Prince from the next generation whilst arguably eligible sons are still alive nay have accelerated this process.

At the time of publication, the Kingdom of Saudi Arabia has been led by seven kings. They are:

1953 - 1964 King Saud bin Abdul Aziz was the first King to succeed his father. The accepted consensus was that King Saud was both extravagant and incompetent. He was deposed.

1964 - 1975 King Faisal bin Abdul Aziz was the half brother of King Saud and was seen as the main competitor to the king and the leading force behind his deposition. King Faisal was generally seen as a reformist, putting the Kingdom back on to the path of economic stability and prosperity. He abolished slavery, which was not illegal in the Kingdom until 1962. King Faisal also implemented the oil production controls of the early 1970s that impacted the developed world's oil consumption and price.

He was also seen as a modernist. Amongst the changes was the introduction of television, which was met with protests as well as being welcomed. This modernist approach probably contributed to his eventual assassination by a nephew, who was amongst the anti-television protesters.

1975 – 1982 King Khalid bin Abdul Aziz assumed the leadership of the Kingdom upon the assassination of his half brother. He focused on the improvement of the domestic infrastructure of the Kingdom. Major events during his reign included the transition of full control of Saudi Aramco, which had previously been shared with the US.

It was also during his reign, in 1979, that Saudi protestors took over control of the Grand Mosque in Mecca, the holiest site in the Islamic world. This was perceived as a direct threat to the Ruling family. The protestors were quickly executed. It was also the pivotal point when the Kingdom reverted to a more conservative set of domestic and social policies. King Khalid died of a heart attack in 1982.

1982 – 2005 King Fahd bin Abdul Aziz became the next King upon the death of his half brother. He adopted the title of Custodian of the Two Holy Mosques, favoured over the sole title of King. King Fahd was the eldest of the Sudairi Seven brothers.

King Fahd implemented several conservative policies that also strengthened the position of both the military and the religious police during the early days of his reign. Further reforms were ended, especially as funds originally planned for education, medical and infrastructure were diverted.

King Fahd also made declarations of the strength of the bond with the United States whilst clarifying that the social path of the Kingdom was not to emulate that of the West. Many would see this as a response to the events in Mecca of 1979 as well as the perceived concerns in the aftermath of the Iranian revolution, also in 1979.

King Fahd suffered a serious stroke in 1995 and was effectively incapacitated. Day to day affairs were mostly managed by then Crown Prince Abdullah. King Fahd died from complications from stroke and other health problems in 2005.

2005 – 2015 King Abdullah bin Adbul Aziz became the next King after the death of his half brother. As Crown Prince, many expected King Abdullah to continue many of the policies of King Fahd.

However, King Abdullah was a reformist. He focused on the state of Saudi education and promoted the scholarships of many young Saudi nationals to study abroad, where their educational prospects were greater than at the time within the Kingdom.

KAUST, the King Abdullah University of Science and Technology was established in 2009. With the expertise of board members and academics from globally respected institutions, KAUST is also a social experiment whereby gender segregation, dress code, and other related behaviours are relaxed.

He was also a strong proponent of girls' and women's education. For example, the new campus of Princess Noura bint Abdul Rahman University was established in 2011 and is currently the largest women's university in the world.

King Abdullah also managed the beginnings of civil unrest that could have accelerated in the Kingdom in light of neighbouring Revolutions and unrest often referred to in the West as the Arab Spring that began in 2011.

Reforms lessening the powers of the religious police, formalising these changes with the appointment of a new head of the Committee for the Promotion of Virtue and Prevention of Vice, also known as Haia, in 2013. Social reforms even went as far as ignoring some public gender segregation practices, although these are not enshrined formally.

Although an absolute monarchy, Saudis have recently gained limited voting rights for electing municipal councillors which took place in late 2015 after his death. Women were also appointed to the Consultative Assembly, also known as the Shura Council for the first time in 2013.

From a business perspective, it was under the reforms of King Abdullah that allowed foreign business women to obtain business visas in revolutionary numbers compared to before. Most foreign businesswomen, if they are otherwise qualified, are now routinely able to visit and work in the Kingdom if they are willing to comply with the rules of how to dress and behave socially.

King Abdullah died on 23rd January 2015 at 90 years old from pneumonia after suffering from a number of back ailments and other health problems.

Current King

The current king is King Salman bin Abdul Aziz al Saud. He assumed power in January 2015 after the death of his half brother. He is another of the Sudairi Seven brothers and is considered to hold views that are more conservative than King Abdullah. He is also supportive of business, including Western businesses.

At the time of publication, several significant actions have been taken by King Salman. They include the first ever naming of both a Crown Prince and Deputy Crown Prince from the next generation of the House of Saud. He has made several changes to top level government positions, often involving extended family members.

Under the rule of King Salman, internal unrest, whilst mostly controlled by his predecessor, was treated very differently by the current king. Within the first year of his ascension to power, King Salman's rule has been responsible for more than 150 executions in 2015, more than have taken place annually in the past 20 years in the Kingdom, with 2016 continuing at an accelerated pace. Several other high profile cases, including political and social protestors remain in limbo at the time of publication.

Under the leadership of King Salman, Saudi Arabia has intervened in the conflict in Yemen, and is involved in rhetoric against Iran, Syria and Iraq, all neighbouring countries with significant or outright Shi'a majority populations. Saudi Arabia is continuing to demonstrate discomfort over internal Shi'a activities in the Eastern Province and along its Southwest border with Yemen.

King Salman was born in 1935 and has a history of chronic and recent health problems.

Crown Prince and Deputy Crown Prince

In April 2015, King Salman broke with Saudi tradition for the first time in its modern history and replaced Crown Prince Muqrin, his half brother, with the first two members to hold these titles from the next generation. They are Crown Prince Mohammed bin Nayef, a nephew of his full brother and Deputy Crown Prince Mohammed bin Salman, a son.

The Crown Prince, born in 1959, is US educated has a long career in the ministry of the interior.

The Deputy Crown Prince, born in 1985, is Saudi educated and was named defence minister shortly after his father became king. The author reminds readers that this information is provided from a Western perspective and is not necessarily the author's personal opinion. The Deputy Crown Prince is perceived to be a favourite son of the King and is very possibly being groomed to be the next Saudi King in spite of his relative youth, inexperience and position to the Crown Prince. He is seen as responsible for the current military activities in Yemen. He is also promoting future business practices to diminish the Kingdom's heavy reliance on oil revenues, most notably with the announcement of Saudi Vision 2030.

Brief Political Overview

Absolute Monarchy

The Kingdom of Saudi Arabia is a unitary Islamic absolute monarchy that, as seen in the paragraphs above, is hereditary through a consensus of male descendants of the first king, ibn Saud. It is underpinned by Shari'a Law. The Qur'an and the Sunnah – the traditions of the Prophet Muhammed - are the country's constitution, also known as Basic Law of Saudi Arabia.

Shari'a law

Shari'a Law is based on the Qur'an and Hadith – the ways and the sayings of the Prophet Muhammed. Application of Shari'a Law in the Kingdom is determined through *ulema*, religious scholars from the Hanbali school of thought. This is the branch of Sunni Islam predominant in the Kingdom.

The prominent family leading the ulema is the al Shaikh family, who are direct descendants of the al Wahhab family. The al Saud and al Wahhab families have had a power sharing agreement that was enacted in 1744 and remains in effect to the present time.

Shari'a Law rules on all matters of day to day life, including business, politics, banking, contracts, family issues including marriage, divorce, child custody, death and inheritance, all manner of behaviour from sexuality to diet to entertainment to human rights issues. It also rules on criminal matters.

Shari'a Law can impact the Western business professional. It's a good idea to have at least a general awareness for those circumstances that may involve Westerners.

Saudi Arabia's interpretation of Shari'a Law is at the root of many social restrictions that the Western business professional is likely to encounter. This includes the absence of entertainment facilities such as the cinema or live music performances. Of course, it also impacts the segregation of the sexes in public and dress codes as well.

Western business professionals should ensure they have a working understanding of Shari'a Law if they are involved in drawing up a business contract or partnership agreement. They should also be aware that, in the case of a dispute, the only formal legal resolution is through Shari'a Law practices.

There are also serious considerations that should be taken into account if entering into an agreement that places a Westerner or their organisation into debt. For example, defaulting on a debt, including something as simple as a bounced cheque, has serious legal and criminal ramifications throughout Saudi Arabia.

Consultative Assembly – Shoura

The Consultative Assembly, also known as the Shoura Council, is the advisory body of 150 members appointed by the King. It has limited power in interpreting laws, which are exclusively approved by the King.

The Council is chosen to proportionally represent the population, are drawn from each of the Kingdom's 13 provinces and are elected to terms. Under King Abdullah, it has been decreed that at least 20% of council seats are held by women.

The Consultative Assembly currently consists of thirteen committees

- Islamic, Judicial Affairs
- Social, Family, and Youth Affairs Committee
- Economic Affairs and Energy Committee
- Security Affairs Committee
- Educational and Scientific Research Affairs Committee

- Cultural and Informational Affairs Committee
- Foreign Affairs Committee
- Health and Environmental Affairs Committee
- Financial Affairs Committee
- Transportation, Communications, Information Technology Committee
- Water and Public Facilities and Services Committee
- Administration, Human Resources and Petitions Committee

Major global organisation memberships

The Kingdom of Saudi Arabia is a member of the United Nations since its founding in 1945. It is also a member of the IMF (International Monetary Fund), the World Bank and, since 2005, the World Trade Organisation and the G-20.

It is also a founding member of:

1945 Arab League
1960 OPEC (Organisation of Petroleum Exporting Countries)
1962 Muslim World League
1969 Organisation of Islamic Cooperation
1981 Gulf Cooperation Council

Regional geopolitics

Geopolitics in Saudi Arabia can be difficult to capture as events continue to unfold in a notoriously volatile part of the world where allegiances can shift, sometimes unpredictably.

The reader should note that the following information is provided in the most general of terms and is valid at the time of publication. It is written for a business orientated Western audience who may only be interested in the very basics.

It is also written with the intention of portraying the country or organisation's politically stance in a neutral manner. Many countries' populations may generally disagree with their own government as regards their relationship with the Kingdom.

Readers with a keen interest in this topic looking for a deeper understanding should find additional resources that address these issues more thoroughly.

Selected countries and important political organisations:

Current Friends

In general, these countries are on good diplomatic terms with Saudi Arabia, although they may have occasional skirmishes. Recent examples include Sweden due to a public human rights dispute and Qatar, where the Saudis withdrew their ambassador for a period of time over Qatar's perceived support of the Muslim Brotherhood. Additionally, although the Bahraini Ruling Family is on good terms with the Saudi Ruling Family, Bahrain's Shi'a majority population has a more mixed opinion.

Algeria, Australia, Bahrain, Canada, China, Egypt, most European Union Countries, India, Jordan, Kuwait, Morocco, New Zealand, Oman, Pakistan, Qatar, Tunisia, Turkey, United Arab Emirates, USA

Conditional friends or friends of convenience

In general, these countries are on less stable diplomatic terms with Saudi Arabia. Iraq presents difficulties due to the increased role of Shi'a leadership. Lebanon is often problematic due to internal political uncertainty. Palestine is split between two political parties that Saudi regards differently. Russia is regarded as close to Syria.

Iraq, Lebanon, Palestine, Russia

Current Enemies – not war definition of enemy

In general, these countries are on difficult terms or at war. Iran is seen as the other main power in the region and represents the heart of Shi'a interests that are an anathema to Saudi Arabia. Israel is still technically regarded as in a state of war. The Syria diplomatic relationship was terminated in 2012 with the closure of its embassy in Damascus and the expulsion of the Syrian ambassador in Riyadh. At the time of publication, there is an ongoing active military campaign being conducted in Yemen.

Iran, Israel, Syria, Yemen

Additionally, Saudi Arabia considers several regional political organisations to be terrorist organisations. They include

Al Nusra Front, Al Qaeda, Hezbollah, Houthis, Islamic State/ISIL/ISIS, Muslim Brotherhood.

The Saudi relationship with Hamas is also a difficult one although not declared a terrorist organisation.

Stability and reform issues

Although the House of Saud is known to Western governments all over the world, it is on the cusp of venturing into new territory. The current generation of leaders is rapidly coming to an end, with the transition to the next generation seemingly beginning with the appointment of the Crown Prince and Deputy Crown Prince in April 2015. Whilst some assessments of this transition indicate an acceleration of modernisation in the Kingdom, others point out an increasing uncertainty and unpredictability. In reality, it is unclear what direction the House of Saud will take after King Salman is no longer in power as the next generation presumably assumes power.

The Kingdom of Saudi Arabia, a Sunni dominant country, and the Islamic Republic of Iran, a Shi'a dominant country, are the main regional powers. The state of their diplomatic relationship will continue to have a great impact on the region.

The Kingdom is making inroads to diversify its economy beyond its dependence on oil and continue to rely on Western and other foreign expertise in spite of Saudisation programmes. Whether a smooth transition will ultimately occur depends on education reforms within the Saudi population as well as the cautious replacement of expatriate labour with genuinely qualified Saudi talent willing to put their skills to practical use in the work force.

Western organisations are often keen to promote reforms in the Kingdom, especially from the perspective of their values and ethics.

Many of these reforms are focused on human rights issues as well as equality and inclusion. Thus, common challenges for many Western organisations include but are not limited to:

- Gender and other diversity issues
- Discrimination, including along the lines of nationality, pay, and opportunity
- Perception of work ethic and work life balance that is often misunderstood between Saudi Arabia and the West
- Capital and corporal punishment and many other human rights issues
- No separation of religion from everyday life
- No meaningful secular law
- No real representation of the people's will in the form of democracy or similar system
- Questions about clandestine and even some transparent support of fundamentalist religious organisations that are seen as anti-Western and in some instances supportive of terrorist activities from facets of the Saudi population

Geography

The Middle East
The modern day Middle East includes the countries of the Arabian Peninsula, along with adjacent countries to the north of the peninsula that border or nearly border the Eastern Mediterranean referred to as the Levant. Core countries of the Arabian Peninsula: Bahrain, Kuwait, Oman, Qatar, Saudi Arabia, United Arab Emirates, Yemen

With the exception of Yemen, the countries of the Arabian Peninsula are also known as the Gulf Countries, due to their border with the body of water known both as the Persian Gulf and the Arabian Gulf, found between the Arabian Peninsula and Iran. Although most Westerners have been taught to refer to these waters as the Persian Gulf, the politically neutral way to refer to it is simply 'The Gulf'.

The GCC Countries

Countries of the Arabian Peninsula, again with the exception of Yemen, also belong to the GCC (Gulf Cooperation Council). In everyday language, it is common to refer to these countries collectively as the GCC. The GCC has aspirations not dissimilar to the European Union in terms of common market and other economic policies.

The Levant and Egypt

The Levant

Historically, the Levant has included Anatolia in Turkey, parts of Sinai Egypt, Cyprus and sometimes Southeast Europe, including parts of the Balkan Peninsula, although these geographies are not considered a part of the Middle East.

Conventionally, it is agreed that the following countries are part of the modern Levantine Middle East. Countries: Iraq (in part), Israel (although not generally mentioned in the Arab world), Jordan, Lebanon, Palestine, Syria

Egypt

Although technically located in North Africa and the Sinai Peninsula, Egypt is in many ways the heart of popular culture in the Arab world. Thus, unlike Turkey or the rest of North Africa, where other identities prevail, Egypt is considered to be a very important part of the Arab world regardless of its geographical realities.

Saudi Arabia and its Regions

Saudi Arabia is the largest country in the Middle East and the thirteenth largest country in the world, with an area of 2,149,690 km². Saudi Arabia is mostly desert, and contains Rub al Khali, the world's largest sand desert.

Saudi Arabia is comprised of 13 separate regions known as provinces: Al Jouf, Northern Borders, Tabuk, Ha'il, Medina, Qassim, Mecca, Riyadh, Eastern Province, Al Bahah, Asir, Jizan and Najran.

Sometimes, Saudi Arabia can be regarded by its previous provinces – the Eastern Hesa Province, Central Nejd Province, Southern Asir Province and Western Hejaz Province, and the North. Many Saudis will identify regionally by these distinctions. The Eastern Province and Hejaz Province have the reputation of being more relaxed than the other regions, perhaps in part by their relative familiarity with outsiders over a longer period of time. However, the Eastern Province has been the focus of recent unrest between Sunni and Shi'a communities, and is currently notably less relaxed than in the recent past.

Major Cities

Most expatriates and business travellers are likely to be working in Riyadh, Jeddah or one of the cities of the Eastern Province. Smaller numbers of expatriates and business travellers may also be working in the industrial city of Yanbu, or more recently in King Abdullah Economic City or King Abdullah University of Science and Technology, all located to the north of Jeddah on the Red Sea coast.

Riyadh

As the largest city in Saudi Arabia as well as its capitol city, most businesses are likely to have a presence in Riyadh, especially those with significant dealings with the government. Greater Riyadh has an estimated population of about 7 million.

Many Western expatriates favour the north of the city and often live in compounds in these areas. The Diplomatic Quarter, to the west is also popular and contains most embassies.

Olaya Street and nearby thoroughfares are the main business district, although there are additional business zones being developed. Its two most famous landmarks are the Kingdom Centre and the Faisaliyah Centre.

The old city, although still in existence, has generally fallen out of favour, although there is a museum in the Masmak Castle, with the old Batha *souq* nearby. This and most other *souqs* are no longer a way of life for most Saudis or Westerners (other than for a touristic diversion), although less affluent expatriates, often from the Indian subcontinent or the Philippines continue to shop there for inexpensive, everyday goods.

Riyadh has an excellent infrastructure, with all of the modern amenities expected by Western visitors and residents, including quality hotels, restaurants and shopping.

Eastern Province Cities

As Saudi Arabia's centre of the oil and gas industry, many businesses with these interests are likely to have a presence in the Eastern Province. The four main cities of the Eastern Province of likely interest to Westerners each have their own identity.

Greater Dammam, which also includes Dammam, Al Khobar and Dhahran has a population of more than 4 million people. Each city has its own collection of compounds and residential neighbourhoods that could appeal to expatriate residents.

Al Khobar is the most popular residential area for Western expatriates, with several upmarket compounds generally located near the beaches. Many of these expatriates are employees of Saudi Aramco, but may also be employed by other organisations. It is the most relaxed of the Eastern Province cities. There is a traditional trading district in Al Khobar as well. Al Khobar also offers substantial recreational activities (from a Saudi perspective) and a popular Corniche. It is also the city nearest the King Fahd Causeway, which links Saudi Arabia to Bahrain by road.

Dhahran is the location of Saudi Aramco headquarters as well as the Saudi Aramco Residency Camp, a residential compound for Saudi Aramco employees and their families. It is now multicultural rather than specifically Western in orientation.

Dammam is Saudi Arabia's second largest port city after Jeddah and is more a more popular residence for Saudi nationals than it is for Western expatriates. It has fewer compounds and many more apartments catering more often to Saudi nationals or expatriates from the Indian subcontinent. It also has substantial shopping. The Eastern Province's major international airport, King Fahd International Airport (KFIA), is the world's largest airport by land mass and is located to the northwest of Dammam.

All three cities in Greater Dammam have an excellent infrastructure, with all of the modern amenities expected by Western visitors and residents, including quality hotels, restaurants and shopping.

Outside of Greater Dammam but still in the Eastern Province, some Westerners may be working in Jubail. Located approximately 90 kilometres north/north east of KFIA airport, it is the Kingdom's and the

Middle East's largest industrial city, with a major presence of companies such as the Saudi manufacturing conglomerate SABIC.

Unlike the other major cities described above in the Eastern Province, Jubail has excellent road infrastructure, but a more limited selection of modern amenities expected by Western visitors and residents. Basic shopping, including food shopping is satisfactory, but other shopping needs may require a trip to Dammam and points south. However, more shopping centres are being built, so the situation should improve in the near future. Restaurant choices are better. There are a limited number of high end hotels; the Intercontinental is by far the most popular hotel for Western expatriates.

Jeddah

Traditionally, Saudi Arabia's leading commercial city and trade hub, many businesses, especially those in the private sector are likely to have a presence in Jeddah. Greater Jeddah has a population of over 5 million people.

Many Western expatriates favour the north of the city or west of the airport and often live in compounds in these areas. Many Western expatriates also belong to one or more private members' clubs with access to the beach and water sports. Most of these are located north of the Jeddah airport in the district of Obhur. Most Western countries support consulates in Jeddah.

King Abdullah Street and Tahaliyah Street are the main business districts, although there are additional business zones being developed. Jeddah also has a major industrial zone and port to the south of the city. Its most famous landmarks are the Corniche along the seafront and the old city, which has recently been named a UNESCO World Heritage Site. Jeddah will also be home of the Kingdom Tower, designed to become the world's tallest building at 1000 metres high once completed.

Jeddah is also the gateway to Muslim pilgrims to both Mecca and Medina. As a result, the city and surrounding area earns substantial revenue from religious tourism as well.

Jeddah has an excellent infrastructure, with all of the modern amenities expected by Western visitors and residents, including quality hotels, restaurants and shopping. However, much of its infrastructure is older than Riyadh and grew with little planning. Thus, Jeddah can be much more congested, especially on its roads.

Mecca and Medina

Non-Muslims are not permitted to travel anywhere within the officially recognised limits of Mecca. Check points exist on all routes into Mecca. Your paperwork will be inspected and as your visa indicates your religion, you will be turned away if you are not Muslim.

Non-Muslims are not permitted to travel anywhere near the centre of Medina, although they are allowed on the outskirts of the city beyond the Al Haram boundaries. This includes the airport and a small number of hotels and other facilities used by business travellers. Whilst not as rigorous as in Mecca, do expect to be challenged if you appear to be non-Muslim if you enter any area near the Prophet's Tomb.

Organisations that have business in Mecca or Medina must take these restrictions into consideration when selecting their employees for work in either location. The author would not wish to formally verify the rumour that some non-Muslims with highly sought after and difficult to find skills receive special dispensation to travel into the restricted areas of these cities under very specific conditions.

Yanbu

Yanbu has excellent road infrastructure, but a more limited selection of modern amenities expected by Western visitors and residents. Basic shopping, including food shopping is satisfactory, but other shopping needs may require a trip to Jeddah. Restaurant choices are wide enough to satisfy the casual diner. There are a limited number of high end hotels; the Movenpick, Radisson Blu and Holiday Inn are by far the most popular hotels. Most Western expatriates prefer to live in compounds. The most popular are The Cove, located in the prestigious Royal Commission enclave, and Arabian Homes in the older, port area of Yanbu.

Other cities

Some Westerners may travel or live in other parts of the Kingdom, especially is they are in the defence industry or are on location for natural resources. Tabuk and Taif are likely destinations for the former. Natural resources may be found in very remote locations. Outside of expatriate compounds, both Tabuk and Taif are considerably more conservative than other cities frequented by expatriates in the Kingdom. However, the availability of most amenities of interest to Westerners in these cities continues to improve.

Although there are cities located in the southwest of Saudi Arabia, they generally attract much less interest for the Western business traveller. In recent times, some of these locations have an escalated safety risk as they are located near the Yemen border. Many of the Saudis living in this part of the Kingdom may be both politically and socially connected more toward Yemen than to Riyadh, especially within the not insubstantial Shi'a communities found in the region.

Economic basics

Overview and current realities
The Saudi Arabian economy remains heavily reliant on oil and gas and their related industries. In 2014, approximately 70% of the GNP and 95% of export revenue was derived from the oil and gas sectors.

Economic reforms
As oil and gas are finite resources, the Saudi government recognises the need to diversify their economy in preparation for the eventual decline of oil, gas and related resources. In recent years, this need has perhaps been accelerated by the growing practice of hydraulic fracturing commonly known as fracking, a technique that allows extraction of natural resources in geographies that were previously not cost effective to process. This has reduced the reliance on Saudi oil and gas, especially by the United States, and at the time of publication, has hit the Kingdom's economy hard. In May 2016, an announcement was made stating that Saudi Aramco is considering selling bonds for the first time in its history to raise revenue for the Saudi government.

Although most of the remainder of the Saudi economy is currently focused on providing infrastructure via the construction and building trades, or via small family run businesses, the government is encouraging new business, from large scale manufacturing to banking and finance, telecommunication and a variety of services. Most important

Saudi owned businesses are traded on the Tadawul, the Saudi Stock Exchange, which was established in its present form in 2007.

Substantial railway projects are unmissable even to the casual observer visiting the Kingdom. For example, the Haramain High Speed Rail project is building a system to link Jeddah, Mecca and Medina. Saudi Railways Organization (SRO) operates the only long standing railway line from Riyadh to Dammam and has plans to interconnect all major points within Saudi Arabia. The Riyadh Metro development is now underway and will have six separate lines upon completion. Once the Jeddah Metro design plans are complete, construction is expected to begin. Mecca Metro plans have also been announced, which will compliment the Al Mashaaer Al Mugaddassah Metro system, which opened in 2010 and transports pilgrims between major holy sites. Plans have been announced in 2014 to build a Dammam Metro, linking Qatif, Dhahran and Dammam.

Additionally, the Saudi Railway Organisation has announced plans to link the Kingdom's railway system into the larger Gulf Cooperation Council (GCC) Railway Project, designed to connect to systems being developed in Kuwait, Bahrain, Qatar, the UAE and beyond to Oman.

Saudi Vision 2030

Saudi Vision 2030 was announced by Deputy Crown Prince Mohammed bin Salman in April 2016. It is designed to project the Kingdom forward through the themes of A Vibrant Society, A Thriving Economy and An Ambitious Nation.

The goals of Saudi Vision 2030 are described as follows:

- Transformation of the Saudi Sovereign Fund to strengthen investment
- Freedom from economic dependency on oil revenues
- IPO for up to Aramco stock to fund the Sovereign Wealth Fund
- Green Card system for Arabs and Muslims wishing to live in Saudi Arabia
- Plan to open tourism for all in line with the values and beliefs of the Kingdom
- Increase pilgrim number to 30 million

- Private sector goals – increase women in the labour market to 30%, reduce unemployment to 7%, and increase private sector GDP to 5.7%.
- Government owned military industry
- Restructure and improve housing projects
- Anti-Corruption measures

Further information can be found in English on the Saudi government website http://vision2030.gov.sa/en

The government plans are to continue to accelerate diversification through special economic cities, which are currently under development.

In addition to businesses interested in supplying infrastructure products and services to the Kingdom, organisations in the fields of education, medicine and finance are particularly well positioned to benefit from Saudi Vision 2030.

Special Economic Cities

King Abdullah announced the Saudi Arabian General Investment Authority's plans to develop a number of separate economic cities in 2005. These cities are located throughout the Kingdom and are intended to facilitate the diversification of the Saudi economy through private sector enterprise. The cities will not only contain industry, but will also support housing, hotels, restaurants and recreational facilities that are intended to make them attractive for people to both work and live.

The economic cities and their locations are as follow:

King Abdullah Economic City (KAEC) – Jeddah Province

Prince Abdulaziz bin Musaid Economic City (PABMEC) – Ha'il

Knowledge Economic City (KEC) – Medina (inside Al Haram area – Muslims only)

Jazan Economic City (JEC) – Jizan

There are indications of plans for further economic cities located in Tabuk and the Eastern Province.

Status

King Abdullah Economic City (KAEC)'s development is well underway. Located near the coastal town of Thuwal, approximately 100 km north of Jeddah, KAEC is attracting businesses from all over the world, including many Western businesses. Its economic focus is diverse, with the intention to attract heavy industry and a world class seaport along with finance, education and recreation sectors.

The prestigious King Abdullah University of Science and Technology (KAUST), the Kingdom's first mixed gender university also operating under other somewhat relaxed social codes is also located near KAEC in Thuwal.

KAEC's first hotel is now open for business, as are some restaurants and a small supermarket. Residential properties already have a waiting list.

Prince Abdulaziz bin Musaid Economic City (PABMEC) is planned to cater to agribusiness and natural resources and is also designed to be a logistics and transport centre.

Knowledge Economic City (KEC) is planned to cater to a number of knowledge based Islamic orientated businesses and services

Jazan Economic City (JEC) is also well under development, with a focus on agribusiness, fisheries and a large industrial park.

Public and private sector attractions

Organisations who are considering setting up a presence in Saudi Arabia should be aware of their obligations to comply with Saudisation, which is also known as *nitaqat* in Arabic. Often, the main challenges are not only to find genuinely qualified Saudi nationals with the required skillsets, but to find Saudi nationals who are comfortable working in the private sector as opposed to a government job.

At the present time, only about 2% of Saudi nationals are employed in the private sector. Historically, there have been significant challenges in finding Saudi nationals with the right educational background. This is due to a great extent on traditional Saudi education system concentrating on obedient, unquestioning rote learning, with a strong focus on religious training.

Thus it continues to be difficult for Saudi nationals to fill skilled positions, especially requiring mathematic and hard science skills such as engineering. Soft skills required to manage a multinational work force can also be lacking for those not educated abroad. Many Saudis also would not consider entry level positions that many Westerners would consider paying their dues to gain experience and on the job expertise, especially if they have a modest job title or pay grade.

The remainder of Saudi nationals who are in employment are employed in the government sector as the vast majority of Saudi nationals perceive a government job to be a better fit. Reasons include status, job title and other prestige issues, wages, especially for those with competitive skill level challenges, leadership issues, and a common expectation of generous leave (official and sometimes unofficial) for a variety of reasons, including a higher tolerance for Saudi employees who must also attend to urgent family matters.

Saudisation (nitaqat)

It is estimated that there are only about 3 million Saudi men and about 500,000 Saudi women in gainful employment. Reasons range from a mis-match of skills to what is required for the job to an attitude of entitlement found in some circles.

Other Saudis may wish to work but don't have the right connections all too commonly needed to access many jobs. Yet others may wish to work but would only accept positions with a significantly high job title and other high status criteria, which does not always match the demands of the job market.

Many women also wish to enter the work force but may be held back by factors outside their direct control, even for well educated women and sometimes from their own family. Older women were also much more likely to have suffered from institutional restrictions prior to government reforms that were implemented by King Abdullah's policies.

The Saudi government recognises the need to reduce its reliance on expatriate labour and to increase employment amongst working age Saudis from all backgrounds, even if some Saudis remain more privileged than others. To this effect, the Saudi government have implemented a programme of *nitaqat*, known in English as Saudisation. Saudisation is designed to replace expatriates with Saudi nationals in as many jobs as is possible. Saudisation is discussed in further detail in a later Section.

Population Demographics

Saudi Arabia

According to the Central Department of Statistics, the total population of Saudi Arabia was 30,770,375 people as of 2014. Of these, 20,702,536 were Saudi nationals and 10,067,839 non-nationals. About 51% of the population is under the age of 25. Although Saudis have traditionally favoured large families, the current fertility rate is now estimated to be 2.26 children born per woman. About 90% of Saudi nationals are ethnically Arab. Nearly all of the remaining 10% have an ethnically African or Asian background.

Expatriates

From a Western perspective, it is important to remember that *everyone* who is not a Saudi national is an expatriate, including people from developing countries performing semiskilled or unskilled labour. The only exemptions are other GCC nationals from the neighbouring countries of Bahrain, Kuwait, Oman, Qatar and the United Arab Emirates, who have an agreement with Saudi Arabia that is broadly analogous to residency rights enjoyed by most EU nationals within the EU.

Estimates as to the number of expatriates living in Saudi Arabia vary widely. In this breakdown, the total number is expatriates is approximately 10 million. Respected sources estimate the following numbers of expatriate nationals with a large presence in the Kingdom:

India	2.0 million
Egypt	1.5 million
Pakistan	1.5 million
Philippines	1.3 million
Yemen	600,000
Jordan*	500,000
Syria**	400,000
Lebanon	400,000
Sudan	300,000
Afghanistan	200,000
Bangladesh	200,000
Sri Lanka	200,000

Europeans	150,000
North Americans	50,000
Others	700,000

*This figure includes a majority who are actually Palestinian with a Jordanian passport
**The number of Syrians residing in Saudi Arabia have decreased since the instability in Syria has been perceived to be a political and social threat in many Saudi circles

Traditionally, most Westerners are working in the oil and defence industries. However, as the Saudi economy develops and diversifies, so do the roles diversify for Westerners working in the Kingdom.

The Saudi government announced an end to amnesty for all expatriates who were residing in the Kingdom without the correct documentation in early November 2013. This triggered a mass exodus of mostly less skilled workers, although Western expatriates with incorrect paperwork (sometimes issued without their knowledge or understanding) were impacted as well. This has reduced the number of expatriates, although the specific numbers are unclear and may be temporary as continued demand for outside labour grows, especially for jobs most Saudis shun.

Language

Arabic is the official language of Saudi Arabia. Although English is very likely to be the language of business in many multinational and most Western organisations, Arabic is the language of government business and many Saudi-owned businesses as well.

Unlike in other countries in the region, where English language skills are excellent, the Saudi population has a wide range of English language skills. Many well educated Saudis and Saudis who travel abroad frequently will speak and understand English well. In fact, it is not unusual to encounter Saudis with British received pronunciation or superb American accents.

However, Saudis who are less well educated or less well travelled may speak English more poorly and with less confidence. This generally includes more of the elderly, rural population as well as a disproportionately high number of women, although the gender gap is closing.

Business travellers and expatriates who speak another language common to large expatriate communities found in Saudi Arabia may also be able to converse with others in these shared languages as well.

OTHER BASICS

Capitol City

Saudi Arabia's capitol city is Riyadh.

Date, Time and Time Zone

All of Saudi Arabia is located is UT/GMT +3. It does not observe summer time so does not change its clocks.

Please note that Saudi Arabia officially recognises the *Hijri* or Islamic calendar. The *Hijri* calendar designates the time when the Prophet Mohammed left or emigrated from Mecca to Medina in the 7th Century. Day one of the *Hijri* calendar is the equivalent of 16 July 622AD in the most commonly used Western calendar. In October 2016, it became the *Hijri* year 1438AH

It is important to clarify all references to time in Saudi Arabia to determine whether a Western or Islamic time measurement is being referred to. For example, a Western year is either 365 or 366 days long, depending on whether it is a leap year. An Islamic year is generally either 354 or 355 days long. Months are of varying lengths, depending on a precise citing of the new moon. These points can be of particular importance for bureaucratic purposes, from signing an annual lease to determining the validity or duration of your visa, driving licence, etc.

Work week

In 2013, Saudi Arabia officially changed its work week to Sunday – Thursday. Friday and Saturday is the Saudi weekend.

Friday is the holy day in Islam. However, many retailers are now opening their shops on Friday afternoons, after the end of the late afternoon *asr* prayer. This includes supermarkets and many other retailers, especially in the big shopping malls.

Traditional working hours

Government sector businesses generally work from 07.30 or 08.00 until about 14.00 or 14.30 hours. Thus, anyone with government business should keep this in mind and plan to conduct their business in the morning.

Private sector business often work a traditional split day, with office hours from about 08.00 – 12.00 and then again from about 17.00 – 20.00. Timings may vary somewhat between different businesses and during different times of the year, and may correspond with specific prayer times.

However, many private sector businesses continue to adopt the more Western style working hours of a straight day, i.e. working from about 08.00 – 17.00 or 09.00 – 18.00. This is especially true for multinational organisations or for any organisation doing a lot of business abroad, especially with Europe and the Americas.

Work weeks are up to 48 hours, after which additional pay, time off and other adjustments are meant to be made for the employee. Work is officially reduced to a maximum of six hours per workday during the month of Ramadan.

Weather

It is not always hot in Saudi Arabia! In fact, it gets downright cold in the desert in the winter. This includes evenings in Riyadh. It can snow in the mountains in the northwest and southwest of the country. The winter months are generally pleasant in Jeddah and the Eastern Province.

In the summer months, it can easily reach 50C, with high humidity on both coasts as well. It remains in the mid 30s throughout the night. Riyadh and other cities at higher elevation are often several degrees cooler and usually at lower humidity.

Most rain falls in the winter months, usually between December and February, although some years may not see any significant rain at all in parts of the Kingdom.

Sand storms can occur in Saudi Arabia, often in the spring months. They generally originate from Iraq and work their way south, often affecting the Eastern Province and Riyadh. Sandstorms are generally less frequent in Jeddah and along the Red Sea Coast.

Both rain and sandstorms can be debilitating to the rhythm of daily life in Saudi Arabia, especially on the road, where accidents increase. Floods quickly develop with any significant rainfall. Sand storms can drop visibility to only a few metres. It is remarkable how sand can penetrate in places one never imagined possible, from eyes and ears to gadgets and homes. Precautions should be taken to minimise both health and material damage.

Electricity

Historically, Saudi Arabia has used both a 127V and the 220V/230V/240V systems. Plug configurations in common use are North American, British and Continental European terminators. In 2010, the Saudi authorities announced that, over the next 25 years, the electrical standard throughout the country will be 230V.

From a practical point of view, expect to find the following pattern: The American system is more prevalent in the Eastern Province. The British system is more prevalent in and around Riyadh. The European system is more prevalent in and around Jeddah.

This is only a general guideline and many exceptions can be found. Sometimes, the nationality of the building's architects will have a direct influence. It would be wise to travel with an assortment of adapters that can be used for all common mains socket styles.

Money

The Saudi Riyal is the official currency of Saudi Arabia. It is officially pegged to the US Dollar and is fully convertible abroad. There are 100 halalas to the riyal, although they are not commonly used. It is important to confirm that only current banknotes are accepted as previous series will not be accepted.

Official rates of exchange:

1 US Dollar = 3.75320 Saudi Riyal

1 Saudi Riyal (SAR) = 0.26644 US Dollar (USD)

Riyal banknotes are issued in denominations of 1, 5, 10, 20, 50, 100, 200, 500 riyals. There are *halala* coins in denominations of 5, 10, 25, 50, and 100 *halala*.

Please refer to the Money chapter in the 'Preparing for Travel to Saudi Arabia' section for further practical information.

Telephone country code and dialling codes

The country code for dialling all Saudi telephone numbers is +966.

Saudi telephone numbers work like most other countries in the world outside of North America. When dialling from abroad, dial the international access code (eg. 00 from Europe, 011 from the US), then the country code, then drop any reference to 0 immediately after the country code if present, then dial the remaining city code/mobile code followed by the 7 digit telephone number.

When dialling another Saudi telephone number from within the Kingdom, drop the access and country codes, add the leading zero if not present, then dial the remaining city code/mobile code followed by the 7 digit telephone number.

Dialling codes for major cities land lines

Recent changes to Saudi landlines include the addition of a '1' in front of the previous city code. Thus, the Riyadh dialling code has changed from 01 ---> 011, the Jeddah dialling code from 02 ---> 012 etc. If you have a telephone number in the old format, such as on an older business card, use the same formula to update to the new, correct dialling code as the old number will no longer connect.

Here are the dialling codes for Saudi landlines:

011 – Riyadh and the region
012 – Jeddah, Mecca, Taif and the region
013 – Eastern Province, including Dammam, Dhahran, Al Khobar, Jubail and the region
014 – the Northwest, including Yanbu, Madinah, Tabuk, al Jouf, Sakaka and the region
016 – the Centre, including Qassim, Buraydah, Ha'il and the region

017 – the Southwest, including Asir, Jizan, Abha, Najran and the region

Dialling codes for Saudi mobiles
All Saudi mobile telephones begin with 05x, followed by 7 digits.

STC mobiles – start with 050, 053 or 055
Mobily mobiles – start with 054 or 056
Zain mobiles – start with 058 or 059

Emergency and other service numbers
Telephone operators answering emergency other service numbers do not all speak English. If you do not speak Arabic well enough to hold a conversation in the language, you may need to find someone who does or to try to convince the operator to locate a colleague who does speak English. The most common emergency and other service telephone numbers are:

959 – Mobile Customer Service Centre - Zain
1100 – Mobile Customer Service Centre - Mobily
902 – Mobile Customer Service Centre - STC
904 – Telephone Customer Service Centre for Subscribers - STC
905 – Saudi Telephone Directory
906 – Internet Service Centre - STC
907 – Telephone Customer Service Centre - STC
909 – Telephone Enterprise Services Call Centre - STC
933 – Saudi Electricity Customer Services
939 – Saudi Water and Sewerage Services (Eastern Region)
940 – Saudi Municipal Services
966 – Saudi Natural Disasters
985 – Saudi General Intelligence Presidency
989 – Saudi Public Security
990 – Saudi Telephone Service for Security Issues
992 – Saudi Passport
993 – Saudi Traffic Police Force
994 – Saudi Border Checkpoint
995 – Saudi Anti-Narcotics
996 – Saudi Highway Traffic Police Force
997 – Saudi Red Crescent

998 – Saudi Civil Defense

999 – Saudi Police Force

Internet code

The internet code for Saudi Arabia is .sa

Driving

Driving is on the right.

Saudi Arabia is the only country in the world where women are not allowed to drive. Men who are resident in the Kingdom must be 18 to obtain a full Saudi driving licence. Men must be 25 years old to hire a car from most internationally recognised car hire companies.

Seatbelts are required for the driver and front seat passengers. Using a hand held mobile phone whilst driving is illegal. Both of these rules are widely ignored.

Driving in Saudi Arabia is much more dangerous than in most of the rest of the world. With low petrol prices, excellent quality roads and powerful vehicles, high speeds often go hand in hand with reckless drivers who often have a very fatalistic attitude, an attitude of entitlement, or both. In some extreme cases, young men play a road game of *tafheet* or 'drifting' where even more dangerous manoeuvres are attempted, including driving a vehicle on two of its four wheels at high speeds, often whilst spinning and sliding. Innocent as well as not so innocent road users have been killed when this activity goes wrong.

In addition, most traffic laws are not enforced – at least, until an accident occurs. As a result, over 7000 road accident fatalities and approximately 40,000 serious injuries are recorded every year, making Saudi Arabia's roads amongst the most dangerous in the world (some say Saudi Arabia is *the* worst).

Although the *Saher* speed camera system has been installed several years ago, it is widely avoided, often by clever use of technology. Other Saudis find ways around their fines, also defeating their purpose as a deterrent.

Petrol pricing is amongst the least expensive in the world. It is approximately 1/6 the price in the US and 1/14 the price in the UK.

More detailed driving information is found in subsequent Sections.

SECTION 3

UNDERSTANDING ISLAM IN SAUDI ARABIA

UNDERSTANDING ISLAM
IN SAUDI ARABIA

The fundamentals

Islam is more than a religion – it is a way of life and a moral code. It is important that Western business professionals have an elementary knowledge of Islam if they intend to spend any time working in Saudi Arabia.

Islam is a monotheistic, Abrahamic religion that shares its roots with Judaism and Christianity. A Muslim is a person who believes in Islam.

Islam follows the teachings of the Prophet Mohammed, who Muslims believe was the final prophet. These teachings are known as the *sunnah* – the traditions and practices of the Prophet. The *hadith* refers to the oral traditions regarding the words and deeds of the Prophet. There are some distinctions between the *sunnah* and *hadith* amongst various Muslim groups.

Muslims believe that the *Qur'an* is the Islamic holy book. Only the Arabic language version is considered to be pure. The *Qur'an* is used as a source of Islamic Law known as Shari'a Law. Shari'a Law is comprehensive, addressing everything from punishment for criminal activity to providing guidance for everyday civil matters.

A mosque (*masjid* in Arabic) is a place of worship for Muslims.

Adherent Muslims pray five times per day. These prayers are called *salat*. Prayer times are determined by the movements of the sun, and will vary from day to day and from location to location. Muslim men are expected to pray in a mosque for the Friday mid-day prayer but may pray anywhere that is clean if away from a mosque during other prayer times.

The *azan* or *adhan* is the call to prayer. *Wudu* are a proscribed set of ablutions that must be performed prior to prayer, regardless of where a Muslim is praying. Shoes must also be removed before entering a mosque and before praying.

The *Ka'aba*, located in Mecca, is the holiest site in Islam. It is believed to have been first built upon by Abraham, and was the site of prayer for the Prophet Mohammed. It is the large gold-trimmed black cube-shaped monolith seen in the media that is often encircled by faithful pilgrims. It is now surrounded by the mosque known as the Masjid al Haram. Muslims around the world face the *Ka'aba* in Mecca when they pray.

Prayers are performed by following a specific set of rituals and reciting specific words. Daily prayers may be performed at a mosque, prayer room, at home, or even in transit. Generally, prayers last for about 20 to 30 minutes when praying with others. Praying is considered serious business, especially for men.

If praying with others, people are segregated by gender, regardless of where they are praying. Mosques are segregated by gender. Women pray in a separate part of the mosque to men. This may be a separate room, a section of the prayer hall roped off for women, behind men, or in another part of the mosque inaccessible to men. In Saudi Arabia, women have no access to many of their local mosques. This is not the case in many other Islamic countries.

Friday is the holy day throughout the Muslim world. It is expected that Muslim men attend mosque during the Friday mid-day prayer. The Friday mid-day prayer is called *Jumu'ah* and is the most important prayer of the week.

A *madrassa* is a place of learning, i.e. a school. A *madrassa* can teach at all levels, from the Western equivalent of primary education through higher education in specialised fields, including mathematics, science, medicine and literature. There are many *madrassas* throughout Saudi Arabia.

Some provide a full curriculum of subjects, leading to a high standard of education. However, there are also some *madrassas* that focus on memorisation of the Qur'an and sometimes little else. *Madrassas* also hold a diverse range of political thought, often reflecting the political views of their benefactors.

The five pillars of Islam

Most mainstream Muslims, including all Sunnis, recognise five pillars of Islam. Other groups have additional beliefs as well, including Ibadi, Druze, Alawites, Ismailis and some Shi'a.

1. *Shahada*

Shahada means the profession of the faith that there is only one God and that Mohammed is his prophet. The *shahada* is recited every day by religious Muslims. In English, the recitation is 'There is no God but Allah, and Muhammed is his messenger.' The script found on the national flag of Saudi Arabia is the *shahada*.

2. *Salat*

Salat is formal Muslim prayer. Prayers are performed five times per day by practicing religious Muslims. The *azan* or *adhan* is the call to prayer heard from mosques that announce a prayer time. Modern Saudis who wish to be advised of prayer times no matter where they are will often install an app on their mobile.

- *Fajr* (dawn)
  Not to be confused with sunrise, the *fajr* prayer occurs at the first sign of changing light at the end of night. Very religious Muslims believe they need to complete this prayer before sunrise (*shurooq*) begins.
- *Dhuhr* (early afternoon)
  Dhuhr occurs just after the sun peaks in the sky, and is replaced by *Jumu'ah* on Friday.
- *Asr* (late afternoon)
  Asr occurs according to a calculation of the size of an object's shadow relative to its true size. From a practical point of view, it is the time when many people can just start to detect a change in the heat of the day.
- *Maghrib* (sunset)
  Maghrib, as the name suggests, occurs at sunset.
- *Isha* (night)
  Isha occurs at the end of twilight, when the night sky arrives.

3. *Zakat*

Zakat means the giving of alms, or charity. *Zakat* is calculated by using a formula applied to a person's wealth based on their savings and assets. *Zakat* has other conditions as to when and where it is paid. *Zakat* is often visible during Ramadan and both Eids.

4. *Sawm*

Sawm means fasting. It is practiced during the month of *Ramadan*, which is the ninth lunar month of the Islamic calendar. *Ramadan* is also known as Ramzan in some parts of the worlds including the Indian sub-continent, so do not be surprised to hear this term, especially from Pakistanis and Bangladeshis. *Sawm* lasts for the duration of Ramadan, usually 29 or 30 days.

During Ramadan, all followers must not eat, drink (including water), smoke, chew gum, or engage in sexual relations from dawn to sunset. They must also strive to think good thoughts and do good deeds.

People who are exempt from *sawm* include anyone where fasting would cause them physical harm: very small children (usually to the age of puberty, but younger in some conservative cultures), infirm elderly people, people with certain medical conditions such as Type 1 diabetes, pregnant women and nursing mothers.

Older children who have not yet reached puberty will often start practicing fasting, but are allowed to break the fast as necessary. Menstruating women must not fast during this time. Travellers (not normal commuters) are also exempt – airlines will be fully catered during Ramadan, including Middle East based carriers. There are rules of compensation for not fasting for most of these exemptions. For example, observers may fast on another day(s) after Ramadan is over to make up the 'missed days' not fasting. Charitable donations are often made by people who may never be able to fast.

5. *Hajj*

The *Hajj* is also known as the Pilgrimage to Mecca. It is an act of devotion to Allah. Every Muslim who is physically able and has the financial means to do so is obligated to perform Hajj at least once in their lifetime. This applies to men and women.

Hajj is held on 8 – 10 *Dhu al-Hijjah*, the twelfth and last month of the Islamic calendar. Thus, Hajj will occur in a little over two months after the end of Ramadan.

Ihram is the state of being a person experiences whilst performing *Hajj*. A series of rituals will be practiced by pilgrims in a set sequence. Many Muslims believe that their past sins are forgiven, but this is not universal.

Ihram clothing is worn during the pilgrimage. Westerners travelling to Jeddah – the gateway airport to Mecca - may be surprised the first time they encounter pilgrims wearing *ihram* clothing. It is usually in the form of two pieces of simple white cloth as worn by a man. Women will often wear a simple white robe. The purpose of *ihram* clothing is to make all pilgrims of equal status.

Umrah is a pilgrimage to Mecca that takes place at any other time of the year. It is encouraged in Islam, but does not take the place of *Hajj*.

Background and demographics

Islam is considered to have begun when the Prophet Mohammed left or emigrated from Mecca to Medina in the seventh century. The exact date corresponds to 16th July 622 in the Western calendar. It spread throughout the Arabian Peninsula in just a few years, and through the influence of traders, could be found from Spain to India within 100 years. Islam also became the dominant religion of modern day Malaysia, Indonesia, Brunei, and much of North and East Africa a bit later, also introduced by Arab trade.

Today, Muslims can be found in nearly every part of the world. It is estimated that there are up to 1.6 billion Muslims worldwide, representing approximately 22% of the world's population of about 7.3 billion people.

Only 20% of the world's Muslims live in the Middle East. Another 50% live elsewhere in Asia, including 30% in the Indian subcontinent and 16% in the Far East. About 4% live in the West, mostly in Europe, although Muslim populations are growing in the Americas. Most of the remainder live in Africa.

All Saudi nationals are Muslim. The vast majority, over 80%, are Sunni Muslims. Most of the remainder are Shi'a.

Sunnis and Shi'a

Shortly after the beginning of Islam, the religion split into two main factions, Sunni and Shi'a. Between 80% and 85% of the world's Muslims are Sunni; most of the rest are Shi'a.

After the death of the Prophet Mohammed, there was no clear-cut successor to lead people who embraced Islam. A simple way to think of the main difference between Sunni and Shi'a is the interpretation of who should lead them – through consensus or through lineage.

Sunnis believe in following the *Sunnah*, the way of life of the Prophet Mohammed. They believe *caliphs* are successors to the Prophet, and should be chosen from the Muslim community, subject to a number of qualifications. A *caliph* is the head of an *ummah* or religious community.

According to Sunnis, Abu Bakr was the first caliph, followed by Umar, Uthman and Ali. The division between Sunni and Shi'a is the result of a dispute in the lineage of subsequent caliphs; the division was permanently deepened when the third caliph Uthman was murdered. His death set off a series of events that led to the eventual split of the Islamic community into the two main sects that exist to this day.

Shi'a believe that Ali should have been the first caliph. Shi'a do not believe that *caliphs* are the holders of power within Islam. Instead, they believe this power is transferred through the lineage of Ali, the Prophet Mohammed's son in law. Ali's wife Fatima was the daughter of the Prophet and his wife Khadija.

There are also relatively small numbers of Muslims who are neither Sunni nor Shi'a. From a Saudi perspective, nearby Oman has the largest population – Ibadis - who follow beliefs that are not wholly Sunni nor Shi'a. Some Muslims may regard these groups as not entirely Muslim. Indeed, some Saudis also believe that Shi'a are also not true Muslims; others are more tolerant.

Salafis (Wahhabis)

The perception of tolerance and religion in Saudi Arabia are not always closely associated, especially compared to most neighbouring countries in the region. This perception – and often reality – exists due to a movement and agreement that goes back to the early part of the 18th Century.

Back in the 18th Century, there were two powerful families living in Diriyah, located in the Najd region of what is now the centre of Saudi Arabia. These were the al-Wahhab and al-Saud families. The al-Wahhab family, lead by Muhammad ibn Abd al-Wahhab, believed a reform was needed within Islam that brought its beliefs and practices back to basics. His beliefs spread widely throughout the region and became the predominant form of Islam found amongst many Saudis today, including many prominent families. Indeed, an alliance was formed between the al-Wahhabs and the al-Saud family, the latter family becoming the Saudi ruling family. This alliance remains in force to the present time.

Salafists are Sunni Muslims who believe in strictly following the teachings of the *Qur'an* and the *hadith*, emulating the way of life found during the first years of Islam during the time of the Prophet Mohammed. It is considered by *Salafists* to be the purest form of Islam. Many other Muslims disagree, including many other Sunnis.

Salafism is the dominant sect of Islam in Saudi Arabia, and is responsible for the rules, regulations and restrictions found in everyday Saudi life, including those placed on Western business professionals.

Wahhabism is often described as being synonymous with *Salafism*; others make the distinction that *Salafism* is a group of ultra-conservative Islamic sects, of which *Wahhabism* is prominent. It should be noted that many people who practice *Wahhabism* do not like to be known as *Wahhabis* and prefer to be called *Salafis*.

Unlike most followers of Islam, *Salafism* cannot be described as tolerant of other religious beliefs, including other Islamic beliefs. It believes that all non-Muslims and Muslims holding other beliefs are *infidels* – someone who has no religious faith – including Shi'a Muslims. It also believes in absolute, unquestioning adherence to the interpretations of their religious scholars.

Some adherents to the most extreme interpretations of *Salafist* beliefs have become prominent in the news in recent years. This includes the extremist political groups with *Salafist* ties such as al Qaeda and ISIS/ISIL. There is continuing evidence to suggest they are gaining popularity and influence in many other geographies outside Saudi Arabia and the Middle East, including parts of Europe, the Indian subcontinent and sub-Saharan Africa.

It is important to acknowledge that not all *Salafists* are extremists or condone violence. It is equally important to acknowledge that there are extremists who hold other Islamic beliefs and their interpretation – and indeed others who are not Muslim. Islam, politics, and tolerance come in many forms.

Common distinctions found in *Wahhabi* male dress and appearance can include *thobes* worn short enough to expose the ankles, wearing a *ghutra* without an *agal*, and wearing an ungroomed beard that is grown to fist length. It is also characteristic of the dress code of the *muttawa*, the Saudi religious police.

Wahhabi women's dress can include wearing an unadorned, plain *abaya* and headscarf combined with the wearing of the *niqab*- a face veil that comes in many designs and covers all of part of the face, and often wearing opaque hosiery to conceal the feet and gloves to conceal the hands.

Impact on visitors and residents in Saudi Arabia
Salafist beliefs have a massive impact on daily life for everyone in the Kingdom, including visitors, who must also abide by these strict religious practices. Visitors and especially potential expatriate residents must give these issues serious consideration in determining whether working and/or living in Saudi Arabia is suitable for their personality as well as their own moral code.

Restrictions include but are not limited to: No live music, dance, or many board and card games, no alcohol, gender segregation in many public settings, strict dress code requirements for women and men, mandatory prayers for Muslim men, no tolerance of other religious practices, and no idol worship, which can extend to the worship of images of people, animals, birthdays, and anything that could potentially become a shrine.

As with any other human behaviour, some people are stricter in their interpretation of what is acceptable, tolerated and forbidden; Saudis are no different. A description of practical behaviour and how it is changing follows later in the Section and elsewhere in this book where relevant.

Significance of Mecca and Medina

Mecca and Medina are the two holiest cities for all Muslims, regardless of sect.

Mecca is the birthplace of the Prophet Mohammed and is the location where the Qur'an was revealed to the Prophet. Muslims face the Ka'aba in Mecca whilst praying. The Ka'aba is located inside the centre of Islam's holiest mosque, Al-Masjid al-Haram. Mecca is located about 70km southeast of Jeddah. Mecca is the primary location where all Muslim pilgrims travel for *hajj* or *umrah*.

Medina is where the Prophet Mohammed died and is the location of his burial tomb, contained in the Mosque of the Prophet, Al-Masjid al-Nabawi. Medina is the base from where the Prophet's first four successors continued to develop the Muslim community.

In Saudi Arabia, the title Custodian of the Two Holy Mosques has been used in recent times, including by King Fahd, King Abdullah and now King Salman. It is common to see this title used in many publications when referring to the Saudi King.

Both Mecca and Medina are restricted cities. Non-Muslims are forbidden to travel to Mecca. There are checkpoints along all routes into the city. Non-Muslims travelling to or from Jeddah to locations such as Taif must take a more circuitous route (often cheekily known as the 'Christian by-pass') to avoid Mecca. Non-Muslims are also forbidden to travel to the centre of Medina, although they do have access to the outskirts of the city as well as the airport. Restricted areas are clearly signposted but do not have the same rigorous checkpoint system as in Mecca.

The impact of Islam and other religions on everyday life in Saudi Arabia

Understanding religious expectations and restrictions

There is a strong expectation that all visitors and residents in Saudi Arabia respect Islamic practices throughout the Kingdom. This has been traditionally enforced by authority figures in the Kingdom, including by the *muttaween*, also known as the *muttawa*, or religious police.

Unlike in the recent past, where many expatriates could tell stories from pettiness to horror about some encounters with the *muttawa*, visitors to Saudi Arabia are much less likely to encounter the *muttawa* at all and if they do, they are much more likely to be treated with respect.

However, it is still strongly advised not to draw attention to the *muttawa* by either your appearance or your behaviour, especially during

Ramadan. Do be aware that the religious police could become more active in times of political and social upheaval in regions of the Kingdom where these challenges are most acute.

Islamic values do not include proselytising (converting people to their religion), although people who come to the religion of their own free will are welcomed. Western business professionals will not generally encounter pressure to convert to Islam, although they may receive comments about living according to Muslim values, especially about drinking, sex or the perceived breakdown of the Western family.

Islamic items you may find in your hotel room

A *sajjada* (prayer rug) is often stored in a closet or drawer. It will measure about 100cm x 60cm. It will often be woven to contain geometric designs or an item found in a mosque. It should be treated with respect or left alone by guests who do not use it for prayer.

A *qibla* is a sign, sticker or other indication used to assist people as to the direction of Mecca. A *qibla* sticker can be found on desks or affixed to the ceiling in hotel rooms, published in *salat* schedules, or even displayed on video screens on airline flights. It may be a simple arrow, or it may be a degree reading on a compass. Like *salat* times, *qibla* information can also be found on many websites, and can be texted to a mobile or found in an app.

A copy of the *Qur'an* is often found in a desk drawer. This book should be respected in the same way as a Bible, Torah, or any other religious holy book.

Attitude to other religions and no religion

Many observers may note that there is a paradoxical attitude toward other religions in Saudi Arabia. On one hand, there is an expectation that everyone has a specific faith. The concept of agnosticism or atheism is alien and generally not tolerated or even sometimes believed. As Westerners, most people will be assumed to be Christian unless something specific in your background or surname indicates otherwise.

However, there is no religious tolerance for practicing other faiths within Saudi Arabia. This means there are no churches or other places of worship other than mosques. Holding religious services in private is also technically illegal. It must be noted that some expatriate compounds may discretely hold religious meetings in the privacy of someone's home. Although the risk is currently low that this will cause difficulties, it does remain possible.

Apostasy and proselytising

Westerners or anyone else who may be keen to convert Muslims to Christianity should be aware that in Saudi Arabia, the penalty for apostasy (renouncing one's religion) for someone to convert from Islam to another religion, including Christianity, is death.

Islamic and cultural taboos - *halal* and *haram*

Halal simply means something is permitted. Many Westerners are familiar with *halal* butchers. In this case, it simply means that the butcher is selling meat that is permitted to be eaten by observant Muslims. *Haram* means forbidden. Thus, an observant Muslim must avoid a *haram* item or practice.

The following information explores the most common situations encountered by visitors and expatriate residents of Saudi Arabia, and may be either religious or cultural in nature.

Pork

Pork is not eaten by practicing Muslims. Nor are pork products used, such as items made out of pig skin. Although some neighbouring countries may sell pork in controlled, licenced environments, pork products are completely illegal in Saudi Arabia, including their importation.

Other meat and poultry

Meat and poultry that is not *haram* must be slaughtered and prepared in a specific way as outlined in the Qur'an and Sunnah before a Muslim can consume it. No blood can remain in the meat. All meat sold in Saudi Arabia is *halal*.

Fish with scales are considered *halal*. Other fish are considered by some sects as *halal*, and others as *haram*. Many Muslims permit consumption of some or all shellfish; others don't. However, it's best to err on the side of caution in the company of very religious people and choose scaly fish if you are unsure.

Alcohol

Alcohol consumption is forbidden in Islam. It is completely illegal throughout Saudi Arabia, including in top end hotels and in expatriate compounds, including those catering to Westerners. The only exception to this rule is on the grounds of foreign embassies who wish to serve alcohol to their invited guests.

Public intoxication is also illegal, including upon arrival at the airport and leaving foreign embassies. In practice, many travellers to the Kingdom do consume alcohol on their journey, but they must ensure they do not appear to be intoxicated or behave in a manner that would draw unwanted attention by the airport authorities. Do note that airlines that serve alcohol will only do so when they are not in Saudi airspace. Embassy visitors should give serious consideration about their transport when leaving the grounds if they have consumed any alcohol at all.

The left hand

The left hand is considered dirty throughout the Middle East, as it is in most Asian cultures. The left hand has traditionally been used for unclean functions, including removing shoes and for the toilet. This will be an ongoing challenge for left-handed people no matter how long they work in Saudi Arabia.

The left hand should not be used when eating with the hands, such as when eating a sandwich. Never take food from a communal serving plate or bowl with your left hand, even when using cutlery. Approach buffets with the right hand only. Cutlery for individual use can be held in the left hand, as can pens and sporting equipment.

The left hand should never be used for passing items to another person. This includes food, an item in the office, business cards, money and bank cards, and gifts or other purchases. Items should be passed with the right hand, or with both hands when necessary.

The soles of your feet

The soles of the feet or shoes are considered dirty in Saudi Arabia and throughout the Middle East, most of Asia and much of Africa. They should never be seen by another person. Unlike the left hand issue, where a violation is looked upon as bad manners, exposing the soles of one's feet or shoes is actually offensive.

Western business professionals should not sit with their legs crossed at the knee, as the sole of your foot will inevitably be seen by someone else in the room. Westerners should also be prepared to sit on low cushions or even on the ground in a manner that does not show the bottoms of their feet. This is much trickier than it sounds, and may require quite a bit of dexterity. Bring a wrap or some other item to cover your feet if you cannot otherwise manage a suitable position.

Western business professionals should also be prepared to remove their shoes when entering a person's home. Slippers may be offered for indoor wear, but it's always a good idea to make sure the quality of your socks or tights are of sufficient standard.

Pornography

Islam is in agreement with other religions and most moral codes about the unacceptability of pornography. However, the definition of pornography may differ quite significantly from that of the West. Images of men and especially women who are not modestly dressed may be considered pornographic.

In Saudi Arabia, images may be considered pornographic or unsuitable that would not get a second look in the West, including advertising, sports figures in action, or even innocuous features in newspaper supplements and business publications.

A small army of censors are employed in Saudi Arabia whose sole job is to monitor and 'correct' pornographic images. In the examples above, the images would probably still be allowed into the Kingdom, but only once black markers have done their work on the offending component of the image.

Although both printed and electronic material is rarely inspected by Saudi customs as it once was in the past, it's still best not to give the officials a reason to draw their attention to you.

If you are preparing marketing material for use in Saudi Arabia, it's important to keep all of the above in mind. Also consider your company logo as to its suitability – scantily dressed women, pigs, dogs, crosses, stars and many more examples could be problematic.

Other inappropriate images

Many of the most conservative branches of Islam, including *Salafists*, consider images of other living things as *haram*. This includes photographs and other reproductions of people, animals and anything else that can be worshipped. Photographs of women are particularly frowned upon.

From a practical point of view, photographs found in your corporation's annual report and other photos that are clearly of businesspeople conducting business will be tolerated. More care should be given to photographs used in advertising and presentations. Photographs of women in Saudi newspapers, once banned, are becoming more common.

Public displays of affection between a man and a woman

All public displays of affection between a man and a woman should be avoided throughout Saudi Arabia. This includes between people married to each other. Innocent gestures common in the West that should be avoided are hugging, touching any part of the other person's body, holding hands and greeting someone of the opposite sex by kissing on the cheeks. Paradoxically, these behaviours can be commonly observed between Saudi men.

Dogs

Dogs are considered dirty in Islam. Whilst many people will keep guard dogs in Saudi Arabia, they are unlikely to have dogs as pets. Western business professionals who are considering a move to Saudi Arabia are able to import their dog but should consider Western compounds as the only real, practical option that would tolerate the family pet.

Gambling and lotteries

All forms of gambling are *haram* in Islam. However, like with many other issues, the definition of gambling is open to interpretation.

Activities where money is exchanged for the sole purpose of a win based on chance is forbidden. This is most likely to include betting and lotteries. Many card games often fall into the same category. Gambling and lottery websites from your home country are likely to be blocked.

Horse racing and camel racing proliferate throughout the Middle East. Interestingly, many religious scholars site various *hadith* that allow competitions with horses and camels.

Gold, silk and diamonds for men

Islam forbids men from wearing items that are considered an excessive display of wealth, which includes gold and silk. Some Islamic scholars will also consider these items to be feminine, and thus *haram* for men. There are many opinions as to whether this includes gemstones, especially diamonds.

Many Saudis observe these beliefs, although others interpret their jewellery options differently. Thus, although a Western man is unlikely to be criticised for wearing a gold wedding band or even a gold watch, it is suggested that they refrain from openly wearing a gold necklace or any other gold jewellery, at least in the company of very religious Saudis.

Visiting mosques if not Muslim

Rules vary throughout the world as to whether non-Muslims can visit mosques. In Saudi Arabia, it is forbidden for non-Muslims to visit any mosque throughout the Kingdom.

Travel to Mecca and Medina for non-Muslims

Western business professionals who are working in Saudi Arabia should be aware of additional restrictions surrounding travel to Mecca and Medina, Islam's two holiest cities located in the West of the country. Only Muslims are allowed into all of Mecca and the centre of Medina. These restrictions are strictly enforced, with several road blocks and check points along the way to Mecca. Roads leading to restricted areas are clearly sign posted in Medina. It is sensible advice for even the most intrepid traveller not to try to break this taboo, as penalties are severe and enforced.

Non-Muslim religious symbols in Saudi Arabia

Non-Muslim religious symbols and artefacts are not allowed into Saudi Arabia and should be left behind if travelling to the Kingdom for work or relocation. Saudi authorities can interpret what qualifies in vague and sometimes random ways.

It is strongly advised that these items in particular are not worn or brought into the Kingdom: Christian crosses and similar, bibles (although this is where e-books can come in handy), Christmas ornaments and other decorations, anything associated with St Valentine's

Day, any Judaica, Sikh turbans or any of the five K's, Hindu god statues, artefacts and other symbols, including the *kalava* thread, Buddha bells and prayer wheels, even as souvenirs, or anything else from any other religion that could be interpreted as suspicious.

Capital and corporal punishment

It is true that Saudi Arabia's interpretation of the Qur'an and application of Shari'a law means that a strict attitude is taken over a number of crimes against Islam. Saudi Arabia practices both capital and corporal punishment. Saudi Arabia's position on capital punishment means it may execute its own citizens or anyone else who commits a capital crime on its soil. Capital crimes in Saudi Arabia include murder, rape, apostasy, blasphemy, armed robbery, illegal drug smuggling, repeated drug use, adultery, sodomy, homosexual sexual activity, witchcraft, sorcery and terrorism. Saudi Arabia's usual method of execution is by beheading.

Most of the world's practitioners of capital punishment are found in China, Iran, Iraq, Yemen, Sudan, Afghanistan, North Korea and the United States, with China the most prolific by far. With the death of King Abdullah and the arrival of King Salman in January 2015, there has been a clear upswing in the implementation of executions. In 2015, Saudi Arabia executed more than 150 people.

Although all visitors to the Kingdom should have a healthy fear of capital punishment, in reality, most people who suffer this fate have been involved in the illegal drug trade or have become entangled in very messy personal relationships with Saudi nationals, both situations that can be easily avoided. Sadly, many maids and other service workers, including those who have been horrifically mistreated may also find themselves in dire straits if they ultimately commit an act of violence against their sponsor.

Others were involved in terrorist activities as interpreted by the Kingdom. This includes al-Qaeda members and others who have been accused of invoking terror within the Kingdom. Most, but not all, have been Saudi. The case of Nimr al-Nimr, considered by some to have been a fiery advocate for Shi'a minority rights and by the Saudi authorities as accused of terrorist activities was perhaps the most famous person to be executed in early 2016.

Western expatriates are not exempt from the consequences of capital crimes. Western embassies cannot protect its citizens from Saudi law. However, many Westerners or their wealthy employers may be able to negotiate a punishment to avoid execution by agreeing to a blood money figure called *diyya* to compensate for their crime in lieu of execution. *Diyya* is paid to the aggrieved party or their survivors in a capital case and can allow the accused to go free as payment for their crime. *Diyya* settlement should never be assumed even if it is possible financially as the aggrieved party may never agree to it or the crime may not qualify.

Corporal punishment in Saudi Arabia is also used for certain crimes. Punishment for the accused, seen as an eye-for-an-eye retribution for their victim's suffering, range from flogging to amputation or other method designed to inflict intentional pain and suffering for the crime committed. *Diyya* can be paid for corporal crimes as well. Official figures as to the frequency of their occurrence are difficult to come by. Anecdotally, they occur most often amongst the least well-connected members of Saudi society or expatriates from developing countries with few options to extract themselves from the situation.

Prayer times

Unlike any other country in the world, Saudi Arabia enforces mandatory prayer times, where businesses, shops, restaurants, and all other commerce and other activities stop for the duration of each prayer. You will be asked to leave shops, which will then be shuttered. If you are in a restaurant, supermarket or other large shop, you have the choice of being locked in or locked out before the establishment is also shuttered.

Prayer times also dictate when shops close for their long afternoon break. Many open until *Dhuhr*, the midday prayer and only reopen again after the *Asr* prayer in the late afternoon.

Prayer times, including performing ablutions and prayer rituals, takes about 20 minutes when praying in a group. However, in Saudi Arabia, it is prudent to expect prayer times to last closer to 30 or even 40 minutes overall before retail businesses reopen. This is because many people who have just finished praying will have a smoke or a chat with friends.

Expectations and behaviour

It would be wise for all visitors to and residents of Saudi Arabia to learn each day's specific prayer times so you can plan your day accordingly. This information is available from a wide number of sources, from most newspapers to your hotel to downloading an app on to your smart phone. Prayer times are determined by the position of the sun, which means they will be slightly different every day and also slightly different from city to city. Unlike so many other facets of life in Saudi Arabia, prayer times are precise.

Muslim men, regardless of nationality are expected to pray during each prayer time, although this does not always happen. Religious police in many locations, including Riyadh, used to be very vigilant toward men complying with prayer times, expecting them to find the nearest mosque or prayer room. Although the religious police can still be seen 'collecting' random men during prayer time and questioning their religious affiliation, this is a much less frequent occurrence than only a few years ago.

On occasion, it is possible to see Muslim women praying, quite often in public places like in the middle of a shopping centre or sometimes in women's public toilet facilities. This is because many prayer rooms and mosques are male only in Saudi Arabia.

Non-Muslim men and women are expected to stop what they are doing and wait quietly and patiently until prayers are over. Although a quiet conversation or use of non-disruptive technology would not generally be problematic, acting with respect is recommended and appreciated.

Prayer times and business

As in public, businesses are also required to close during each prayer time. In practice, some business may be conducted discretely and quietly during prayer times if the owner is not particularly religious, is of sufficient status in the community, and has rooms in the office that cannot be seen by the general public.

It is important to be aware of prayer times when working in Saudi Arabia, especially whenever you are working with religious Muslims. Try to avoid scheduling a meeting during prayer times, although the imprecision of timekeeping means that this may happen on occasion anyway even with the best of planning. If you are responsible for organising a day-long event, it is expected that you will accommodate meals and breaks to coordinate with prayer times.

For those organisations working a split day, it is traditional to return to work at the end of *Asr* prayers.

Ramadan

Saudi Arabia enforces fasting during the month of Ramadan. This includes all public venues and can be enforced in private venues as well. Other public behaviour such as immodesty, swearing and public displays of affection is watched more carefully during Ramadan as well.

Expectations and behaviour

Visitors and expatriate residents, including non-Muslims, must also fast in public, including in hotels, although room service can be organised. It is also possible to purchase provisions from a supermarket during daylight hours, where you can bring them back to your hotel room or compound.

Those people who are exempt from fasting, such as diabetics or pregnant women, should also refrain from eating or drinking in public during Ramadan. In addition, never smoke or chew gum in public during daylight hours. There may be limited tolerance outside of Western orientated compounds for infants and very small children, but even then, offering a small child a drink or food should only be done with the utmost discretion.

Western orientated compounds are not expected to enforce the rules and behaviour of Ramadan, including fasting and modest dress. However, residents of Western compounds must observe the rules of Ramadan whenever they leave the compound and venture outside.

During Ramadan, dress codes become more conservative for both men and women. Men should ensure that their arms and legs are fully covered. On occasion, it may be just about ok to roll up your sleeves to expose your forearms, keeping the elbow covered. Women should wear an *abaya* with minimal decoration. Western women who don't often wear a headscarf in Saudi Arabia during the rest of the year may find it more comfortable wearing one during Ramadan in more venues.

More information about the dress code for all visitors and expatriates are detailed in relevant Sections throughout this book.

Ramadan and business

As in public, the rules of fasting, public behaviour and the dress code apply in a business environment as well. Ramadan is not generally a good time to travel to Saudi Arabia for business from an efficiency perspective, unless the nature of your trip is so important that it can't wait. A good way to look at Ramadan is as a time where business should be kept ticking over, but not a time to expect to make important business decisions, implement a new policy or programme, conduct training, or formally establish a brand new business relationship.

During Ramadan, Saudi Arabia often seems to function in reverse time to the rest of the year. People who are fasting can become lethargic and often grumpy during the day, but lively during the night. And as many people tend to stay up throughout much of the night, they may be tired when they arrive in the office the next morning. You should plan the pace of your business accordingly.

If you are an expatriate resident in Saudi Arabia, it is still important to set your expectations for lower efficiency during Ramadan. Businesses will set their hours so that Muslim employees work a schedule does not exceed six hours. In practice, many people work significantly less than this, especially if they have been celebrating during most of the evening and into the late night hours.

If you are working in the Kingdom during Ramadan, one way to join in the festivities and to perhaps enhance business relationships is to participate in an *iftar*, which is the meal eaten at sunset to break the fast.

Iftars are elaborate and are held in all of the major top end hotels. As a guest, it is an honour to attend an *iftar*. As a host, an *iftar* can be an excellent event to sponsor for important clients and business partners with whom you wish to strengthen your business relationship. It's also possible to make new connections.

Iftars can also include extended family and friends, who may be breaking their fast at home or in a restaurant. *Iftars* are also held and hosted by charities for the poor in several public venues such as parks and near mosques.

Contrary to logic, many people actually gain weight during Ramadan, especially if they are partaking in too many *iftar* celebrations.

Finally, it is important to take note that most shopping malls and other retail outlets will only reopen during Ramadan after the *iftar* is over. This is usually about 90 minutes after sunset. They will generally stay open until the early hours of the morning.

The Islamic calendar

Definition and how it works

The Islamic world has its own calendar; it is known as the *hijri* calendar. The *hijri* starts when the Prophet Mohammed fled or migrated from Mecca in the seventh century. It corresponds to 16th July 622 in the Western Gregorian calendar.

The *hijri* operates on lunar cycles. There are twelve lunar months in the *hijri* calendar. Days begin and end at sunset. Each month starts and ends when the new moon is spotted at sunset. Thus, *hijri* months are typically twenty-nine or thirty days long. As a result, the Islamic year is ten to eleven days shorter per year than the Western calendar.

In early October 2016, it became the year 1438 AH in the Islamic calendar. AH is used in a similar to using AD in the Gregorian calendar; AH comes from the Latin anno Hegirae (*Hijri* year).

Important Islamic dates and holidays

Islamic religious holidays correspond to dates in the Islamic calendar. Because it is not in synchronisation with the Western calendar, Islamic holidays will occur ten to eleven days earlier than in the previous year.

It is not possible with complete precision to predict the date on which an Islamic holiday falls until shortly before the actual date. This is because traditional rituals are used in spite of the availability of more accurate modern technology as it is believed to more accurately reflect the will of Allah.

Ramadan is a case in point. The start of Ramadan is observed by a physical sighting of the new moon on the 29th day of the 8th month of the Islamic calendar. If it is seen, Ramadan begins the following day; if it is not seen, then there is one more full day before Ramadan starts. Thus, religious holidays in particular will only be officially declared shortly before the actual dates. They may also vary slightly from country to country, as each country recognises their own religious authorities.

Here are the names and a brief description of Islam's religious holidays that are most likely to impact the Western business professional:

Islamic New Year occurs on *1 Muharram*, the first day of the first month of the Islamic calendar. It is a normal work day in Saudi Arabia.

Mawlid is the Prophet Mohammed's birthday. Sunnis recognise this holiday on *12 Rabi al-awwal*, the third month of the Islamic calendar. However, as *Salafists* do not generally recognise birthdays, this is a normal business day in Saudi Arabia, although some other Saudis may discretely observe the date in private.

The entire month of *Ramadan* is a special time in the Islamic calendar. Ramadan is discussed in further detail in relevant sections throughout this book.

Eid al Fitr is held on *1 –3 Shawwal*. It is a public holiday throughout the Islamic world, including Saudi Arabia, and immediately follows Ramadan. *Eid al Fitr* is a time of feasting and celebration. Many people will buy new clothes to mark the festivities, with special attention paid to children. It is the smaller of the two Eid holidays and may also be known as Sweet or Sugar Feast.

The *Hajj* is held on 8-10 *Dhu al-Hijjah*, and is described throughout this book.

Eid al Adha starts immediately after the Hajj has completed descent from Mount Ararat at the end of the Hajj, and lasts for four days in Saudi Arabia, although it is not unusual for some organisations in Saudi Arabia to declare a longer Eid break during some years. *Eid al Adha* is also known as the Big Eid or the Feast of the Sacrifice. Traditionally, a sheep, goat or camel is slaughtered, with the meat distributed between family, friends and the poor. It's also another time when people will wear their finest clothing.

Other important dates

The Saudi National Holiday is a fixed public holiday and falls on 23rd September each year. It may be celebrated on the nearest working day if it falls on a weekend day.

No other public holidays are recognised in Saudi Arabia.

SECTION 4

PREPARING FOR TRAVEL TO SAUDI ARABIA

HUMAN RESOURCES
AND DIVERSITY ISSUES

It is important to understand that Saudi Arabia has very different views toward diversity, inclusion and tolerance that have become familiar to employees and their management in most European, North American and other Western environments. For some, the biggest challenge to working in Saudi Arabia is not the weather, the dress code or the pace of work but ethical and moral challenges, especially when they clash directly with an individual's personal beliefs.

Employees and employers alike should understand the practicalities of working and living in Saudi Arabia, as there are very specific behavioural expectations for all visitors and expatriates living in the Kingdom.

Practical considerations for employers

EU, UK, US and other Western employment laws do not apply in Saudi Arabia. Whilst an employer may wish to implement an open policy driven by merit and experience, this may not always be possible to implement for anyone travelling to or living in Saudi Arabia. Careful consideration must be given to what HR policies are put into place if an otherwise qualified employee cannot or will not work in Saudi Arabia.

In addition, the definition of an expatriate remuneration package must be taken into account. In recent years, the Saudi Arabian economy has been robust. Even with the recent volatility in the oil industry and the impact of the *nitaqat* or Saudisation programme where Saudi nationals are favoured over others, expatriate amenities are often in short supply. This is especially true for suitable accommodation in Western orientated compounds and in the schools.

Although it is impossible to anticipate all problems that could be encountered for work in Saudi Arabia, it is important to understand the most common issues for employees working in the Kingdom.

Age

It is commonplace for Saudis to discriminate on the basis of age. Jobs are often advertised for people of a specific age range; candidates not falling into this age range will most probably never be considered no matter what other qualifications they may have for the job.

Employers must be aware that candidates for secondment in the Kingdom must be less than 60 years old. Older candidates are unlikely to successfully complete the process for a residency visa, although they may be eligible for a business visa. This removes the possibility of living in the Kingdom but will allow them to work for short periods of time.

Women are successfully applying for Saudi visit, business and residency visas in their own right more than they ever have before. However, it remains difficult for women under the age of 30 to obtain a visa to the Kingdom. Young women intending to work in Saudi Arabia should ensure they have a job title that indicates high professional status and responsibility to increase their chances of success, as well as ideally having a sponsor who strongly advocates their presence in the Kingdom.

Gender

As mentioned above, it has become commonplace to see Western businesswomen in Saudi Arabia. However, employers and women themselves do need to be aware that this is a recent change from just a few years ago when businesswomen were rare on the ground.

Women should be aware that there are many practicalities that are different in Saudi Arabia to any other country, including other Middle East countries. This includes a strict adherence to the dress code, which includes wearing an *abaya* and at times, wearing a headscarf as well. More detailed information about the dress code can be found in a following Section.

Happily, more Saudis than ever are supporting the presence of businesswomen. A woman can be sure she can work successfully in the Kingdom as her sponsor is responsible for facilitating her visa in the first place.

However, we must keep in mind that public behaviour expectations are modest and genders have been segregated until very recently (and still are in some situations). Whether we like it or not as women, we are still being judged by our behaviour and if it becomes uncomfortable for too many Saudi men, it could easily jeopardise future prospects of us being able to continue to work effectively in the Kingdom.

Religion

Saudis expect everyone to have a faith. Agnosticism and atheism make Saudis feel very uncomfortable, as if you declared yourself an immoral person simply by a lack of faith. Thus, it is strongly recommended that all visitors to Saudi Arabia refrain from directly challenging these faith issues. This begins at the visa application process, where questions will be asked about the applicant's faith. It is prudent to enter a specific faith, although there are cases where Westerners have been successful in obtaining a visa simply by declaring 'non-Muslim'.

Westerners are generally expected to be Christian – Christian is enough, with no need to specify any further detail – unless their name makes it clear they are likely to have a different faith.

Whilst there is no specific taboo against Jewish visitors to Saudi Arabia, there are increased chances of visa applications being denied for applicants declaring Judaism as their faith. This is distinct from Israeli passport holders, who are not eligible to travel to Saudi Arabia on their Israeli passport.

Muslim Westerners may have some difficulties applying for a business or visit visa in the lead-up to the Hajj. Those who already have a visa will also be restricted from some travel to Jeddah during the same time period.

People of all religious faiths other than Islam must understand that they cannot enter Saudi Arabia with any religious books, artefacts, jewellery, etc.

Nationality

It is an unpleasant reality that the Saudi job market discriminates by nationality. There is a strong expectation that certain jobs are performed by certain nationalities and not by others. Whilst nationals of Western countries, tend to benefit from mostly highly paid, prestigious jobs, most other nationalities do not.

In addition, some Western nationalities are held in higher regard than others, further complicating a number of HR issues. As a rule of thumb, passport holders of countries in North America, Antipodes, or European countries that were in the European Union (adding Switzerland, Norway, and Iceland) prior to EU expansion in 2004 are held in higher regard than other Western nationalities. South Africans can fall somewhere in the middle. Dual nationals should use the passport that gives them the highest status within the Kingdom if at all possible.

Nationality can impact anything from the speed of obtaining a visa to the conditions and duration of the visa. Nationality also has a very strong correlation to pay and other remuneration benefits.

Visible diversity

There are times that Saudi Arabia can be challenged by 'visible diversity'. This can mean anything from someone holding a nationality that does not match their expectations to physical disability. Common examples of the former include Westerners who are also visible ethnic minorities in their home country or mixed race people. Examples of the latter include people who may be deaf, dependent on a wheel chair, or have acute healthcare requirements.

Although times are changing and there is increased tolerance, travellers to Saudi Arabia should be prepared that, on occasion, people who are visibly different may experience occasional unpleasant behaviour or unwanted attention, at least until they work out their nationality.

Practical considerations for employees considering business travel to Saudi Arabia

Many short term visitors are willing to look at many of these issues in a flexible way, showing their own ability to be tolerant of an intolerant situation. For example, gay employees often choose to hide their sexuality, including for the purposes of small talk, referring to family in the vaguest of terms. In another example, the female author drives everywhere else in the Middle East and would do so in Saudi Arabia as well if she could but reluctantly accepts her reliance on drivers.

Whilst there is no one correct approach to these issues, it is strongly advised that all business travellers to Saudi Arabia consider that changes in attitude are often gained more effectively in slow increments. The author has personally seen a massive difference in attitudes toward businesswomen in the Kingdom that are real progress compared to conditions on the ground – and in Saudi minds - in the 1990s.

Additional considerations for employees considering an assignment in Saudi Arabia

In addition to the information describe earlier in this section, employees who are considering an expatriate secondment may wish to take into account additional factors about life in Saudi Arabia before making their decision.

Sponsorship rights and restrictions as defined by the Saudi authorities can be in conflict with many Western lifestyles. These include the following:

Partnerships

Westerners considering a secondment in Saudi Arabia will generally qualify to be able to sponsor their partner, children and household help whilst on their residency visa. A main qualification is they are paid at least a certain amount per month, which is achieved by nearly all Westerners and is stated in their employment contract.

However, the only partnership recognised by the Saudi authorities is a heterosexual, married couple who can produce a marriage licence. Although the days of carrying around a marriage licence in the Kingdom when men and women are out in public together is not longer routinely necessary, producing a marriage licence is mandatory in order to sponsor your spouse to live with you in Saudi Arabia.

Gay marriages and civil partnership ceremonies are not recognised in Saudi Arabia. Unmarried couples in any gender combination are not recognised. This applies to everyone falling into one of these categories, including couples with children.

Children

Western expatriates have the right to sponsor their children to live with them in Saudi Arabia as above, although there may be some instances where they may not wish to do so. From a practical perspective, they may have accepted an assignment in an area of the Kingdom that does not have other expatriate children living nearby. The opposite problem is also common, where there are so many children that the expatriate family is unable to secure a place in an acceptable expatriate school. Yet others may have concerns about special needs children who may not get the services they require in the Kingdom.

Another consideration is with older children. Although younger children tend to adapt well to a new culture, some older children do not, especially if it is their first experience living abroad. Unlike younger children, some teenagers may find life more difficult in Saudi Arabia, especially if they are used to a level of autonomy back home that is unsuitable or impractical in the Kingdom. Others worry about rebellious children who might be testing their boundaries, especially as regards social matters such as sex and drugs (and rock 'n roll).

Finally, it must be noted that it is very difficult to sponsor boys over the age of 18 in the Kingdom unless they are in full time education or a few other exceptions that are unlikely to apply to Westerners. Family visit visas for an older child can be obtained, but they can take a long time to be processed. Older daughters can be sponsored beyond the age of 18 unless they marry.

Health issues

There are no specific health checks for short term visitors to Saudi Arabia, although a good travel or employee insurance plan is strongly advised to cover the entire country. Do keep in mind that travel to any part of the Kingdom that is included in an official government advisory from your home country may make your insurance invalid.

However, for employees considering an assignment to live in Saudi Arabia, they must be aware and be prepared to submit to a health examination that tests for a number of conditions. If any of these conditions are found to exist – including indication of pregnancy for unmarried women - then a residency visa will not be granted in most circumstances. These conditions include: HIV/AIDS, liver function, syphilis, tuberculosis, Hepatitis A,B,C, bilharzia antibodies, malaria antibodies, and a pregnancy test for women. Married women who are pregnant remain eligible for a residency visa. All expatriates must have private health insurance as a condition of their residency visa to cover all family members, including any sponsored domestic help.

BASIC TRAVEL PREPARATION
FOR ALL TRAVELLERS TO
SAUDI ARABIA

Getting ready

Travelling to Saudi Arabia should not be considered as arduous as, say, India. However, there are some precautions and sensible planning tips that can make your journey to the Kingdom more pleasant.

Health and jabs

Western business professionals who are preparing for short term travel to Saudi Arabia should consult with their government's official website for health advice about travel to Saudi Arabia. The World Health Organisation website also has useful information. Expatriate residents should also refer to the Daily Living Section for the more extensive list of requirements applicable to them.

The usual precautions should be taken for hepatitis, tetanus, typhoid, and rabies. Although most of Saudi Arabia is outside a malarial zone, there is a published risk of malaria in the border areas with Yemen, including Jizan and Najran. There is no yellow fever anywhere in Saudi Arabia. However, you should be prepared to show a yellow fever certificate if you are arriving from an affected country in Africa or South America.

Middle East Respiratory Syndrome, known by the acronym MERS, was first identified in Saudi Arabia in 2012 and is thought to be a viral infection somehow associated with camels. Although there is no known vaccine, it is believed that transmission to humans is low unless in the prolonged presence of camels or in very close contact with someone who has been.

Western business professionals must ensure they have sufficient medical coverage for travel to Saudi Arabia. It is a requirement for all expatriate residents in their terms of employment and residency. Medical facilities geared toward and used by Western expatriates in Riyadh, Jeddah and the Eastern Province are of excellent standard, with most medical staff trained in the West and who speak excellent English. Standards of hygiene are high.

The weather

It is not always hot in Saudi Arabia! In fact, it gets downright cold in the desert in the winter. This includes evenings in Riyadh. It can snow in the mountains in the northwest and southwest of the country. The winter months are pleasant in Jeddah and the Eastern Province.

In the summer months, it can easily reach 50C, with high humidity on both coasts as well. It remains in the mid 30s throughout the night. Riyadh and other cities at higher elevation are often several degrees cooler and usually at lower humidity.

Most rain falls in the winter months, usually between December and February, although some years may not see any significant rain at all in parts of the Kingdom.

Sand storms can occur in Saudi Arabia, often in the spring months. They generally originate from Iraq and work their way south, often affecting the Eastern Province and Riyadh. Sandstorms are generally less frequent in Jeddah and along the Red Sea Coast.

It is important for both men and women to dress for the weather. Clothing made of breathable fabric that lets the air circulate, such as cotton and linen, are a great idea. Women should choose a lightweight *abaya* for warmer temperatures and give consideration as to what to wear (or not!) under her *abaya*. Everyone should note that, even when the weather is extremely hot outside, Saudi buildings are typically air conditioned to a very cool temperature – to the point where a jumper might be appreciated.

What not to pack

Whilst the Saudi authorities no longer search every camera or storage device, it is important to remember that they can do so at any time if they so choose. Thus, it is important not to draw unnecessary attention to yourself in the first place if you wish to avoid an ad hoc inspection.

Pork, pork products and alcohol must not be brought into the Kingdom. Other items that are banned include any religious artefacts of all descriptions from any religion other than Islam and pornography. It is important to keep in mind that the definition of pornography may differ quite significantly from that of the West and may even include something found in the magazine or newspaper you purchased for the journey at your home airport.

Men should avoid wearing any article of clothing that could be perceived to be military, including camouflage designs, and should never wear any T-shirt containing military content or anything politically or socially contentious. (Women are already covered up by the *abaya*).

Although mobile phones including smart phones are perfectly fine to bring into the Saudi Arabia, it would be wise to leave satellite phones, binoculars, professional specification cameras and powerful camera lenses at home. In fact, bringing in even a basic camera for personal use is not always a good idea as photography is generally regarded with suspicion in most of the Kingdom. You can use the camera in your phone discretely if you must.

Do keep in mind that all baggage, both checked and hand luggage, are x-rayed upon leaving the airport throughout Saudi Arabia.

Toilets, tampons and tummy troubles

First time visitors to Saudi Arabia who have also never travelled outside of the West may encounter toilets different to what they are used to for the first time. Squat toilets happily co-exist alongside Western toilets in most public venues, including airports and shopping malls. They are also found in many office buildings, especially those that are older.

Women who are expecting to frequent squat toilets should seriously consider their choice of clothing. Whilst trousers are often a sensible choice of clothing under her *abaya* in Saudi Arabia, they are not very practical when confronted with a squat toilet, especially one that hasn't seen a cleaning brush or bleach for a while. Footwear should also be carefully considered, in part because you will need to have a good sense of balance.

However, sit down toilets in Saudi Arabia are also different to those found in the West. Firstly, most sewer and septic systems are simply not equipped to accept loo roll. Forget about disposing tampons, sanitary towels or anything else down the toilet. Instead, a bin will be found near the toilet, usually placed on the left side when sitting that is meant for used loo roll (and the rest). Visitors should also follow this convention, as toilets will otherwise quickly become blocked.

Secondly, loo roll is not always found in toilets in the Kingdom regardless of style. This is because it is traditional to attend to personal cleanliness with the left hand and water. In fact, many people from the region actually consider the use of loo roll to be unsanitary! If you do not prefer to adapt to traditional Saudi hygiene practices in the toilet, you may want to consider carrying an emergency supply of loo roll or tissue with you at all times.

Thirdly, many toilets in the Middle East do not flush as robustly as they do in the West. Both squat and sit down toilets may also come equipped with a bucket – not to be confused with the refuse bin. There will also be a tap mounted on the wall of the loo. This bucket should be filled with water that is available from the handily supplied tap. Simply dump the water down the toilet – gravity will take care of the rest. Repeat as required.

Western businesswomen should carry an emergency supply of tampons or sanitary towels with them to Saudi Arabia, even if you do not expect to be menstruating during your visit. Tampons may not always be available in remote areas of the Kingdom.

Whilst tampons are generally available throughout the major cities, it's possible you might need them on a Friday morning, when all of the shops are closed, including hotel gift shops. If this does happen to you, it is highly recommended that you find a female or other sympathetic employee of your hotel to make a discrete request for assistance.

Most Western business professionals should not have any health problems related to tummy troubles whilst travelling in Saudi Arabia if they follow good standards of hygiene and use their common sense. In general, tap water is safe to drink throughout Saudi Arabia, although its taste may be unpalatable as much of the water is desalinated. For this reason, bottled water is strongly recommended, although using the tap for cleaning your teeth is unlikely to make most visitors ill.

Most Western business professionals who are prone to tummy troubles due to water or unfamiliar food would be wise to carry their favourite remedy with them into Saudi Arabia, but only after checking that the item is not banned for importation. For example, never bring a codeine based product into the Kingdom. If you are unsure, it is always safe leave them at home and to go to a Saudi chemist, who will provide you with an over the counter medication for your tummy troubles.

Money

The Saudi Riyal

The Saudi Riyal is the official currency of Saudi Arabia. It is officially pegged to the US Dollar and is fully convertible abroad. There are 100 halalas to the riyal, although they are not commonly used. It is important to confirm that only current banknotes are accepted as previous series will not be accepted.

Official rates of exchange:

1 US Dollar = 3.75320 Saudi Riyal

1 Saudi Riyal (SAR) = 0.26644 US Dollar (USD)

Riyal banknotes are issued in denominations of 1, 5, 10, 20, 50, 100, 200, 500 riyals. There are halala coins in denominations of 5, 10, 25, 50, and 100 halala.

Travellers Cheques

Travellers cheques should be considered a thing of the past; they are not used in Saudi Arabia.

ATMs

It is recommended that Western business professionals use ATMs in Saudi Arabia for their cash requirements. In addition to being safe, withdrawing funds from an ATM abroad often yields a better exchange rate than for cash. Travellers should ensure that their bank does not charge additional fees for using their bank cards abroad as this could negate exchange rate benefits, especially if ATMs are used frequently for relatively small withdrawals.

Many Saudi ATMs provide services in Arabic and English. For those travellers who already have an account at HSBC, the Saudi bank SABB is HSBC's presence in the Kingdom.

Customers can often withdraw substantially larger amounts from ATMs than they may be able to back home, assuming your bank balance is healthy. They will be in good working order, and will be found pretty much everywhere you would expect.

Acceptance of bank cards

The acceptance of credit and debit cards varies throughout Saudi Arabia. In general, most hotels, restaurants and Western shopping centres accept bank cards with the same level of enthusiasm found in most of the West, especially in Riyadh, Jeddah and the Eastern province, where most expatriates work and live. Very traditional shopping establishments, such as in the few remaining *souqs*, small family owned businesses, and in smaller provincial cities, towns and settlements may only accept cash.

Visa and Mastercard are generally accepted in equal measure. Chip and pin has arrived in Saudi Arabia. Make sure you know your pin number, and make sure it works abroad; check with your bank if in doubt. Cirrus, Plus, Pulse and Maestro are all recognised debit card associations, and are usually accepted in Saudi Arabia as well. At the time of publication, most credit cards issued by American banks have not yet adopted the chip and pin system, although some debit cards include a chip. Americans should ensure they have at least one bank card that works on the global chip and pin system.

Travellers will struggle to use American Express or Diners Club cards (which are not technically bank cards) except in Western owned establishments such as chain hotels or a few other high spend locations. The American card Discover is not accepted in the Middle East.

Foreign bank card holders may be asked if they wish to complete a transaction in Saudi riyals or in their home currency. It is generally advisable to choose Saudi riyals, but check with your bank if foreign transaction fees negate any gain from the merchant's exchange rate on offer.

Bureaux de change

Using bureaux de change in Saudi Arabia is possible for anyone wishing to convert cash in another currency to Saudi riyals. There will be no problem changing US dollars, euros, British pounds, or other GCC currencies into local currency. Western business professionals coming from Australia, Canada, New Zealand, South Africa or from a European country outside of the Euro zone should consider carrying one of the currencies listed above prior to arriving in the Kingdom, as they may suffer from poor exchange rates. Exchange rates vary. As usual, hotel rates are often worse than kiosks or banks, but not always.

Be careful with the quality of the bank notes you plan to exchange, as many bureaux de change and merchants will not accept notes that are torn, excessively worn, or written on. Generally, large denomination bank notes in pristine condition are best. It is always recommended that the traveller obtains a receipt for their transaction.

As a general rule, although most bureaux de change in the Middle East will readily exchange other GCC currencies, they are less likely to accept currencies from elsewhere in the Middle East and will probably refuse to exchange non-convertible currencies from the region, including Egyptian and Syrian pounds.

Personal communication and technology

Laptops, data storage and personal entertainment devices
Saudi Arabia will allow the Western business professional to temporarily import laptops, data storage devices such as external hard drives or memory sticks, iPods, iPads and other tablets. Business professionals are unlikely to be stopped for further inspection upon arrival or departure, unless it appears that you have an inordinately high number of items that it could appear you intend to resell them. In addition, it is always a good idea not to attract too much attention from the authorities wherever possible. For example, carrying a dodgy magazine may prompt a more thorough search through all of your luggage, as would the strong smell of alcohol on your breath.

Mobile phones and smart phones
Saudi Arabia is a subscriber to the GSM 900/1800 standard. This is the same system in use throughout the West, with the notable exceptions of the United States and Canada.

Mobile phones are ubiquitous throughout Saudi Arabia, including amongst service employees such as drivers and maids. They are also a status symbol, with many people using customised, blingy devices. Smart phones are popular amongst everyone who can afford them. 4G services have been enabled for several years.

In general, mobile phone coverage is excellent throughout Saudi Arabia, including all population centres and along the roads connecting them. People travelling into the desert may not always get a signal once they are away from the road, depending on exactly where they go. Signal quality is generally excellent, often better than in some Western countries.

At the time of publication, the main mobile phone service providers in Saudi Arabia are STC (Saudi Telecom Company), Mobily and Zain. All provide roaming services that will depend in part on your home carrier. It's always a good idea to check with your home service provider before you travel to learn what services and roaming charges you will encounter when using your mobile phone abroad.

Many Western business professionals who plan to visit Saudi Arabia on a regular basis should consider obtaining either a second mobile phone or at least a local SIM card. Both options provide the business professional with a local or regional mobile telephone number. In addition to greatly reducing roaming charges, which can be very expensive, having a local telephone number shows your commitment to the region. Not only are your local contacts are much more likely to call you on your local number, but it also looks good on a business card. It is possible to purchase a SIM card without an *iqama* or residency visa. The retailer will simply use your id number hand written in your passport on your business visa page at immigration to register your SIM onto the system.

Internet access

Internet access is reasonably open in Saudi Arabia; much more so than in China for example, where many popular websites used by business professionals are routinely blocked. In general, websites are blocked in Saudi Arabia if they are anti-Islamic, anti-royal family or anti-government, or are considered to be pornographic as defined by the local authorities. Saudi Arabia may also block websites that reference alcohol, gambling, some music and other forms of entertainment, the promotion of religions other than Islam, homosexuality, most political websites, and any website promoting Israel or having an Israeli website domain name ending in *.co.il. On the other hand, many Saudis are enthusiastic users of social media, most of which are open to use in the Kingdom. They have also found many clever ways around many internet restrictions.

For the Western business professional, the use of proxy websites (and robust security) should be considered if access is important when travelling to Saudi Arabia.

Monitoring communications

The author is not in a position to make official comments about the monitoring policies of communications in Saudi Arabia. However, a very good policy is to assume that all of your communications may be monitored by the local authorities and possibly other interested parties at any time during your visit to the Kingdom. For those Western business professionals who are particularly concerned about this issue, it is strongly recommended that you seek the advice of reputable organisations that supply professional standards of security measures.

Mains terminators/electrical plugs

Historically, Saudi Arabia has used both a 127V and the 220V/230V/240V systems. Plug configurations in common use are North American, British and Continental terminators. In 2010, the Saudi authorities announced that, over the next 25 years, the electrical standard throughout the country will be 230V.

From a practical point of view, expect to find the following pattern: The American system is more prevalent in the Eastern Province. The British system is more prevalent in and around Riyadh. The European system is more prevalent in and around Jeddah.

It would be wise to travel with an assortment of adapters that can be used for all common mains socket styles.

Surge protectors

Power surges can occur throughout Saudi Arabia, particularly if it rains. It is strongly advised that all Western business professionals have a plan to protect their electronic devices when travelling to the region. Surge protectors are strongly recommended if you are unsure of the quality of the power supplies you will be using, including in your hotel or compound.

Your passport

There are a few common sense preparations the Western business professional should consider before travelling to Saudi Arabia. Your passport should have plenty of blank pages, as your visa will require two full pages of your passport every time a new visa is issued. Your passport will be stamped each time you enter and leave Saudi Arabia.

Saudi Arabia also requires that your passport is valid for a further six months after the end of your visit to Saudi Arabia. If your passport is getting close to its expiry date, it would be wise to renew it prior to applying for your Saudi visa.

Your passport should also be in reasonably good physical condition. Passports that are excessively worn or have pages that are beginning to peel, especially on the page with your photograph or around the biodata chip, may attract extra attention and could be cause for further investigation at passport control. If the authorities are not satisfied with your passport, you could be refused entry.

You *must not* have any evidence of having travelled to Israel or even the intention of future travel to Israel when travelling to Saudi Arabia or even applying for a Saudi visa. Although recently the Israeli authorities have stopped routine stamping of passports at their airport, there is no guarantee that this practice will continue.

Travellers must also *not* travel overland between Israel and either Jordan or Egypt, where a stamp from either of these countries showing entry from a shared Israeli land border is also considered evidence of travel to Israel. This applies to Egypt's Taba crossing as well as Jordan's crossings at Aqaba and at the Sheikh Hussein Bridge (not to be confused with the King Hussein/Allenby Bridge). There are special circumstances in play at the Allenby Bridge crossing which *may* allow some travellers to circumvent this problem, but only with expert advice and only if they are also lucky.

Many countries, including the UK and US, allow their citizens to carry a second passport that will allow them to enter Israel on a passport separate to the passport they use for Saudi Arabia. Dual nationals often choose to use the nationality that is easier to travel on to Saudi Arabia and throughout the Middle East, using their other nationality for entry into Israel. It is important to note that it is illegal to have two passports whilst in Saudi Arabia, making this a risky option. If the business professional chooses to take this risk, they must always keep the two passports separate and never let the Saudi authorities discover the second passport.

Finally, anyone who was born in Israel will be automatically denied entry to Saudi Arabia, even if you are a citizen of another country. The author does not have any advice as to how to circumvent this issue.

Choosing a flight

There are ever expanding choices of flights to Saudi Arabia, both direct and with convenient connections. Common factors in choosing a flight include cost, available classes of service, reputation of the carrier's customer service, frequent flyer programmes and alliances, and convenience of flight schedule departures and arrivals. It may also be dictated by your company's travel policy.

Who should I fly with to and from Saudi Arabia?
Western business professionals have a choice of European, Middle Eastern and Asian and African carriers when travelling to Saudi Arabia.

Saudia is the Kingdom's national carrier and flies from most European capitals as well as to a few North American east coast cities and from a number of destinations in Asia and Africa. Travellers should be aware that no alcohol is served on Saudia regardless of destination. They should also be aware that if the flight contains many people who wish to pray, the toilets can become so wet from *wudu* that they are effectively unusable.

Many Middle East carriers, including Emirates, Etihad and Qatar, enjoy some of the best reputations in the sky, with attentive, luxurious service in premium classes and a tolerable way to fly in economy, at least for routes serving Europe, North America and Australia. Most of these carriers also include ground transport as a benefit of first and business class service at departure and arrival airports. This means the Western business professional will be collected from their home or office on both ends of their journey, thus eliminating the hassle of organising transport to and from the airport. All three carriers continue to expand their network, including long haul flights into an increasing number of North American cities. For those Western business professionals choosing a Gulf airline, they will undoubtedly enjoy an experience superior to that offered on a North American carrier.

Middle East carriers based in the Levant and Turkey have had a long history of serving Saudi Arabia, connecting to some North American destinations as well as the main European capitals and business destinations through their home countries. Service reputations vary from acceptable to 'avoid wherever possible'.

Some Western business travellers prefer to fly on their national carrier or on a carrier that supports their favoured frequent flyer programme. Choices abound.

First time visitors to Saudi Arabia and anyone travelling to Saudi Arabia on a new visa *must fly* into the city listed on their visa application. Most Western business travellers enter via Riyadh or Jeddah; some enter through the Dammam airport. Visitors with multiple entry visas can return to Saudi Arabia through any airport that handles international traffic. They can also make a subsequent return visit on the same visa over the King Fahd Causeway from Bahrain.

Finally, it is strongly advised that Western business professionals consider flexible airfares, as the nature of some business in Saudi Arabia will routinely include the need to stay in the region later than originally planned.

Flights within Saudi Arabia

Both Saudia and Flynas fly to major cities and regions within Saudi Arabia. Saudia, the full service national carrier, covers the widest range of domestic destinations. Flynas is a popular, Saudi based budget carrier that continues to expand its service to domestic and regional destinations. It works similar to airlines such as easyjet.

Are there any times I shouldn't go to Saudi Arabia?

There are generally fewer travellers to Saudi Arabia during the summer months. Although unpleasant from a weather perspective, the main reasons are that many decision makers are not in the Kingdom, making business travel less necessary. In addition, many expatriates take advantage by also leaving the Kingdom for their main holidays during this time.

However, there is another time that business travellers should take into account when planning a trip to Saudi Arabia. In the lead-up to the Hajj, although it is business as usual from a commercial perspective, logistically, millions of pilgrims are travelling to the Kingdom. For approximately six weeks, there is a steady increase in traffic, first to Jeddah and, once these routes have reached capacity, then to other major gateway Saudi cities. This means that flights are full or very expensive, as are many hotels, especially in Jeddah.

It is also important to note that anyone flying to Jeddah at this time must prove they either hold a *Hajj* visa or, if they are travelling on a business visa, that they are *not* Muslim. This procedure has been put into place by the Saudi authorities to prevent Muslim visitors from travelling into the Kingdom for reasons at cross purposes with business and the *Hajj*. This policy can easily impact Western Muslim business travellers, who may find it very difficult to work in Jeddah during this time. Western Muslim business travellers may continue to enter Saudi Arabia through the Riyadh airport as per usual during this six week period.

PREPARING TO TRAVEL SHORT TERM TO SAUDI ARABIA

Travel to Saudi Arabia is never straightforward. It is important to be prepared from both a bureaucratic and a practical perspective. The following information is accurate at the time of research. It is always prudent to double check any travel requirements and advice for any changes that may have occurred since this book was published. It is believed that the following information will be useful to all travellers to the Kingdom even if prices have risen or a formality has changed.

Obtaining a visa

Although some of the information pertaining to obtaining a visa to Saudi Arabia is also discussed in the Human Resources and Diversity section, the information provided in this section will describe the visa process in greater detail.

All visitors and residents to Saudi Arabia, other than GCC nationals, require a visa in advance of travel to Saudi Arabia. Visas must be sponsored by a Saudi national and approved by the Ministry of Foreign Affairs (MFA).

Visa types
Visa types can be categorised as work related or non-work related visas. Although limited numbers of tourist visas have been issued in the past, non-religious tourist visas are not being issued at the present time. An occasional exception can be found through some specialised agencies offering very high cost tours that are often organised around an academic, cultural or other educational justification.

Work related visa types for short term visitors

Visit visas

The main types of work related visas available to business travellers to Saudi Arabia include a commercial visa, short term working business visa, and work visa. A work visa is generally issued with the right to apply for a residency visa for the worker and certain family members for most Westerners.

1. Commercial visa

   A commercial visa allows the business traveller to enter Saudi Arabia for the specific purpose of attending business meetings and similar. They do not allow the visitor to perform a job that is located in Saudi Arabia, such as filling in for a business colleague who is on holiday.

   Single or multiple entry business visit visas may be granted by the Saudi authorities. It does not always matter what you have requested on your visa application form. Business visit visas are often granted for 180 - 730 days, although there are many instances where they have been granted for only 30 or 90 days. Others have received business visas for longer than 180 days, but not very often in recent times, other than some US American passport holders. Your nationality often has an influence on what duration you receive, with many but not all Western nationalities benefitting from longer visa validity than most other nationalities. Anecdotally, so does evidence of previous trouble-free visits.

   Business visits are usually restricted to 30 - 90 days per visit, even for people who have obtained a multiple entry visa. Never exceed the 30 day limit per visit or you could become ineligible for future visas to the Kingdom. It is possible to leave Saudi Arabia for only one day and immediately return, thus starting the next duration of up to the maximum stay.

2. Short term working business visa

   A short term working business visa is more robust, allowing the visitor to work, albeit with limitations, whilst in Saudi Arabia. It is not possible to obtain a residency visa on a short term working business visa. Popular reasons to obtain a short term working visitor visa is for rotational workers such as many employees in oil and gas jobs, consultants on medium term projects, and similar.

Most short term working visitor visas are granted for 180 - 730 days, but with a limit of 30 - 90 days per visit. However, as with a business visit visa, it is crucial to check your individual visa's specific conditions. Never become angry is your visa is different to colleagues who seem to have similar credentials to yours. It is ultimately up to the MFA to determine all visa approvals, rejections and conditions.

Eligibility practicalities for a commercial or short term working business visa

As with so many other elements of Saudi bureaucracy, your chances of obtaining a business visa depends on your personal profile, your connections in the Kingdom and sometimes luck.

Factors that often influence the outcome of a visa application include your age, gender, religion, nationality, job title, employer and the level of enthusiasm of your Saudi sponsor's wish for you to visit Saudi Arabia.

The most important considerations for most Western business travellers are as follow:

Age is not generally a problem if you are between 21 and 60 for a man or between 30 and 60 for a woman. Older travellers are increasingly successful in obtaining a commercial visa.

Very young women may struggle to obtain a visa, although some nationalities may have a better chance than others, especially combined with a very prestigious job title and a sponsor with good connections with the MFA.

Jewish people may struggle to apply successfully for a Saudi visa, even with a Western passport. Jewish people or indeed anyone else with evidence of having travelled to Israel regardless of nationality will be refused a visa. People who officially declare no religion may also run the risk of rejection.

Although Westerners tend to be favoured in Saudi Arabia over most other non-Arab nationalities, some Westerners are regarded differently than others. Do not be surprised if you obtain a more favourable visa if you are North American, Northern or Western European, or

Antipodean. Unfortunately, Eastern Europeans and some Southern African nationalities may not share the same benefits from a bureaucratic perspective, although exceptions certainly exist. People born in Israel are not eligible for a Saudi visa.

The visa application process for a commercial or short term business visa

The application process for either type of business visa is more rigorous than for most other countries. The applicant must first obtain an invitation letter from the Saudi organisation you will be visiting or working with. They will need your passport details. Ideally, it is recommended that the passport page containing your personal details is scanned and sent to the contact through whom the invitation request is being made.

Your passport must be valid for more than six months from the time of travel to Saudi Arabia and must contain at least two fully blank pages face to face that can receive the Saudi visa.

Once the invitation letter has been received from your Saudi sponsor, then several additional steps must be taken. Women should ensure that the Saudi organisation also sends a copy of their CRA, a document declaring their legal trading status that is often required as a part of a businesswoman's visa application.

The next steps are to complete a standard visa application form precisely as instructed (including details such as ink colour) and a visa order form required by the visa processing organisation that is recognised by the Saudi authorities. Your employer must also provide a supporting letter describing why travel to Saudi Arabia is required. This letter must now be officially stamped by the Chamber of Commerce or equivalent organisation in your country of application to validate it. Additionally, applicants must take out medical insurance from an approved Saudi supplier, even if they are already covered by another policy.

It is wise to ensure that the applicant declares a job title with the highest status possible that does not misrepresent the applicant. Make sure that any professional qualifications such as Engineer or Doctor are noted as this will greatly enhance the traveller's chance of a successful application.

Western nationals working and living in other GCC countries must also ensure that their job title on their Saudi visa application matches the job title found in their official documents in their secondment country or they will almost certainly have their Saudi visa application rejected. Other GCC paperwork must be in order, including a minimum of six months remaining on their work or residency visa.

Western nationals working and living in any other country other than the country of their nationality, other than most EU nationals living elsewhere in the EU, should be prepared to prove their legal status in their country of residence. Thus, it is advised that they include a scan of their work or residency visa with their Saudi visa application. They may also be required to present their birth certificate.

The Saudi business visa application also includes many personal questions that most other countries do not require. These include your religion and sect. It is strongly advised that non-Muslim Western business professionals answer 'Christian' for their religion and 'Protestant' or 'Catholic' for their sect. Other Western business professionals have also successfully applied for their visa by answering 'non-Muslim' to these questions. All other personal questions should be answered completely, including the names of relatives requested who are no longer living.

Many visitors can run into difficulties if they state one city on their visa application form as their port of entry but then arrive at a different city during the first use of their visit visa. It is of critical importance that once a visa application has been lodged, entry into the Kingdom is through that city only. Otherwise, it is possible that the traveller will be detained for several hours before their paperwork is sorted out. In some instances, the Saudi immigration authorities may choose to deny entry other than through the originally declared city, necessitating an additional, inconvenient flight.

Entry into Saudi Arabia cannot be made over the King Fahd Causeway from Bahrain for the first use of a Saudi visit visa. However, anyone with a multiple entry Saudi visit visa can enter through any legal airport on subsequent visits, and is also allowed to cross the Causeway as well.

In addition to all of the above, two passport photos and the usual (very expensive) visa application fees are required.

In addition to the visa application, prospective travellers to Saudi Arabia will also be required to sign a declaration form demonstrating that they understand several rules that must be followed for entering the Kingdom, including the fact that smuggling illegal drugs into Saudi Arabia attracts the death penalty.

Time and timing

It is not unusual for first time applicants to receive their visa very shortly before travel to the Kingdom – sometimes within 24 hours of travel. Happily, applicants who travel regularly to Saudi Arabia often see their visa process completed in a matter of a few days.

Caution: It is especially difficult to obtain a business visa in the six week lead up to Hajj. This is because the Saudi authorities are preparing travel documents and other formalities for up to three million pilgrims, all of whom will travel to the Kingdom within a specific band of dates in a short period of time. In general, Hajj pilgrims' travel requirements will take precedence over your business visa application unless your sponsor has sufficient *wasta*, i.e. connections in the appropriate government ministry.

Work visa

A Saudi work visa is required for long term expatriates who will be working in Saudi Arabia permanently for a contracted period of time, often two or three years or even longer. Unlike shorter term visas, bureaucratic requirements for a work visa are substantially more complicated. Details pertaining to a work visa can be found in the Preparing for Daily Living Section of this book.

Non-work related short term visa types

1. *Hajj visa*
   Hajj visas are issued to Muslim visitors who are performing the obligation of Pilgrimage to Mecca and other religious sites during a specific time in the Islamic calendar. This visa is effectively issued for religious duties, restricts where a pilgrim can travel within the Kingdom, and does not permit any work related activities.

2. *Umrah*
   Umrah visa are issued to Muslim visitors who are visiting Mecca and other religious sites during any other time of the year. As for the Hajj visa, this visa is effectively issued for religious reasons, restricts where a pilgrim can travel within the Kingdom, and does not permit any work related activities.

Western Muslim visitors who have entered Saudi Arabia on a Hajj or Umrah visa should never consider working in the Kingdom on either visa.

3. *Family visit visa*

Saudi Arabia does issue visas for close family members of employees who are resident in the Kingdom. However, this visa does not include the right to work. More information can be found in the Daily Living Section of this book.

Visa expiry dates and renewals

It is important to note that all dates are calculated in the Islamic calendar. Although this is straightforward for visas that specify the number of days, it is less so for visas containing monthly or even yearly validity. Thus, a visitor may find that their validity has expired a few days before they thought, especially if they are calculating months or years in the Western calendar. It is strongly advised that visitors do not miscalculate or overstay their visas as the Saudi authorities can penalise, fine or even ban future entries into the Kingdom.

Commercial visas and short term business visas cannot be extended. However, new visas can be applied for if your sponsor has an ongoing need for you to visit the Kingdom. At the time of publication, a new visa can be applied for and obtained once the current visa has less than two weeks' validity.

Although in theory, it should be possible to enter the Kingdom at the end of the visa's validity and stay until the visit validity period is over (typically 30 days), it is not advisable to do so as some Saudi immigration officials may not accept this.

Flight options

There are ever expanding choices of flights to Saudi Arabia, both direct and with convenient connections. Common factors in choosing a flight include cost, available classes of service, reputation of the carrier's customer service, frequent flyer programmes and alliances, and convenience of flight schedule departures and arrivals. It may also be dictated by your company's travel policy.

Who should I fly with to and from Saudi Arabia?

Western business professionals have a choice of European, Middle Eastern and Asian and African carriers when travelling to Saudi Arabia.

Saudia is the Kingdom's national carrier and flies from most European capitals as well as to a few North American east coast cities ns from a number of destinations in Asia and Africa. Travellers should be aware that no alcohol is served on Saudia regardless of destination.

Many Middle East carriers, including Emirates, Etihad and Qatar, enjoy some of the best reputations in the sky, with attentive, luxurious service in premium classes and a tolerable way to fly in economy, at least for routes serving Europe. Most of these carriers also include ground transport as a benefit of first and business class service at departure and arrival airports. This means the Western business professional will be collected from their home or office on both ends of their journey, thus eliminating the hassle of organising transport to and from the airport. All three carriers continue to expand their network, including long haul flights into an increasing number of North American cities. For those Western business professionals choosing a Gulf airline, they will undoubtedly enjoy an experience superior to that offered on a North American carrier.

Middle East carriers based in the Levant and Turkey have had a long history of serving Saudi Arabia, connecting to some North American destinations as well as the main European capitals and business destinations through their home countries. Service reputations vary from acceptable to 'avoid wherever possible'.

Some Western business travellers prefer to fly on their national carrier or on a carrier that supports their favoured frequent flyer programme. Choices abound.

As a reminder, first time visitors to Saudi Arabia and anyone travelling to Saudi Arabia on a new visa *must fly* into the city listed on their visa application. Most Western business travellers enter via Riyadh or Jeddah; some enter through the Dammam airport. Visitors with multiple entry visas can return to Saudi Arabia through any airport that handles international traffic. They can also make a subsequent return visit on the same visa over the King Fahd Causeway from Bahrain.

Finally, it is strongly advised that Western business professionals consider flexible airfares, as the nature of some business in Saudi Arabia will routinely include the need to stay in the region later than originally planned.

Buying an *abaya* for a woman's first visit to Saudi Arabia

All women in Saudi Arabia must dress modestly according to local social conventions, regardless of nationality or religion. This means covering all of the body other than the feet, hands, face and sometimes hair. Although there have been times in the past where a few female visitors have adopted their own style of compliant, modest dress, women now wear the *abaya*, including Western business women.

Women who are planning their first business trip to Saudi Arabia are strongly encouraged to purchase an *abaya* prior to arriving in the Kingdom. Many women may resent this requirement; some women are curious and find the opportunity interesting; yet others simply put up with it. The author suggests that Western businesswomen think of their *abaya* as a 'Saudi business suit' or a uniform.

There are a number of *abaya* styles that denote anything from religious sect to the latest fashion. It is recommended that a visiting businesswoman purchases her first *abaya* in a style that looks like a loose, black dressing gown with wide sleeves rather than an *abaya* that is cut in a tent shape. Most *abayas* found in the West will be of the recommended design.

Some *abayas* are affixed in the front, usually with a series of snaps – these are called open *abayas*. Other *abayas* are sewn up in the front and are worn by placing them over your head, where the garment is cut wide enough and then closed at the neckline – these are called closed *abayas*. Either option is fine.

Abayas are black, although some modern garments contain designs in contrasting colours on a black background. There are very elaborate, 'bling-y' *abayas* that are acceptable in some cities and in some business environments, but not others. It is recommended that a woman's first *abaya* is a modestly designed garment that can be worn throughout the Kingdom. A good example of modest design would be the addition of understated decoration at the end of the sleeves, also in black. An *abaya* is usually purchased with a matching headscarf. Headscarves are also sold separately.

A woman should take two measurements before buying an *abaya*. The first is her circumference at her bust line in centimetres. The second is the distance from her shoulders to the floor – in inches. The second measurement is often found on a label sewn into the *abaya*.

It is beyond the scope of this book to identify *abaya* shops in all major Western cities. However, they are more common than you might think, especially in European cities with large Muslim populations. For example, the author recommends Shepherd's Bush in London. There are stand alone shops along the Uxbridge Road near the Underground station as well as many stalls in Shepherd's Bush market. Other areas include Edgware Road, Upton Park and Whitechapel, although many of these shops in the latter two neighbourhoods sell garments more suitable to the communities of the Indian subcontinent. There are numerous on line shops that sell and ship *abayas* as well.

Visiting businesswomen should carry their *abaya* in their hand luggage on their flight to Saudi Arabia. They can put it on at the end of the flight and thus be ready to enter the Kingdom properly dressed. The author uses the '20 minutes to landing' announcement as the signal to put hers on.

There is additional information about the *abaya* and the dress code for women in the Women's Daily Living Section found later in this book.

Upon arrival – setting expectations

First time visitors to Saudi Arabia are often curious as to what to expect. Some people hear horror stories; others arrive with no previous information – and sometimes no warning, either. Although business travellers' experiences will vary for a number of reasons including when they are travelling, with which flight or carrier, and into which city, it's still advisable to set realistic expectations.

Travellers to Saudi Arabia should note that new terminals are being built in both the Riyadh and Jeddah airports. Thus, information in this section is very likely to change quickly.

In the immigration hall
If you are very lucky, you will arrive at your destination to an empty immigration hall. For most visitors, this is only a dream, although the

Dammam airport can be significantly less busy than Jeddah and Riyadh.

More often, there are large numbers of passengers who have arrived on flights prior to yours and are waiting to reach an immigration officer at passport control. There can be a sense of chaos and a distinct lack of discipline as perceived by visitors from countries with a strong queuing culture.

Saudi airports do not generally operate on a strict first in, first out system. Saudis and often Arab nationals of other countries tend to go to the front of the immigration desks and expect to be processed ahead of anyone else who may already be waiting. Many Saudi authorities monitoring the hall encourage this as well.

Once Saudis are through, then the authorities are very likely to walk through the crowds and choose certain people to advance to the front of the immigration desks. Broadly speaking, this will include a collection of Westerners: single women, families with children, and people who look Western, especially if they are also well dressed. People who are Western but may be considered a visible minority of their country might find it helpful to have their Western passport on clear display in the immigration hall as treatment of Western visible minorities is inconsistent.

The Saudi authorities are also likely to be making a judgement as to your physical condition, including your choice of dress and personal grooming, perceived possibility of intoxication, and your general attitude. Looking the part of a Western business executive can be very advantageous in a crowded hall where it is clear that other less fortunate arrivals have been waiting, sometimes literally for hours. Impatience – never a good trait in Saudi Arabia – is your enemy in the immigration 'queue'.

Entering Saudi Arabia on a new visa

In the Riyadh airport, recent changes mean that there are now separate queues for people who are arriving on a new visa and those who are arriving on a visa that has been previously used. If you are entering on a new visa for the first time, you must join the new visa queue. It doesn't matter if you are a first time visitor to the Kingdom or if you have been travelling to the Kingdom for years. At the time of publication, this was relatively clearly defined at the Riyadh airport, where the new visa queue is to the left when looking directly at the immigration desks.

Entering Saudi Arabia subsequent times on a multiple entry visa

If you have already entered Saudi Arabia at least once before on your current visa and it is a multiple entry or residence visa, then you should join one of the general immigration queues.

At the passport control desk

Once the visitor has reached the passport control desk, the process includes inspecting your visa for validity, and for first time visas, taking an image of your iris, and submitting to a fingerprint scan. Once this is complete, travellers on a visit or business visa will receive a handwritten 10 digit number that serves as an internal identification number whilst in Saudi Arabia. This is usually placed near your visa, along with an entry stamp. Once this is in place, you are ready to proceed to the baggage claim area. There is usually another Saudi authority checking your passport in between the immigration desk and the baggage claim area.

On occasion, single women, especially those at the Riyadh airport, might be asked at this stage where their sponsor is, but not always. Should this happen to you, simply tell the authority that they are waiting for you outside and ideally, be prepared to look like you are about to ring them on your mobile. Western women travelling alone rarely have any further challenges, although this is very different from only a few years ago, where our sponsor or *mahram* (male guardian) was expected to 'collect' us at this point.

Exiting the airport

Travellers with checked luggage will see monitors indicating the baggage carousel number for their flight. Those who wish can use a porter or they can take a trolley if necessary.

All luggage, both checked luggage and hand luggage, is subjected to a final x-ray scan prior to leaving the baggage hall. All passengers must submit to this check. Westerners are generally left alone to go on their way unless the scan suggests they may be carrying in an item banned in Saudi Arabia. This is usually a suspicion of alcohol, but it could be other items such as pork or other material inappropriate to Islamic values. If you are stopped and are polite, patient and not carrying contraband, you are very likely to be on your way in minutes.

In the arrivals hall

Once past customs, you will now enter the arrivals hall where the general public can wait for their friends, family and business associates. The arrivals hall often has a feeling of chaos and is often noisy. The arrivals halls of all three main international airports – Riyadh, Jeddah and Damman – have most of the usual amenities, including ATMs, bureaux de change, mobile phone kiosks (a good place to purchase your Saudi SIM), food and beverage vendors, and car hire companies for men.

You will generally see a large scrum of professional drivers holding placards containing their clients' names. It is likely that your sponsor or hotel will do the same if you have made arrangements in advance.

Transport from the airport

Most Western visitors prefer to organise transport prior to arrival in Saudi Arabia. Often, this will be taken care of by their sponsor. Many visitors also organise transport via their hotel, although this should ideally be done 24 hours in advance of arrival as many hotels struggle with last minute or ad hoc transport requests.

In either case, the traveller simply needs to find the placard with their name on it to meet their driver in the arrivals hall and off they go. The driver or his assistant, if there is one, will almost certainly take the burden of looking after your luggage and deliver it safely into your vehicle. This is safe, although some travellers prefer to keep in possession of their money, passport and expensive technology. Always ensure that you have at least one local mobile phone contact number in case your driver has been held up in unavoidable traffic delays, which are common throughout all urban areas of Saudi Arabia.

For Western visitors to the Kingdom who have not made local transport arrangements or for whom their arrangements have fallen through (it does happen), there are a number of options. Some airports have secure taxis and a taxi manager who will organise a fair rate and a (somewhat) safe vehicle and driver. There are general taxi ranks which some people use when there are no other alternatives.

The challenges presented by general taxi drivers are less about personal safety and more about the condition of the vehicle (and sometimes the driver), a reasonable chance of a language barrier, and the passenger's ability to know the going rate to their destination and their ability to haggle well. Women can expect drivers, especially taxi drivers, to move up the front passenger seat as a gesture of respect for the woman.

Other visitors prefer to wait if it is a matter of fixing the transport problem that was originally arranged. Local public transport, where is does exist, is *not* recommended for Western visitors. At the time of publication, there are no train services to any airports in Saudi Arabia, although there are future plans for all three major international airports.

Self drive for men

The basics
Driving is on the right.

Saudi Arabia is the only country in the world where women are not allowed to drive. Men who are resident in the Kingdom must be 18 to obtain a full Saudi driving licence. Men must be 25 years old to hire a car from most internationally recognised car hire companies.

Seatbelts are required for the driver and front seat passengers. Using a hand held mobile phone whilst driving is illegal. Both of these rules are widely ignored.

Driving in Saudi Arabia is much more dangerous than in most of the rest of the world. With low petrol prices, excellent quality roads and powerful vehicles, high speeds often go hand in hand with reckless drivers who often have a very fatalistic attitude, an attitude of entitlement, or both. In addition, most traffic laws are not enforced – at least, until an accident occurs. As a result, over 7000 road accident fatalities and approximately 40,000 serious injuries are recorded every year, making Saudi Arabia's roads amongst the most dangerous in the world (some say Saudi Arabia is the worst).

Drivers should be aware that road signs are not always in English; some are only in Arabic.

Petrol pricing is amongst the least expensive in the world. It is approximately 1/6 the price in the US and 1/14 the price in the UK. As of July 2014, the average petrol price in Saudi Arabia is US$0.12 per litre.

Hiring a vehicle

Most multinational car hire companies can be found in the arrivals hall of the Riyadh, Jeddah and Dammam airports as well as in most regional airports. Car hire is also possible in offices found in the central business district of most cities and can often be organised through top end hotels as well.

Men with driving licences from Western countries should have their driving licences accepted by multinational car hire companies. International driving licences are no longer readily recognised in many Gulf countries. Men with driving licences from other countries should check with their chosen car hire company in advance of travel as to driving licence requirements.

It is strongly recommended that men who choose to hire a vehicle consider their safety. This includes many factors, including the size of the vehicle, the driver's confidence in challenging driving conditions, and their defensive driving abilities. Ideally, they should only consider self driving once they become familiar with the road system of the city after several visits.

Comprehensive insurance is strongly advised. The driver should have immediate access to the car hire company if they are involved in a road traffic accident (known as RTA throughout Saudi Arabia). Ensure you have telephone contact details before you drive away. 993 and 996 are the telephone numbers for the Saudi Traffic Police.

Drivers should never underestimate the need for assistance to deal with the system if they are involved in a RTA. It is important to double check that your employer back home allows you to hire a car in Saudi Arabia, as many corporations' health and safety policies often have specific rules and restrictions about driving permissions in certain parts of the world. If you are permitted to hire a car and are involved in a RTA, you will probably have an additional insurance policy as well as a procedure to follow in case of occurrence. You must still contact the Saudi authorities, but you may also wish to make urgent contact as instructed by your organisation as well.

Never sign anything unless you can read it and agree to what is written, keeping in mind that the document will be in Arabic. Ideally, you should have a robust travel policy in place that includes dealing with the Saudi authorities.

Meet and greet services

Many Western business people who travel to other countries in the region may be familiar with 'Meet and Greet' services, such as the Marhaba services available at the Dubai airport.

It is beyond the scope of this book to describe services available to VIPs, VVIPs, diplomats, etc. However, there are limited options for the Western business traveller who may wish to arrange a smoother experience upon arrival to Saudi Arabia.

Meet and greet services can facilitate anything from a speedy and relatively comfortable experience through immigration, passport control and customs to organising ground transport.

In Saudi Arabia, meet and greet services are in their infancy and are offered by a limited number of organisations. At the time of research, they are available for use at the Riyadh airport, where they can greet the traveller at the end of the jet bridge and facilitate their journey through all airport formalities if arranged by the traveller. Meet and greet services are not available at the Jeddah airport at the present time, although they have been in the past. Local belief is that meet and greet services are not necessary at the Dammam airport.

Budgets should be considered when organising meet and greet services. Costs of about £100, excluding transport, are to be expected.

Accommodation

Accommodation considerations should be a very high priority for the Western business visitor to Saudi Arabia. Your accommodation is your sanctuary from which to escape some of the social pressures of being in public, so it should be comfortable. You should also take the location of your accommodation into consideration to minimise unnecessary travel time and to avoid traffic jams wherever possible.

Hotels

Hotels in Riyadh and Jeddah are plentiful, with most of the usual Western brands and many non-Western luxury brands available.

In addition to the usual five star international hotels, Saudi Arabia has its own luxury brands as well. Examples include Hotel Khozana and Hotel Faisaliyah in Riyadh, as well as the Qasr al Sharq and the Rosewood Corniche in Jeddah.

It is important to check the condition of hotels in both cities. Some continue to modernise both the infrastructure and service levels of their hotel; others seem to rest on their earlier reputations; a few don't seem to care very much in spite of Saudis' reputation for hospitality. This is where the value of recent experience pays off. Do check the opinion of colleagues who have stayed in the property recently. Read travel websites and social media in addition to the hotels' own websites to get a feel for the hotel's standards and conditions.

Western business visitors should also be aware that their choice of hotel is important to their Saudi counterpart, as they are often judging their visitors by their choices and behaviour whilst in the Kingdom. You will be expected to stay in a 4* or 5* hotel; anything with a lesser reputation will probably send the wrong message to your hosts and colleagues. Very low end hotels are unlikely to accept Western men and almost certainly will not accept women.

Upper end long stay hotels and apartments are available for visitors staying for blocks of time in the same city. They often have kitchen facilities and are more comfortable and more budget friendly than a standard room in a hotel.

Western business visitors should note that they are expected to adhere to the Saudi dress code in all public facilities within the hotel other than in gender segregated facilities such as the health club or swimming pool. It should be noted that Saudi hotel swimming pools are for the use of men only

Riyadh now has a high end, women-only hotel that caters to businesswomen. Popular with Saudi and many other Arab and Muslim business women, the Luthan hotel will also accept Western female guests. This gives women the opportunity to relax the dress code and to freely mingle and use all of the facilities of the hotel without restriction.

Some hotels in Jeddah are also affiliated with private clubs with access to the beach and water sports. Most of these are located north of the Jeddah airport in the district of Obhur and can take an hour or more to reach from the hotel. However, they are also open to women and operate a relaxed dress code.

A slightly more limited selection of hotels suitable for Westerners can be found in the Eastern Province, including Dammam, Dhahran and Al Khobar. Westerners travelling to Jubail should note that most visitors opt for the Intercontinental Hotel. It has the additional benefit of a private beach open to women, families and male guests of the hotel.

Short stay on Western expatriate compounds

Some Westerners who are new to travel to Saudi Arabia may wish to consider the option of a short stay on a Western compound.

Of course, this option is only available if you already have a connection with one of the compounds and only if the compound has availability. As this option can be popular, visitors can expect rooms to be full at short notice during popular times. Prices for rooms that may not always have the same amenities as a 4* or 5* hotel may still be commensurate with 4* or 5* rates. You may also be required to organise payment in cash or via bank transfer.

On the other hand, Western business visitors staying on a Western expatriate compound will have access to all of the same facilities as compound residents. They often include a restaurant, robust sporting facilities, a swimming pool open to all, small market, and organised social activities. Western dress codes prevail in the compounds.

Further information about compounds can be found in the following Section.

SECTION 5

PREPARING FOR RESIDENCY AND DAILY LIVING IN SAUDI ARABIA

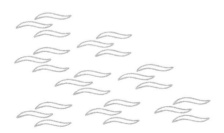

PREPARING FOR RESIDENCY AND DAILY LIVING IN SAUDI ARABIA

Understanding the sponsorship (*kafala*) system

Saudi Arabia already has strict controls on who can enter the country and under what circumstances. These controls are even stricter for expatriates who intend to live in the Kingdom for a specified period of time whilst employed by a Saudi based employer.

For much of its modern history, Saudi Arabia has needed to import labour due to a variety of reasons. For most Western expatriates, they are invited to work and live in the country because they bring a skill that does not exist within the Saudi working population.

Anyone who is considering a secondment must understand that they effectively become a dependent of the *kafala*, or sponsorship system, whereby their rights, restrictions, and even their movements can be controlled by their Saudi sponsor, including the ability to leave Saudi Arabia without permission. Thus, the Saudi sponsor is in effect the legal guardian of their employee, including Western employees. This is a much more stringent system than is applied to business professionals who simply enter the Kingdom on a business visit or short term work visa.

However, becoming resident in Saudi Arabia also offers benefits that are not available to short term visitors. These benefits include, but are not limited to sponsoring close family members' own residency in the Kingdom, the right to participate in everyday life such as renting a property, opening a bank account, obtaining a long term mobile phone contract, securing a school place for your children, accessing routine medical care through private insurance, owning a vehicle and, if you are male, driving it as well.

Eligibility practicalities for a residency visa

Just as a number of factors can influence those who are simply travelling to Saudi Arabia on a short term visa, prospective expatriates will have a greater chance of being successfully sponsored as residents due to who they are. This includes but is not limited to their nationality, country of birth, age (young and old), gender, job title, and religion. It also depends on your job title and professional qualifications, although these are rarely factors that prevent most Westerners from becoming resident.

Most Westerners are generally treated relatively well, with most sponsors willing to ensure that bureaucracy is sorted to the satisfaction of the expatriate, even if it may not always seem so at the time. However, politics between your home country and Saudi Arabia can also have an impact on how willing the Ministry of Foreign Affairs may be in facilitating the visa process.

For example, Swedish passport holders were unable to obtain a business visa for Saudi Arabia or to get their residency visa renewed for several weeks in early 2015. This was due to an ongoing diplomatic dispute over human rights and gender issues, publically discussed by the Swedish foreign Minister. During the previous year, the Kingdom had a temporary ban on issuing visas to Dutch nationals for allegedly anti-Islamic behaviour by a Dutch politician. Most British passport holders report that their multiple entry business visit visas were reduced from 180 to 90 days for a few weeks in late 2015. This was in response to the British government and the then Prime Minister publically cancelling a bid for a contract to help train Saudi prison staff over human rights complaints.

Poor diplomatic relationships and/or suspicion also have an impact on passport holders from several countries, including Iran, Syria, Iraq, Yemen and some people from Lebanon. People planning to travel to Saudi Arabia on these passports may not always be successful in their visa application.

Israel and Saudi Arabia have never established a diplomatic relationship. Israeli passport holders are not eligible to apply for any type of visa to travel to Saudi Arabia, other than for Hajj or Umrah visas for Muslim Israeli passport holders and then only under strict circumstances that do not include work or residency. Nor will any other passport holder of any nationality who was born in Israel.

This restriction is distinct from people who are Jewish and have no outward ties to Israel. Theoretically, Western passport holders who are also Jewish are eligible for travel and residency in Saudi Arabia, although there may be additional bureaucratic efforts to overcome in some situations.

It is very difficult for most employees over the age of 60 to obtain a residency visa unless their sponsor can successfully claim special circumstances that are recognised and accepted by the Ministry of Foreign Affairs.

Most Western women who are eligible for a business or residency visa due to their job title will find the rate of acceptance significantly higher than it was only a few years ago. The remaining difficulty is often the married woman's ability to sponsor her husband unless he is eligible for travel or residency in his own right. A woman will have little difficulty sponsoring her minor children.

Medical certificate

A health examination is required prior to becoming eligible for a residency visa. This includes the employee and any family member who will be a resident dependent over the age of 15. The health exam includes several procedures, which can change over time.

If any of these conditions are found to exist – including indication of pregnancy for unmarried women - then a residency visa will not be granted in most circumstances. These conditions include: HIV/AIDS, liver function, syphilis, tuberculosis, Hepatitis A,B,C, bilharzia antibodies, malaria antibodies, and a pregnancy test for women. Married women who are pregnant remain eligible for a residency visa.

Medical certificates can only be issued by approved medical professionals recognised by the Saudi authorities.

Many expatriates prefer to conduct their health exam in their country of residence. However, even if this is done precisely, it is not at all unusual for the Saudi authorities to demand another complete health exam after arrival in Saudi Arabia.

Negotiating a deal for becoming resident in Saudi Arabia

As with many other life changing decisions, only the employee and their family can decide whether making the commitment to become resident in Saudi Arabia is beneficial to them on a personal level and is beyond the scope of this book to attempt to do so on their behalf.

If you come from a country where your nationality is unlikely to prevent you from obtaining a Saudi visa and you are able to pass the required medical examination, then the next steps are to decide how serious you are about relocation and working in Saudi Arabia. For most people, once they sort out personal matters, it's often a matter of money and whether the lifestyle is compatible or can be compromised to make living in the Kingdom work.

Considerations on what to negotiate in your labour contract

For those who are giving the idea serious thought, many considerations should be taken into account when preparing to negotiate their labour contract. Most Western expatriates, especially those working for a prestigious Saudi, Western or multinational organisation will generally expect the following matters to be covered in a mutually satisfactory way.

The basics

- Salary and other remuneration
- Where and how salary paid, what currency
- Bonuses and end of service benefits, how and when they will be paid
- Realistic support and options for spouse's ability to work where required
- Tax assistance where necessary in the secondee's home country
- Robust private medical insurance to cover all family members resident in Saudi Arabia and abroad where necessary
- Agreed range of acceptable accommodation provided by the sponsor, including budgetary, realistic choice of expatriate compound where desired, and other expectations

- Transport – corporate car or car allowance, driver or travel budget for women and any other secondees unable or unwilling to drive
- Paid travel back home for secondee and family over a reasonable period of time and at least annually
- School arrangements in Saudi Arabia and travel arrangements for (usually older) children who are being educated back home
- Support for pet relocation and transport, including cats and dogs

Other important considerations

- Agreement about holding passports
- Agreement about issuing multiple exit/re-entry visas
- Mutual expectations for renewing employment contract
- Employee's right to change jobs, terms and conditions of compliance
- Clear understanding of how to resolve problems and disputes
- Clear understanding of what the sponsor considers as banning infractions
- Anything else that can impact your legal, financial and other important matters

Obtaining a residency visa

For most Western professionals, their current employer and Saudi sponsor will generally manage the bulk of this bureaucracy for obtaining a residency visa and eventually the residency visa required for any family members also living with the employee. It is also beyond the scope of this book to provide costs and fees for these services as they vary by nationality and are constantly subject to change. However, it is important to understand the basics of the process to know what to expect in broad terms.

Please note that visa regulations are under constant review and may change with little or no warning. The following information is provided as a guideline and should be only taken under consideration with other sources of information, including your employer, Saudi sponsor, professional BPOs and only after a thorough review of your personal circumstances and options.

An employee who intends to live in Saudi Arabia will need a wide range of documentation in order to start the process of obtaining their residency visa. Most of this documentation will also be required for many other processes whilst living in Saudi Arabia, and can range from opening a bank account to securing a school for your child.

- Your passport with at least 6 months' validity and at least two blank pages facing each other. Ideally, many expatriates find it easier to start with a new or a nearly empty passport with as much time possible beyond the expected length of the secondment. As a reminder, any passport with evidence of having travelled to Israel will void eligibility to live in or even travel to Saudi Arabia

- It should be highlighted that the possession of a second/additional passports is illegal in Saudi Arabia regardless of nationality

- Passport size photographs – recommend about 30 to complete the process

- Appropriate fees, which are often but not always paid by the sponsor

- Contract of employment

- Evidence of your professional credentials such as an engineering degree

- Evidence of your academic qualifications such as a degree

- Evidence of private health care insurance

- Medical certificate as evidence of successful completion of a medical examination

- Possibly a police report from your own country attesting no criminal record

- If you are sponsoring your family, then you will also require as applicable o Marriage certificate

o Children's birth certificates

o Evidence of successful completion of a medical examination for family members over the age of 15

Do not be surprised if these documents must be formally attested or notarised, especially if they are not in English or Arabic.

Please note that prospective expatriates who are currently living in a country that is different from their passport nationality may need to allow considerably more time to obtain these documents. There have also been anecdotal stories of some third country nationals being required to return to their country of nationality to complete this process.

Working visa types

Work visa

Most expatriates who are about to become resident in Saudi Arabia enter on a full work visa, supplied by their Saudi sponsor, as the process to obtain a residency visa can take weeks or, in some circumstances, months. This visa is different from a short term work visa as it is usually valid for the duration of the employee's work contract (up to 2 or sometimes 3 years). Unlike with a short term work visa, there is no need to depart and re-enter Saudi Arabia every 30 - 90 days or less.

Residency visa – 'iqama'

Employees who wish to become resident in Saudi Arabia must obtain a residency visa, known as an *iqama*. An *iqama* is a physical card that contains your personal details as well as all relevant information about your legal status in the Kingdom. Once an *iqama* has been obtained, the employee will have full rights of an expatriate resident. Once an employee has their *iqama*, then they are able to start the process of sponsoring their family if they are otherwise eligible to do so.

The *iqama* is applied for by the employee's sponsor. When all steps to obtain a residency visa have been successfully completed, this will usually require the expatriate to visit the General Directorate of

Passports office, known as Jawazat to complete the process. This is also where *iqamas* are renewed. Depending on the sequence of events in obtaining a work visa and an *iqama*, it is occasionally necessary for the expatriate to depart on their work visa and re-enter the Kingdom on their residency visa. Travel to a neighbouring country is sufficient; there is no specific need to travel to your home country.

It is critical to understand that many sponsors, including employers of Western expatriates, will hold the Westerner's passport in exchange for providing them with their *iqama*. This can make many Westerners very uncomfortable.

Some Westerners choose to negotiate this issue prior to accepting work in Saudi Arabia. However, once an *iqama* is obtained, the process of exiting and re-entering Saudi Arabia is also different compared to someone who travels to the Kingdom on a work or business visit visa. They will require an exit/re-entry visa or, once ready to leave the Kingdom permanently, a final exit visa.

An *iqama* is typically valid for 1 or 2 years and is calculated in the *Hijri* or Islamic calendar. This is an important detail as the Islamic calendar is 10 or 11 days shorter than the Western calendar. Never allow your *iqama* to expire as this attracts heavy fines and can hinder most of everyday life. It is also illegal and could have implications for your present and any future employment in the Kingdom. The Ministry of the Interior website has a tab that allows expatriates to check their *iqama* status and validity.

It is also practical advice to check and make sure all of your details are accurate on your *iqama* as any discrepancies can have a negative impact on getting things done, including for example, issuing an exit visa if your name is not spelt the same on both your *iqama* and your passport.

Please note that your *iqama* will also indicate whether you have permission to work. Of course, this will be present for the employee who is sponsored by the Saudi national bringing them into the Kingdom for employment. A working spouse must gain their own work visa and *iqama* if they wish to work as well. Dependent resident *iqamas*, unlike in some other Gulf countries, do not give dependent family members the right to work in Saudi Arabia.

Finally, your *iqama* will provide a quick way to identify your religion. Green *iqamas* are issued for Muslims regardless of nationality; brown *iqamas* are issued for non-Muslims.

Exit/Re-Entry Visa

Once resident in Saudi Arabia, *iqama* holders must obtain an exit visa from their sponsor in order to travel out of the Kingdom. Exit/Re-entry visas, as the name implies, allows the expatriate resident to leave Saudi Arabia and return on the same visa. The Saudi sponsor must apply for this visa. If the sponsor is holding the expatriate's passport, then common practice is to give the sponsor the *iqama* in exchange for the passport shortly before travel. Upon return to the Kingdom, the passport is exchanged again for the *iqama*.

Exit/Re-entry visas are available for single and multiple entry. Multiple entry visas are most often valid for 6 months but in some instances may be valid for as long as a year. Again, be aware of the Islamic calendar when making these calculations. Most expatriates who have a legitimate reason for frequent or sudden travel are able to obtain a multiple entry Exit/Re-entry visa from their sponsor. Check with your sponsor to be sure this is the case if this is an important issue.

Final Exit Visa

When an expatriate and dependent family members are ready to leave Saudi Arabia permanently, they must obtain a final exit visa from their sponsor. They must also surrender their *iqamas* prior to departure; failure to do so could prevent them from travelling.

Most sponsors will only apply for and issue a final exit visa once they are satisfied a number of conditions are met by the expatriate. These include providing the proper notice stated in your work contract, typically but not always 30 days. It is also necessary that you do not have any outstanding debt or other disputes in Saudi Arabia. As your legal guardian, your Saudi sponsor cannot issue your final exit visa unless you are debt free and have no other legal claims against you.

Most expatriates, even those who have enjoyed a good relationship with their sponsor, still take safeguards to protect themselves, their family and their assets prior to requesting their final exit visa and leaving Saudi Arabia. These typically include the following actions:

- Ensure you have been paid to the present time
- Negotiate a solid payment agreement of end of service payment in cash

- Give notice to terminate housing lease
- Sell car or terminate lease
- Ship personal effects back home or to your next destination
- Sell any remaining possessions to other Saudi residents
- Pay all utility bills, including the cancellation of mobile phone contracts
- Pay off all credit card balances and cancel them
- All other loans and debts must be paid in full
- Withdraw funds from all Saudi bank accounts
- Confirm if there are any outstanding traffic offenses or fines and clear them
- Obtain police clearance certificate
- Some employees ensure their family have left Saudi prior to their own departure

Departing Saudi Arabia without leaving a trail of difficulties can also have an impact on future travel and future employment in Saudi Arabia. It is worth the time to plan and get things right for you and for your Saudi sponsor.

There have been several announcements that the *iqama* is being replaced by a *muqeem* document, starting in October 2015. It has been published that the *muqeem* will replace the *iqama* once it has expired, will be valid for up to five years, and can be renewed annually on line.

Diplomatic visa

People who are working for their country's government may be eligible for a diplomatic passport, which gives them additional rights and protections above those given for a work or standard residency visa. As it is beyond the scope of this book, it is suggested that those employees and their dependents who may be eligible for a diplomatic passport pursue this in greater detail through official channels.

Non-working visa types

Family residency visa

Sponsoring family, visitors and household help

The most important requirement to become eligible to sponsor your family is your official job title on your residency visa. The employee must also earn more than the current minimum monthly salary required by the sponsor and Ministry of Foreign Affairs. .

Most Westerners will be eligible to sponsor their family as well as sponsor live in household help if they wish. A family is typically defined as a spouse and children. Occasionally, elderly parents may qualify. Permission must be obtained by the employee's sponsor that will allow them to sponsor family members.

You must be in a legally recognised heterosexual marriage and be able to produce a marriage certificate in order to sponsor your spouse and close family members. Sons often become difficult to sponsor once they turn 18 years old. It is generally possible to sponsor daughters beyond the age of 18 unless they marry, although the process is more complicated than for daughters under the age of 18. You will need to provide birth certificates for each family member.

Adopted children often require significantly more bureaucracy than children born naturally to their parents. Children from previous marriages or relationships require the permission of both parents to travel to and reside in the Kingdom. Children with birth certificates that do not have one mother and one father listed can also present further questions and may be met with bewilderment. It is advised that professional advice is sought for any of these issues if complications are anticipated.

If you are considering live in household help, you will be required to sponsor your maid, nanny, driver, etc. This is only possible once the employee has obtained their residency visa. It is also important to understand that single status men are ineligible to sponsor female live-in household help.

If you do sponsor live-in help, you must comply with Saudi labour law, which at present includes but is not limited to a minimum monthly wage, a maximum number of hours worked weekly with one day off per week, medical coverage, a room to live in, and a paid airline ticket to the labourer's country of origin, usually once every two years.

If you are considering employing live out household help, you must ensure they are legally resident in Saudi Arabia. Do not feel awkward to ask for their *iqama* and any other paperwork that will substantiate their legal status.

Anyone who is sponsored on the employer's visa is also subject to a medical examination, which must be passed prior to issuing the dependent residency visa.

Dependants of employees who are resident in Saudi Arabia do not normally have the right to work. However, it is possible for a spouse to obtain his or her own working visa if they have the right credentials and a sponsor willing to employ them.

At the present time, although it is routine for a husband to sponsor his wife and children, a woman will find it difficult to sponsor her husband unless he has his own separate *iqama*, although sponsoring her children on her own is fine.

Family visit visa

Saudi Arabia does issue visas for close family members of employees who are resident in the Kingdom. However, this visa does not include the right to work. The employee's sponsor must grant permission and will apply for a family visit visa.

You will be required to provide documented proof of your relationship to the family member being sponsored. Each country has its own nuances as to how this documentation must be authenticated.

It is important to note that the following family members of the employee and their spouse are potentially eligible for a family visit visa: parents, children and their heterosexual spouses, brothers and sisters and their heterosexual spouses, and theoretically grandparents and grandchildren.

Ineligible family members include but are not limited to: uncles, aunts, cousins, unmarried partners of any description, other distant relatives.

ACCOMMODATION

Accommodation considerations should be amongst the highest of priorities for the Western expatriate relocating to Saudi Arabia. Your accommodation is your home away from home. It is also your sanctuary from which to escape some of the social pressures of being living and working in Saudi Arabia – more so than for expatriates in nearly any other country. You should also take the location of your accommodation into consideration to minimise unnecessary travel time to work, children's schools and daily living routines and to avoid traffic jams wherever possible.

Accommodation options should be thoroughly discussed with the expatriate's employer long before an assignment is accepted. This discussion should include but not be limited to costs, including all utilities, how they will be paid (by the employer, reimbursement, housing allowance, etc.), what type of accommodation is suitable for the assignee and any accompanying family members, household help expectations, proximity to school where applicable, and transport arrangements for any female family members. As furnished and unfurnished options are available, negotiations should also include shipment of personal and household goods as well.

It should be noted that any Western expatriate who is expecting to live on a suitable Western orientated compound may need to accept that compounds can be very difficult to get into, with demand far outstripping supply and long waiting lists the norm. The reality of possibly needing to accept interim accommodation before a more permanent arrangement can be made should also be discussed.

Residency options

Western expatriates with a long term work visa and right to a residency visa have several accommodation options. Each option has their pros and cons. In addition, things change quickly. Properties are renovated; others are left in an increasing state of disrepair. New buildings are constructed, making new neighbourhoods more fashionable and leaving other neighbourhoods behind. Extended stay rates rise and may no longer fit an organisation's accommodation budget.

Examples of each option are given at the end of their description. It is not the intention of this book to provide a complete list of facilities, but they will give the reader a flavour of what they might find.

Extended stay hotels and serviced apartments

There are a number of serviced apartments and extended stay hotels that offer the long term resident a number of amenities above and beyond the typical hotel room. Extended stay hotels usually offer a separate bedroom and living area similar to a junior suite. Hotel amenities commensurate with the star rating of the hotel are available, such as room service and gender appropriate access to health club facilities.

Serviced apartments are generally larger than all but the largest hotel suites, with a separate bedroom or bedrooms as well as a living area and additional bathroom. They also generally have a kitchen that allows the guest to cook full meals as well as a laundry facility. Some have a full room service option as well; others may have smaller coffee shop facilities.

Examples of extended stay hotels and serviced apartments in Riyadh include Marriott Executive Apartments, Suite Novotel, Mercure Value Hotel, and Hilton Garden Inn, a number of serviced apartments in the Olaya neighbourhood and several international other brand name hotel properties with suites.

Examples of extended stay hotels and serviced apartments in the Eastern Province include Radisson Blu Royal Suite Hotel, a number of serviced apartments in the Al Salamah neighbourhood, and several international other brand name hotel properties with suites. Some expatriates might wish to explore extended stay options at some of the beach resorts and spas to the north of the airport if their location does not cause too many difficulties commuting to work.

Examples of extended stay hotels and serviced apartments in the Eastern Province include Holiday Inn Resort on Half Moon Bay, Best Western Sand Rose Suite Hotel, and several international other brand name hotel properties with suites.

Compounds

Saudi Arabia recognises that many expatriates may find the strict rules of everyday living in the Kingdom very different to their life style back home. They also acknowledge that these rules can be difficult for some expatriates and their families to follow. However, the Saudi authorities also do not want expatriates to influence their way of life in ways that are against their beliefs and expected behaviour. Living on a compound is an alternative that offers a compromise.

Compounds are large properties usually owned by a developer that contain an array of housing styles and a number of amenities that often include a restaurant, robust sporting facilities, a swimming pool open to all, small market, and organised social activities.

Compound properties are generally significantly more expensive to rent than non-compound properties on the open market. The management of each compound has substantial influence over the composition and reputation of the compound, including the decision as to which nationalities are welcome and which are discouraged from applying for residency. This divide may not only be between Westerners and non-Westerners but also amongst specific Western nationalities. Westerners should not be surprised that, although these practices are undoubtedly discriminatory in the West if not downright illegal, they occur openly in Saudi Arabia.

It should be noted that there are also a number of expatriate compounds that cater to non-Westerners; many are unlikely to be of interest to the Western expatriate for a variety of reasons.

Compounds allow residents and guests to mingle freely regardless of gender and to wear clothing of their choice that they would be comfortable wearing back home. In fact, several Western orientated compounds actually *forbid* national dress from being worn on the premises other than *abayas* for women who are about to leave the compound.

Compounds also tolerate some social activities such as cinema, music and dancing that are forbidden elsewhere. Alcohol remains strictly forbidden, although home brewing is known to occur on some compounds.

Compounds are professionally secured, with high walls, concrete blocks, gates and barricades, guarded checkpoints, and a system in place to check all vehicles including the use of undercarriage mirrors, tyre puncturing strips, and the requirement to open the boot and bonnet of all vehicles upon request.

Compounds also have a strict system in place that only allows access by residents and invited visitors and guests. Formal identification from all visitors and guests are required and must be left at the security office upon entry.

Open market housing

Although Western expatriates are not allowed to purchase property in Saudi Arabia, they do have the option to rent housing in the open market once they have obtained their residency visa.

Open market housing is not for everyone, as residents must respect the daily living social norms and requirements of the neighbourhood just like everyone else. This means some of the relaxed conditions of compound living are not possible in private accommodation. It also means that they must choose a landlord very carefully as a bad landlord will be a nightmare, especially for the inexperienced Western expatriate.

However, there are also several advantages to renting private accommodation in the open market. Rents will be significantly less expensive than for an equivalent property in an expatriate compound that caters to Westerners. There will be a wider choice of neighbour-hoods to choose from, which can significantly improve the commute to work, school, and shopping. Finally, it gives the Western expatriate a much greater chance of meeting and getting to know other Saudi families rather than to rely on an expatriate bubble for your main social network.

Open market housing is not for everybody, and might only benefit the more adventurous expatriate only after they have been residing in Saudi Arabia for a period of time and thus better understand the advantages and challenges of this housing option.

Styles of housing

A wide variety of housing styles can be found in Riyadh, Jeddah and the main cities of the Eastern Province. Western expatriates relocating to another region of Saudi Arabia may have more limited housing options.

Options include small studios, modestly sized one or two bedroom apartments (flats) suitable for single people or a childless couple, luxurious apartments, town houses (attached or semi-attached houses) and villas (detached houses) that range from modest two or three bedrooms to 5+ bedrooms. All but the smallest of studios and flats are likely to have separate quarters for daily help/maid.

Choosing and securing a compound property

It is strongly advised that the prospective expatriate and ideally any older family members who will also be living in Saudi Arabia arrange a house-hunting visit prior to accepting an expatriate assignment. This will give them a more realistic taste of what it will be like to live in the Kingdom for a period of time as well as give them the opportunity to note additional conditions they may wish to negotiate prior to their final agreement with their employer.

Expatriates or their employers should organise their house hunting activities by contacting the compound management office by telephone rather than through email. Arrange for a face to face visit and ask to tour the common grounds and shared facilities in addition to seeing the inside of a selection of properties.

Although compounds are designed to make life more comfortable for expatriates, the style and reputation of each compound means that some compounds may be more suitable for some people than others. There are many factors to consider. Some compounds are more orientated to families; in fact, some may not accept singles at all. Others have a good mix of singles and families. Some compounds have a reputation that favours certain Western nationalities over others, sometimes making it uncomfortable if you are from a less desirable nationality. Other compounds are known as 'company compounds' where the vast majority of expatriates are employed by the same employer; a few are noted below. Some compounds are considered to be suitable for top executives and thus establish their own hierarchy, sometimes to the extent that disparaging remarks can be overheard if a resident 'only' has a more modest job title.

Other considerations are whether the employee is looking for a furnished or unfurnished property. Most expatriates, unsurprisingly, opt for a furnished property and ship over a few personal items to make their home more comfortable. In addition, many Western expatriates may wish to purchase additional small electrical goods and other convenience items. Household items of all descriptions are plentiful in Saudi Arabia, from IKEA to bespoke furniture craftsmen who can make a future family heirloom, often at a reasonable price for superb quality.

It is also important to check the voltage in your accommodation, as Saudi Arabia operates both the 127V and the 220V/230V/240V systems, sometimes in the same property!

Once an expatriate and their family have chosen their preferred compound, they must understand that demand far outstrips supply, especially at the top end. Some employers and relocation organisations have an arrangement with compounds that might facilitate securing a property; other employees must work it out for themselves.

Expatriates may also need to accept that even when a property does become available in their chosen compound, their ideal property within that compound may not be available. Most good Western expatriate compounds are at 100% occupancy, with many running long waiting lists.

Some employees will choose to live in temporary accommodation, waiting until a their ideal property becomes available in their chosen compound; many others believe that it is smarter to accept any suitable property within their preferred compound, with the understanding this also brings them to the top of a waiting list when their desired property becomes available. Finances and the flexibility of both the employer and the compound management must be taken into account.

Once a property has been selected, it is important to understand that the Saudi system means that rents are usually paid one year in advance, although a few compounds may consider a six month period with post dated cheques deposited as a guarantee for the remainder of the rent.

Popular compounds for Western expatriates

The following information is not intended to be a complete listing of <u>all</u> compounds suitable for Westerners. Compiled from a number of sources, it should give the prospective expatriate a place to start their research. Additional websites that might be helpful include:

www.rightcompound.com

www.sauditodayonline.com

www.saudiarabia.angloinfo.com

NB: Compound lists were originally published in part on other websites or blogs and have been edited by the author.

Riyadh

Luxury apartments can be found in the Al Khozama hotel, Kingdom Towers or Al Fasiliyah Residences.

Many Western expatriates who do not favour a traditional expatriate compound yet seek a secure and relatively relaxed living environment in Riyadh opt for a property in Riyadh's Diplomatic Quarter. As with most other desirable housing, there may be a waiting list.

Top end compounds catering to Western expatriates include Al Hamra Oasis Village, Arabian Homes, Arizona Golf Resort, California Resort, Cordoba, Eid Villas, Fal Compound, and Kingdom City.

Here is a more extensive list of Riyadh compounds:

- Akaria Villas (inside the Diplomatic Quarter)
- Al Hamra Oasis Village Compound (British School)
- Al Issa Comound
- Al Jawharra (near Diplomatic Quarter)
- Al Jazeera Badar
- Al Mohaeya Compound (Boeing Compound)
- Al Mostaqbal Homes (inside the Diplomatic Quarter)
- Al Nakheel Residence (near Dallah Hospital, Takhassusi Street)
- Al Ola (Olaya between Thalateen & Tahliah Street)
- Al Romaizon (behind Imam University)
- Al Waha Garden Village (Exit # 10)
- Al Yamamah Village (Eastern Ring Road, Exit # 16)

- Arab Investment Compound (near Diplomatic Quarter)
- Arabian Homes (King Abdullah Street, Al Mursalat)
- Arizona Golf Resort (near British International School off Airport Road)
- AsasCo Village (Olaya District)
- California Report (new, near British International School off Airport Road)
- Cofras Compound (Exit # 30, Dammam Road)
- Cordoba Oasis Village (Near British School)
- Delta # 1 & # 2 (Opposite King Saud University)
- Dabbab Gardens Compound
- Dywidag Saudi Arabia Limited (near Football Stadium)
- Eid Compoound (near British School)
- Euro Compound (near Al Aqariya Building)
- Fal Compound (Exit # 8, Near Arizona)
- Green City Compound (King Abdullah Road, Near Takhas-sussi / Sheraton)
- Jazeera Compound (Olaya behind Al Jazeera Supermarket)
- Khuzama Village Compound (west side of Riyadh)
- Kingdom City (next to Kingdom Hospital, Airport Road)
- Najd Village (near Eid Villas)
- Riyadh Village (Phillips Ericsson compound, near Football Staduim)
- Rabwa Compound (Exit # 13, Eastern Ring Road / Khurais Road)
- Ranco Village (near Exit #13)
- Roc Compound (Al-Sulai, Exit # 16)
- Sahara Towers (Olaya)
- Seder Village (al Khaleej area, Exit #30 off Khurais Road near Granada Mall)
- Summerland Compound (Old Airport Road, Al-Malik Fahad)
- Villas Rosas (near Diplomatic Quarter)

Jeddah

Top end compounds catering to Western expatriates include al Andalus, Arabian Homes, al Basateen Village, Golf Village, Mura Bustan, Nueve Andalucia, Sharbatly and Salmia.

Here is a more extensive list of Jeddah compounds:

- Abdullah Compound (Rawdah district)
- Abir Compound (East gate of Saudia City)
- Al Andalus Luxury Villas (off Tahlia Street, behind the Suzuki showroom)
- Al Aoun Village (off Sitteen Street, near the satellite round-about)
- Al Basateen Village (next to the Continental School)
- Al Hajrayn Village (Al Shatti District, near the Corniche)
- Al Hamra Villas (Hamra district)
- Al Rumaih Compound (Al Shatti District, near the Corniche)
- Al Salam Compound (Al Rehab District)
- Al-Saraya Compound (between Medina Road and Tahlia Street)
- Belleview (next to Jeddah Prep and Grammar School)
- Binzagr Villa Compound (Madinah road, opposite the Juffali Building)
- Continental Village (next to Jeddah Prep and Grammar School)
- Fatma Compound (west of Saudia City, near the Business Park)
- Garden City Compound (Madinah Road next to the new NCB bank building)
- Hiba Compound (Hamra district)
- Kindi Housing Compound (Sitteen Street, near the junction with Hera Street)
- Lotus Compounds Jeddah (Hamra district)
- Mostly Residential Complex (southeast of Mura Bustan)
- Mura Bustan Compound (east of Madinah Road near Sary Street)
- Nada Village (west of Sharbatly village)
- Nueve Andalucia (off Sary Street, behind Jarir Bookstore)
- Oasis I Compound (north of Prince Abdullah Street)
- Oasis II, III Compound (east gate of Saudia city on Prince Sultan Street)
- Rania Compound (next to Siham Compound)

- Rawdah Compound (south of Prince Abdullah Street, Rawdah district)
- Reem Compound (apartments)
- Salmia Compound (Makkah-Madinah Expressway, near Carrefour)
- Saripalms Compound (near cornice)
- Saudia City (Saudi Arabian Airlines compound)
- Shaker Village Compound (Prince Sultan Street, north of History Roundabout)
- Sharbatly Village (Prince Majed Street)
- Siham Compound (next to Rawdah compound)
- Sunset Village (north of H bridge, Madinah Road)

North of Jeddah

- Azzam Compound (on the road to Usfan near the Madinah Road)
- Dive Village (on the waterfront of the Creek in Obhur)
- Golf Village (next to Durrat Al Arus resort, 50 minutes north of Jeddah)
- M&M Compound (north of Obhur Creek, on the Beach Club road)

Yanbu

- The Cove (King Khalid Street along the coast, Royal Commission)
- Arabian Homes (out in the desert past Yanbu old town)

KAEC- King Abdullah Economic City

- Coastal Communities in various phases of completion at the time of publication (Al Waha Village, Al Murooj Golf Community, al Shurooq, Al Talah Gardens, Bay La Sun Residential (Marina and Beach Towers)

Eastern Province - al Khobar, Dammam, Dhahran

Many Western expatriates prefer to live in al Khobar, where the atmosphere is relatively relaxed, shopping is good, there is a selection of beach resorts as well as the Corniche, and the King Fahd Causeway to Bahrain is only a few minutes away if traffic is ok. However, expatriates should choose their compound wisely as traffic patterns should be taken into account. As these three cities have now effectively blended into one metropolitan area, the following list of compounds includes all of these areas. It should be noted that Saudi Aramco operates its own camps, i.e. residential compounds for their employees and families.

Top end compounds catering to Western expatriates in the Eastern Province include Arabian Village, Euro Village, Oasis Compound, Oasis Gardens, Rushaid Village, and Zamil Village.

Here is a more extensive list of eastern Province compounds:

Al Bustan Compound (Al Khobar west of Corniche, next to the British School)
Al Mutlaq (Dammam)
Al Saeed Village (between Al Khobar and Dammam near the beach)
Arabian Village (Al Khobar west of Corniche)
Canary Village (near al Naghi BMW showroom)
Euro Village Compound (Al Khobar west of Corniche)
Golden Belt Compound (between Al Khobar and Dammam near the beach)
Mouhawis Compound (near Mall of Dhahran)
Oasis Compound (Dhahran City, separate from Oasis Gardens)
Oasis Gardens (interconnected with Al Hada, Al Bustan, Al Zahra and Stemco)
Rabwah Village (Saidgroup Properties)
Rehab Village (Saidgroup Properties)
Rezayat (Al Khobar west of Corniche)
Riyadh Compound (Al Khobar west of Corniche)
Rumaih Compound (between Al Khobar and Dammam near the beach)
Rushaid Village (Al Khobar west of Corniche)

Tamimi Compound (Al Khobar west of Corniche)
Zamil Village (between Al Khobar and Dammam near the beach)

Jubail

Most expatriate compounds are located in the Industrial Zone as opposed to Jubail City, as most Western employees are likely to be working in this area. Top end compounds catering to Western expatriates in Jubail include the popular properties of Al Murjan Village and Bajrai Garden Village, although they are often full. Nesma Village and Rezayat Village are less popular options.

Commuting between Bahrain and the Eastern Province

Many Western expatriates make the choice to live in Bahrain and commute to work in Saudi Arabia by driving over the King Fahd Causeway that links the two countries. For employees working in Al Khobar, Dammam and Dhahran, this is a realistic if not always predictable commute. Employees further north may find the commuting time outweighs the benefits of living in Bahrain, or at least may not choose to commute every day. It is also much more realistic for male employees than for females, who would need to organise a driver once she has arrived at the Saudi border if not the entire journey.

It is beyond the scope of this book to fully document the legal requirements of living in Bahrain and working in Saudi Arabia. However, these tips are a starting point for those who are considering this lifestyle and wish to do further research.

In general, the commute from Bahrain to greater Dammam takes less than an hour in the morning, when Causeway traffic is light. However, traffic builds in the afternoons and is especially busy on Thursday evening and during the Eid holidays. Horror stories of crossings taking several hours in these situations are prevalent.

The employee's paperwork should be in order prior to settling in to this commuting pattern. They should have their Saudi *iqama*, ideally a renewable multiple exit/re-entry visa, and ideally their Bahraini Central Population Registry Card (CPR). At the time of publication, holders of British, Irish, American and Canadian passports can apply for a multiple-entry visa (for business only) for 4-week stays which is valid for up to 5 years. Other nationalities may have arranged a multiple entry Bahraini business visa as well if they constantly leave and re-enter Bahrain.

Vehicles driven over the Causeway must also have their paperwork in order to be legally driven in both countries, especially if a bank loan is attached to the vehicle. If it is a company owned vehicle, the employee's sponsor must give approval.

Finally, depending on your budget and frequency of travel, it might be worth applying for a VIP Card, which allows you to use special lanes and avoids having your passport stamped for every journey. More information can be found on the King Fahd Causeway website: http://kfca.com.sa/en/

SETTLING IN

Utilities

Prior to signing a rental agreement, it is imperative to confirm which utilities are included in your accommodation. This includes gas, electricity, water and the very important air conditioning. Most Western expatriates negotiate coverage for all of these items.

Drinking water

Although tap water is not specifically unhealthy in Saudi Arabia, it is also not very palatable. Most people drink bottled water. Most Saudi homes have a system where a large jug of drinking water is placed in a dispensing device not dissimilar to what is found in many offices. Expatriates should check the arrangements for the delivery of new containers of water as well as any schedule where empty containers are collected and ensure the supplier has access if no one is at home at the time of delivery and collection.

Setting up home

Once accommodation has been chosen and secured, expatriates and their families will almost certainly want to set up home so that it becomes functional, practical and feels comfortable to live in. How this is done will depend on the expatriate's taste, budget, what they consider to be a necessity and what might be considered a luxury. Setting up home also depends on factors such as accommodation type and how long the expatriate expects to live in Saudi Arabia.

The following information covers items that most people are likely to do when setting up home in Saudi Arabia.

Small household furnishings

Nearly everyone will be looking for household furnishings once they have moved in to their accommodation. This includes expatriates who have rented furnished accommodation or are staying in extended stay apartments, since most properties will not provide everything to make daily living as comfortable as they might like. For example, many places may not have small electrical appliances such as a kettle. Others may not have enough cutlery, crockery or soft goods such as tea towels or bedding.

Small household furnishings can be purchased in all price ranges and qualities, and can be found in most shopping districts, including traditional souqs, hypermarkets, and specialty shops.

Large household furnishings

Expatriates who have chosen to move into unfurnished accommodation will need to furnish their home. Even those who are shipping their furniture from their home country may find that they may need to make additional purchases. Reasons can range from a much greater amount of space to incompatible furniture sizes (small furniture designed for urban flats are often dwarfed in large Saudi homes) to colour and material incompatible with the Saudi climate.

Although many expatriates may prefer to purchase new furniture, others are happy to source second hand, gently used items. Expatriates who are about to leave Saudi Arabia are a good source and often advertise items for sale, often at considerable savings.

Some places to buy household goods

Shops
Most Western expatriates seems to find their way to IKEA at some point during the settling in process. Large facilities exist in Riyadh, Jeddah and Dhahran. They are all very popular with most Saudis and expatriates from all over the world, so expect them to be very busy during peak shopping hours, especially at the weekend on Thursday and Friday evenings.

Other large shops that are popular with Western expatriates include Habitat, BHS (Saudi House), Marks and Spencer al Hokair, Debenhams,

Extra, Lifestyle at Centrepoint, Home Centre, Pottery Barn and many more.

Cost effective shopping for household goods include hypermarkets including Carrefour, Danube, Hyper Panda, and Lulu. Euromarche also sells a range of inexpensive household items. For an authentic if nearly outdated experience, most of the remaining Saudi souqs offer very inexpensive options for plastic goods and other low value practical household items.

Locations

Riyadh
High end furniture shopping can be found in areas including King Fahd, Olaya Street, Takhassusi St, Prince Muhammed bin Adbulaziz Road (Thalia Street), King Abdullah Road and several others up to Urubah Road, the Northern Ring Road, and the East Ring Road near the Granada mall. Less expensive Arab and Indian inspired items can be found in the Kuwaiti souq and the Deira souq.

Jeddah
High end furniture shopping can be found in areas including Tahlia Street, King Abdulaziz Street and Alrawdah Street neighbourhoods. For a step back in time, less expensive Arab and Indian inspired items can be found in many of the traditional souqs such as al Bawadi, al Shate'e, al Zahra, al Balad souqs.

Eastern Province
High end furniture shopping can be found in areas including King Faisal Street, Khreiji Centre, and Prince Turki Street in al Khobar. Similar districts exist in Dhahran and Dammam, generally near the large shopping malls. Less expensive Arab and Indian inspired items can be found in shops near King Khalid Street and Prince Bandar Street (Al-Suwaikit) and the al Issa souq near the mosque of the same name. Both Dammam and Dhahran also have similar traditional shopping districts.

Further information about shopping can be found in the Shopping section of this book.

Large Electrical Goods

Most large electrical goods can be found in districts near large furniture shops throughout Saudi Arabia. Brands familiar to Westerners are readily available as are other global brands.

There is a thriving used goods market for large electrical goods throughout Saudi Arabia. In addition to the usual cautions for buying online, it is also important to keep electrical specifications in mind as they vary throughout the Kingdom.

Communication and technology

Purchasing a mobile phone

Independent distributors of telecommunication products Axiom sell unlocked mobile phones. Handsets can also be purchased in some service providers such as STC, Mobily and Zain. Jarir is a favourite for computer accessories, and SIM cards for mobile phones in addition to their traditional book and office supplies offerings. Jarir shops can be found throughout the Kingdom.

Pay as you go SIM cards can be purchased by residents and visitors alike, but attract slightly higher calling tariffs. Mobile phone service contracts are available to expatriates who have obtained their *iqama*.

The internet

Although Saudi Arabia blocks predictable websites such as those that are anti-Islamic or promote social practices contrary to social values, the internet is much more open than many people might assume. Most popular social media websites such as Facebook, Twitter, WhatsApp, Snapchat, etc are accessible from Saudi Arabia, although the authorities could choose to close them down at any time.

Many expatriates may wish to access some of these blocked websites or simply access websites that are IP address sensitive, such as the BBC I-Player or other catch-up television. Some expatriates may also be concerned about the privacy of their online presence in Saudi Arabia.

Many expatriates find a workaround to these internet access challenges by installing a VPN that allows them wider access to the internet that a conventional Saudi service provider does not provide. VPNs also generally provide a higher level of security and privacy as well. Whilst the author cannot vouch for the legality of these options, it is possible to confirm that VPN use is popular throughout the Kingdom.

Business professionals may encounter Arabic keyboards, especially when using local office computers or business centres in hotels. They should be aware that using these keyboards for English or other languages may not always be straightforward, and may need to work out shift, control, etc key patterns for non alpha-numeric characters, including the popular @ symbol.

Television

Traditionally, most expatriates have chosen television satellite packages that contain hundreds of channels from all over the world. Whilst this is still possible, more expatriates choose to make use of the internet to access programmes that can make watching television similar to what they are used to back home. Slingbox, Netflix, Apple TV, catch-up television and similar are all in common use in the Kingdom.

Saudi Arabia is in DVD Region 2.

Video games

Video games are available in Saudi Arabia, although titles that are offensive to the Kingdom's social and religious values are banned.

Postal system

The Saudi postal system is not generally relied on by Western expatriates or others. Postal addresses are traditionally PO Box numbers. Post is simply delivered to a depot or collection point from where someone must collect the post. For those wishing to use the postal system, correspondence and parcels are generally sent to their employer's PO box so the item is collected by an employee and brought to their office. Items sent from abroad can be delayed at customs.

Most people send parcels throughout globally or regionally recognised delivery services such as DHL, UPS, FedEx, or Aramex. These services are generally reliable although they can also be quite expensive. Professional courier services can often aid the sender in completing customs forms at the point of origin so that delays are minimised or avoided all together upon arrival in Saudi Arabia.

Online shopping

Online shopping is popular in Saudi Arabia, with the notable exception of food shopping. Popular websites include souq.com as well as individual shops. Amazon does ship to Saudi Arabia, although costs can be considerable. Be aware that items sent to Saudi Arabia, including using Amazon, are subject customs formalities of the Kingdom and must not be on the banned items list.

Banned items

There is a long list of items banned from import into Saudi Arabia. The following list provides a good start for those planning to become resident in the Kingdom. For further information, it is recommended that a professional relocation company is consulted, especially if you have any unusual items that cannot be easily recognised by Saudi authorities who might open and inspect any shipments or luggage containing your personal affects or household goods.

List of prohibited items

- Alcohol-containing items, flavouring extracts, cooking wines, wine making kits, books on manufacturing of such drinks or any foods with alcohol, etc.
- Narcotics
- All kinds of medicines
    - o Medicine MUST be accompanied by doctors prescription and is to be for personal use only
- Radio transmitter/communication equipment (including walkie-talkies, short-wave, VHF, marine, police band equipment, etc.)
- Binoculars or telescopic equipment
- All types of statues
- Objects of human or animal form (statues, figurines, carvings, etc.) NB: Assume this includes children's dolls, teddy bears, etc
- Games of chance (chess, dice, backgammon, etc.)

- All weapons and firearms (real or ornamental), including guns, ammunition, fireworks, spears and other edged weapons, etc. (owner subject to investigation, fines, and/or imprisonment)
- Pornographic material and literature including fashion magazines with people wearing undergarments or swimsuits
- Politically sensitive material
- All foodstuff
- Stuffed animals
- Most artwork, especially depicting anyone or anything with a face
- Articles contrary to Muslim or Saudi Arabian beliefs or morality will not be allowed into the country
- Christmas trees/decorations or any other items (BIBLES) associated with religions other than the Muslim faith
- Military uniforms or equipment of any kind
- Other miscellaneous items (blueprints and designs, artificial pearls, etc.)
- *ALL PRINTED MATTER, BOOKS, PICTURES, RECORDS, FILMS, TAPES, SLIDES, MOVIES, VIDEOS, COMPACT DISCS, COMPUTER SOFTWARE AND DISKETTES, ETC. ARE SUBJECT TO CENSORSHIP AND CONFISCATION (MUST BE PACKED SEPARATELY FOR EASY ACCESS AND CLEARLY MARKED ON THE INVENTORY)
- Such items will be removed from all incoming shipments at the time of Customs clearance and sent to the Ministry of Information for review
- Once censorship has been completed, a separate delivery will be made at an additional charge to the customer
- Cartons containing these articles should be clearly labelled as to contents and must not be mixed with other items
- Any restricted or prohibited items in shipment will cause delays, may be subject to confiscation and may cause possible fines or penalties to customers account.

SCHOOLS

Introduction

For Western expatriates with school age children who are considering a move to Saudi Arabia, one of the most important decisions to make is which school to choose.

Every child's needs are unique; so are parents' expectations. This section provides basic information that is intended to point parents in the right direction to assist them in making decisions that are best for their children.

General information

The Saudi school system is available for all Saudi national children from age 6 to age 18. It contains three main stages: primary school for six years, intermediate school for three years, and secondary school for four years. Primary school starts at age 6; most pupils complete their secondary education at age 18. Kindergarten is available for 3-5 year olds.

Only a small percentage of Saudi children attend kindergarten. Most Saudi children start their education when they enter primary school at age 6. Both girls and boys attend primary school at levels approaching 100%. School is compulsory for nine years starting with primary school. Historically, more boys than girls achieve literacy in Saudi Arabia. However, the gender gap has significantly narrowed in recent years, with school attendance for both boys and girls in the mid 90% range.

Saudi Arabia also has a government sponsored higher education system of colleges and universities. At the time of publication, over 60% of all Saudi university students are women. Additionally, the Saudi government has a history of sponsoring tertiary education abroad through a scholarship system for many of their best and brightest students.

The school year in Saudi Arabia runs from September to June, and is normally divided into two or three semesters, depending on the school. The school week is Sunday to Thursday, with Friday and Saturday being the weekend. School hours in international schools are usually from 7am to 3.30pm. Schools days are shortened during the holy month of Ramadan.

All children, including expatriate children must attend school by age 6.

Saudi Arabia has public schools (used in this book to refer to state schools) as well as a selection of fee paying private and international schools. The Ministry of Education is responsible for all education in the Kingdom, including expatriate education.

Public/state schools in Saudi Arabia

Saudi schools are designed to focus on religious education. Although reforms are being applied, the system is still adherent to a much narrower curriculum than in other Gulf Arab countries and throughout the West. Many employers, including many Saudi employers find that many graduates of the Saudi public school system may not be as well prepared as their expatriate counterparts for certain jobs, especially those drawing on skills such as mathematics, hard science, and the ability to apply critical thinking skills in a work environment. Additionally, English language skills that are almost taken for granted amongst the younger generations of other Gulf nationals do not run deep in Saudi Arabia amongst their contemporaries. This is another area targeted for reform, but it will take time.

Most Westerners will not be eligible to send their children to Saudi schools, as the children must be Muslim and speak Arabic. They are also gender segregated.

Private education

Setting expectations
Education in Saudi Arabia has a mixed reputation. It can also be difficult to navigate. Some Saudi private schools have a good reputation; others are mediocre.

Many schools are oversubscribed, with waiting lists even for siblings of a pupil already attending that school. Families with school age children should work to secure a school place for their children as one of their highest priorities.

Many parents use a 'look-see' or familiarisation visit to meet with prospective school authorities in person whilst in the Kingdom. It is especially important to meet face to face if at all possible as it usually yields more information than what is provided through email or a telephone call. Additionally, schools are often more confident that the child is likely to take up their place when offered.

Expatriate education

All schools in Saudi Arabia are licenced by the Ministry of Education. This includes private and International Schools. Parents should also verify that their child's school is accredited and thus recognised in their home country in the event of repatriation or qualification for further education abroad.

It is illegal to establish and run an unlicenced school in the Kingdom. This includes home schooling. It is beyond the scope of this book to provide further information about home schooling in Saudi Arabia, although some families may be accessing online home schooling advice.

Saudi Arabia's private and international schools are fee paying and are structured around the national curricula of many countries – US, UK, Pakistan, India and the Philippines are especially popular.

Fee paying schools vary. Some are for profit, others are non-profit. Most following a Western curriculum are very expensive. Thus, it is imperative for the expatriate employee to understand what is involved in Saudi education so they can negotiate these details in their expatriate package. Most Western expatriates insist on full education coverage for a good quality school that offers their nationality's school curriculum for each of their school age and pre-school age children.

Traditionally, expatriate schools only accommodated children's education to age 14. In recent years, private schools are available through GCSE or high school level, usually until the child reaches 18 years of age. Expatriate children do not have access to Saudi universities.

There are varying standards amongst expatriate schools. Some parents are known to be less happy with education for older students. Parents of teenage children should take into account the usual teenage social challenges that are magnified and can attract severe consequences in the Kingdom, including pushing dress code boundaries or experimenting with sex, alcohol and other illegal drugs.

A selection of private and international schools

The reader should note that schools close and open at a steady rate in Saudi Arabia. The following information is provided as a robust but not necessarily exhaustive list of private and international schools. The author strongly suggests that parents do their own research on which schools are most suitable for their children's needs.

Most private and international schools provide their own transport in the form of school buses that collect students from their homes.

Riyadh

American International School of Riyadh - American
British International School of Riyadh – British
Kingdom Schools - Global Education Management Systems (GEMS)
Multinational School of Riyadh – Australian
Saud International School – American and British

Other Western schools in Riyadh:
École Française Internationale de Riyad - French
German International School Riyadh - German
Swedish School Riyadh - Swedish

Jeddah

Al Waha International School – British
American International School of Jeddah - American
British International School of Jeddah – British
Jeddah International School – American and French
Jeddah Preparatory and Grammar School – British and Dutch

Other Western schools in Jeddah:
École Française Internationale de Djeddah - French
German International School Jeddah - German
Scuola Intaliana di Gedda - Italian

King Abdullah Economic City (KAEC) -

The World Academy - Global Education Management Systems (GEMS)

Tabuk

British International School of Tabuk - British

Yanbu

Yanbu International School - American

Eastern Province

Children of Saudi Aramco employees are generally offered places in schools run as a part of the Saudi Aramco expatriate package. The schools listed in following Eastern Province cities are open to children whose parents may be employed by other organisations as well.

Al Khobar

Al Khobar International School – British
British International School al Khobar – British
International Programs School (IPS) al Khobar - American

Other Western schools in al Khobar:
Lycée Français MLF d'Al Khobar - French

Dammam

International Schools Group (ISG) – American and British

Dhahran

Dhahran British Grammar School – British
Dhahran Elementary/Middle School – American
Dhahran High School - American
Dhahran Baccalaureate Centre – IB and American

Jubail

International Schools Group (ISG) – American
Jubail Academy International School – British
Al Moattesem International School – British

HEALTH CARE

Introduction

Business visitors to Saudi Arabia do not need to complete a medical examination to enter the Kingdom. Residents will have already completed their medical examination as a condition of obtaining their work visa and *iqama*. More information about their requirements can be found earlier in the residency visa medical certificate section.

In 2005, health insurance was made compulsory for all non-Saudi nationals working in the country under the Cooperative Health Insurance Act.

Your company will almost certainly provide you with good health care coverage whilst living in the Kingdom. A wide array of insurers, including well known Western organisations such as Bupa and AXA are present in the market. However, it is critical that you and your family understand exactly what medical services and procedures are covered and what are exempt as medical care is expensive in Saudi Arabia.

Westerners who are travelling to but not living in Saudi Arabia are strongly advised to have a comprehensive medical insurance policy as well.

General information

The quality of medical care in Saudi Arabia is very good, with a majority of health care professionals educated in the West and with excellent English language skills. The latest technology and practices are present. Facilities are clean. Doctors are typically expatriates from Europe, North America, the Indian Subcontinent, Egypt or the Levantine countries.

Most medicine practiced in Saudi Arabia is conventional. Alternative medical practitioners are not common and may not be approved by the Ministry of Health.

For the most part, Western expatriates are satisfied with the care they receive in Saudi Arabia. However, consideration should be given about medical evacuation coverage is included in your insurance if an exceptional medical condition is anticipated.

Health dangers

Most people who need medical attention whilst living in Saudi Arabia do so regardless of their residency. The need to practice preventative health care and the treatment of both acute and chronic diseases continues whilst travelling to or living in the Kingdom

However, there is an elevated risk of requiring health care due to weather related reasons, including sunstroke and dehydration, especially during the summer months, and breathing difficulties or other irritation due to dust storms when they occur as well. The other unfortunate reason that many people may require medical attention is by becoming a victim of a road accident.

Saudis are amongst the world's highest population suffering from obesity related diseases, especially diabetes. This is probably due to a combination of factors, including a sedentary life style, a culture that does not focus on exercise, a diet heavy in fats and especially sugar, and a social life that relies heavily on feasting. Driving (or riding) everywhere doesn't help. Until recently, many Saudi families considered being overweight a sign of wealth, especially amongst men and often a favoured eldest son.

Visitors and especially expatriate residents should be aware that their dietary and exercise patterns are at risk of changing and take action to prevent falling into a trap of gaining unwanted weight.

Although most of Saudi Arabia is outside a malarial zone, there is a small risk of malaria in the border areas with Yemen, including Jizan and Najran. Dengue fever outbreaks have occurred in Jeddah, Mecca and Taif. MERS (Middle East Respiratory Syndrome) is believed to be a viral infection, although it is believed that transmission to humans is low unless in the prolonged presence of camels or in very close contact with someone who has been.

There is no yellow fever in Saudi Arabia. The Kingdom appears to have escaped from the recent ebola crisis, although there was a question as to whether a Saudi business traveller returning from Sierra Leone during the height of the ebola crisis died of the disease. The Saudi authorities acted swiftly at the time, preventing West African pilgrims from affected countries from travelling to Mecca from the region as a preventative measure.

The Saudi health care system

All medical care is run under the control of the Ministry of Health other than military facilities, which are administered by the Ministry of the Interior.

The health care system is a three-tiered system. Primary care facilities are aimed at preventative care. When these healthcare centres are not sufficient, the patient is referred to a hospital or specialist medical professional that is qualified to treat the specific medical condition. In difficult or complicated cases, the patient may be referred to a specialist hospital if care is to be continued in Saudi Arabia. For most Western expatriates, this often means becoming a patient at the world-renowned and highly regarded King Fahd Medical City in Riyadh.

Government facilities are available to the general public, although in practice, are used mostly by Saudi citizens. However, many have a particularly good reputation in the fields of obstetrics and gynaecology and may appeal to Western expatriates as well. There are additional facilities available to people associated with the Saudi military and security that are unlikely to be used by Western expatriates.

Saudi Arabia also has a wide range of private facilities that cater to Westerners and anyone else who either has robust medical insurance or is willing to spend a lot of money on medical care.

Hospitals

Choosing a specific hospital is a personal matter for the Western expatriate and their family. It will include whether their insurance plan covers the treatment required, where they have been referred, convenience, and perhaps recommendations from other trusted expats.

The following list provides the names of hospitals and specialist centres that are popular with Westerners. There are additional hospitals not listed that may suit some patients.

Riyadh

King Fahad Medical City
King Khaled Eye Specialist
Riyadh Care Hospital (also known as Social Insurance Hospital (GOSI)
Saudi German Hospital
Security Forces Hospital

Jeddah

International Medical Centre
King Faisal Specialist Hospital and Research Centre
Saudi American Clinic
Saudi German Hospital
Soliman Fakeeh Hospital

Eastern Province - Dammam, Dhahran, al Khobar and Jubail

Alamana General Hospital, al Khobar
Dammam Central Hospital
Royal Commission Hospital, Jubail
SAAD Medical Centre, al Khobar
Saudi ARAMCO Hospital, Dhahran & Al Hasa

Yanbu

Al Anseri Specialist Hospital
Royal Commission Hospital

Ambulance

The telephone number for a medical emergency is 997. Unlike much of the Saudi medical system, ambulances are not generally as reliable as in the West. Consider alternative transport if in a position to do so.

Dentists

Most Westerners choose their dentist in Saudi Arabia by obtaining a reference from someone they know and trust. They will also need to match any insurance with a dentist who accepts their plan unless they are willing to pay the dental practice directly. Dentistry can be expensive in the Kingdom.

Modern practices expected by most Westerners are available. Dental clinics are plentiful and meet the same high standards as private medical facilities. Similarly, dentists are most often expatriates from Europe, North America, Egypt or the Levantine countries.

Eye doctors

Similar to most Western countries, people who need a corrective prescription for eye glasses or contact lenses but are whose eye health is otherwise good will usually visit an optical shop that employs an optician. This is also the case in Saudi Arabia. For Western expatriates looking for service they are familiar with, al Barakat, Magrabi, Tabbara, Vision Express, Yateem are well known and well established shops; there are others. They are typically found in upscale malls and shopping districts. Any insurance coverage will need to be discussed with the facility.

Chemists

Chemists or pharmacies are widespread and well stocked throughout the Kingdom and are found in malls and other usual shopping districts. Do note that most chemists close for several hours in the afternoon, reopening for business sometime after the *asr* prayer.

Many medicines requiring a prescription in your home country may be available in Saudi Arabia without a prescription.

Medicines will be authentic, with no worries about counterfeit supplies. However, brand names for generic drugs may be different to those you are familiar with back home. If you are taking medication on an ongoing basis, it is a good idea to have both the generic name and brand name of your drug provided by your doctor back home so there is no confusion when requesting a new supply in Saudi Arabia.

Importing medicines

There are many restrictions to importing medication into Saudi Arabia, including prescription medication. In general, only one month's supply is allowed. Anti-depressants, tranquilisers and a wide variety of similar medications are banned, particularly if they contain codeine or other opiate derivative. If you are caught trying to import a banned drug, it will be confiscated.

It is strongly advised that anyone importing medications into the Kingdom also carries the prescription as well as a letter from your doctor confirming the need to take the medication. Alternative drugs will be prescribed if your usual medication is not allowed in Saudi Arabia.

DAILY LIVING BASICS

Western expatriates who are considering a move to Saudi Arabia are often pleasantly surprised that the modern amenities of daily living are plentiful in the Kingdom. This is particularly true for secondees to Riyadh, Jeddah and the major cities of the Eastern Province. Expatriates destined for the more remote provinces may wish to consider the possibility of periodic travel to larger Saudi cities to stock up on favourites that might not be easily found in their location. Of course, the internet is popular in Saudi Arabia as well, giving expatriates in remote areas the option of ordering many goods on line for local delivery as well.

Banking

The following information is provided for readers to understand the very basics of banking in Saudi Arabia. It is strongly recommended that expatriates seek professional banking advice through their employer or other professionally qualified resource.

Banking in Saudi Arabia is modern and safe. It is controlled by the Saudi Arabian Monetary Agency (SAMA), which is the Kingdom's central bank.

There are a number of major banks in Saudi Arabia which, although owned by Saudi nationals, have close affiliations or business partnerships with banks in Europe, the USA and other Arab countries. In addition to retail banking, most Saudi banks also offer additional services, including investment banking and other premium services for high value clients as well as a full range of corporate banking facilities. Major banks include:

Al Bilad Bank
Al Rajhi Bank

Arab National Bank
Bank Al Jazira
Banque Saudi Fransi (affiliated with Crédit Agricole)
Deutche Bank (German affiliation)
Emirates NBD
Islamic Development Bank
National Commercial Bank
Riyadh Bank
Saudi American Bank (SAMBA – affiliated with Citibank)
Saudi British Bank (SABB – affiliated with HSBC)
Saudi Hollandi Bank (Dutch affiliation)
Saudi Investment Bank

Western expatriates are often in a position to decide where they wish to bank. Some choose to continue banking only in their home country, with Saudi salaries and benefits paid into their foreign bank account. However, most expatriates intending to live in the Kingdom on a long term assignment often choose to have their pay split between a Saudi bank and their home country bank.

All non-GCC expatriates must have their residency visa in place before they are allowed to open a bank account in Saudi Arabia. The family member sponsored by their Saudi employer must also obtain a No Objection Certificate (NOC) from sponsor/employer and then complete the additional routine paperwork to open an account. The family member with the work visa must give permission for any other family accounts, such as for a spouse as they are acting as a sponsor for non-working family members. No interest is earned on Saudi bank accounts in compliance with Islamic banking principles.

Bank branches are usually open from 08.00 – 13.00 and 16.30 – 18.30 Sunday – Thursday. There are a number of banks with women only branches; other bank branches have separate women only counters.

Online and internet banking is popular as it is in the West. ATMs are everywhere and are connected to the global Cirrus, Plus, Pulse and Maestro systems. Visitors using Saudi ATMs should always be aware that any transaction may attract a hefty fee from your bank back home if using a foreign bank card.

Although cash remains popular in Saudi Arabia, even for large purchases, bank cards continue to grow in popularity and can be used in most establishments frequented by Westerners. The chip and pin system is used in Saudi Arabia. Expatriate residents may apply for debit and credit cards once they have established a local bank account – and credit- in the Kingdom.

Expatriate residents may be surprised that cheques are still used for some transactions in the Kingdom, usually for recurring payments such as rent. Bank loans for major items like a purchasing a vehicle are likely to require a series of post dated cheques for repayment.

It is important to understand that unpaid debt is a criminal offence in Saudi Arabia. It can lead to imprisonment, including bounced cheques and late repayments on a bank loan. Never extend your finances to risk finding yourself in these circumstances as Westerners and other expatriates have found themselves in prison in violation of loan or payment terms.

Salaries

For many expatriates a decision must be made whether to be paid wholly in SAR, your home currency or a combination. Some employers will give you an option; others will not and you will be expected to comply with their arrangements.

For those wishing to be paid in your home currency wholly outside of Saudi Arabia, consideration must be given as to how this could impact your tax status. In some countries, you are exempt from paying taxes on your income earned abroad if you do not bring it into your home country. Notably, US Americans are taxed on world wide earnings no matter where they earn or where they receive their salaries. Other countries may have other rules in their tax code. It is thus imperative that the employee seeks professional financial advice if paying no or minimum tax is a main reason for accepting an assignment in Saudi Arabia

Taxes

Employees pay no Saudi income tax on earnings made in Saudi Arabia. This includes Saudi nationals and expatriates regardless of nationality.

There is no VAT or sales tax on any goods purchased in the Kingdom.

Food shopping

Gone are the days where food shopping required a visit to several *souqs* specialising in the sale of certain products, hoping the goods have not sold out upon your arrival. Expatriates living in the major cities will find a wide variety of modern supermarkets and hypermarkets selling everything from fresh meat, vegetables and fruit to a mind-boggling range of imported items from most countries with a large expatriate population.

Western expatriates will find a large selection of familiar goods from North America, Europe, and some items from Australia and South Africa. Hypermarkets also provide the perfect chance to explore new foods from places as diverse as India, the Philippines and North Africa in addition to Middle East specialities.

Popular supermarkets and hypermarkets include Carrefour, Danube, Lulu, Panda/Hyper Panda and Tamimi. They are often located in the newer shopping malls, although many are in stand-alone locations in more upscale neighbourhoods. Although many of the largest shops are open throughout the day and evening, some shops close during the afternoon roughly between *dhuhr* and *asr* prayers.

As a rule of thumb, prices are good for items produced in Saudi Arabia or the Arabian Peninsula, with prices rising when importing goods from a long distance. Bank cards are accepted.

Food quality is of a high standard and is safe. Most products are labelled in Arabic, English and the language(s) of the country of origin. It should be noted that all meat is *halal* in Saudi Arabia.

Supermarkets and hypermarkets also sell a wide range of household goods, from pots and pans to a variety of electrical goods, generally at competitive prices.

Unfortunately, expatriates used to on line food shopping and delivery back home will be disappointed that these services are generally not available in Saudi Arabia at the time of publication.

Household help

Most Western expatriates make the decision to employ household help whilst living in Saudi Arabia. There are a variety of options, depending on your circumstances and expectations.

Live in household help is commonplace with some families, especially those that are already used to live in help. The benefits are many, including: no need to do any household chore as you can task these jobs to your maid or nanny, a built in baby sitter, and someone at home to wait for a maintenance call. Typical tasks include cleaning, cooking, laundry, ironing and childcare – you decide priorities and how the work is done.

The trade-off for employing live in household help is privacy. It is also imperative that all household help is thoroughly vetted, ideally through a personal reference from a previous tenant, a neighbour, or someone at work.

Live in help is sponsored by the family member who is resident on a Saudi work visa, with the permission of their Saudi sponsor. There are many rules, including the provision of maid's accommodation in a wing or annex of the home, food, medical insurance, time off one day per week, and paid trips back to their home country (usually every two years). Some generous sponsors also provide a television and a pre-paid mobile phone, thus controlling telephone costs. There is a restriction banning single men sponsoring female live in help. The current going rate for a live in maid is generally SR1,200 to SR2,000 per month.

Families with older children, no children or who prefer a high degree of privacy tend to opt for daily household help. This can be arranged via professional agencies or through a recommendation from a trusted party. It is imperative that Western expatriates keep up to date on what is and is not allowed when hiring daily household help as these rules are constantly changing.

Ground transport

Transport in Saudi Arabia has been described by drivers and passengers alike as anything from a contact sport to a test of wills (and patience) to a death wish. Expatriates with plenty of experience driving on roads in the developing world experience culture shock on Saudi roads. However, at the time of publication, there are no realistic alternatives to getting around in most of the Kingdom, although substantial public transport is being planned and built. Time will tell how practical it will become.

Driving

The basics

Driving is on the right.

Saudi Arabia is the only country in the world where women are not allowed to drive. Men who are resident in the Kingdom must be 18 to obtain a full Saudi driving licence. Men must be 25 years old to hire a car from most internationally recognised car hire companies.

Seatbelts are required for the driver and front seat passengers. Using a hand held mobile phone whilst driving is illegal. Both of these rules are widely ignored.

Driving in Saudi Arabia is much more dangerous than in most of the rest of the world. With low petrol prices, excellent quality roads and powerful vehicles, high speeds often go hand in hand with reckless drivers who often have a very fatalistic attitude, an attitude of entitlement, or both. In addition, most traffic laws are not enforced – at least, until an accident occurs. As a result, over 7000 road accident fatalities and approximately 40,000 serious injuries are recorded every year, making Saudi Arabia's roads amongst the most dangerous in the world (some say Saudi Arabia is *the* worst).

Drivers should be aware that road signs are not always in English; some are only in Arabic.

Petrol pricing is amongst the least expensive in the world. It is approximately 1/6 the price in the US and 1/14 the price in the UK. As of July 2014, the average petrol price in Saudi Arabia is US$0.12 per litre.

Driving licences

Driving is a way of life in Saudi Arabia. Many expatriate men eventually make the decision to self drive once they become familiar with the rhythm of traffic on Saudi roads. If at all possible, men should ensure they have a valid driving licence from their home country and ideally a lot of practical, law-abiding driving experience before they leave for Saudi Arabia.

Saudi Arabia only allows men to drive on their home country driving licence for the first three months of their residency. It has also been possible for men to drive for the first three months of their residency on an international driver's licence, but do note that IDLs are not always recognised. After three months, they must obtain a Saudi driving licence.

For men with driving licences from many Western countries, their licence is exchanged for a Saudi driving licence without further need for a driving examination. Do expect to provide the usual copies of your paperwork, including copies of your original driving licence (and its Arabic translation) as well as a copy of your *iqama*.

For men who do not qualify for a driving licence exchange, it will be necessary to attend a driving school and complete a driving course.

Driving licences are now issued for a period of ten years. Do carry your driving licence with you whenever you drive.

Your vehicle

An important consideration in Saudi Arabia is vehicle choice. Many first time buyers consider safety factors as their top priority, often opting for large, heavy, high performance vehicles, with the idea of protecting themselves from the worst effects of a potential road traffic accident (RTA). It is also important to note that there are some restrictions in what can be officially purchased in Saudi Arabia, depending on your residency status. For example, only families are officially allowed to purchase four wheel drive vehicles or vehicles that seat more than five people.

Popular vehicles in Saudi Arabia include a wide range of Japanese, European and a surprisingly high number of American-made vehicles. It is very important to ensure that any choice of vehicle includes a robust, reliable air conditioning system.

Company car

Ideally, your relocation package will include your employer offering you a company vehicle. This has many financial and practical benefits, including an avoidance of ownership hassles that exist with car ownership. The employer is responsible for the legalities of vehicle ownership, eliminating much of the bureaucracy for the driver.

Purchase or long term lease

If your employer does not offer the option of a company vehicle, then most expatriates consider the benefits of purchase or long term vehicle lease.

Purchasing a vehicle – whether new or used – involves a significant amount of paperwork and probable frustration. It also places the burden of vehicle ownership onto the purchaser, which can be substantial. Paperwork is handled by the Saudi Traffic Police (*al Morat*), which can be challenging and frustrating for many expatriates, especially if impatient or less tolerant of bureaucratic inconsistencies. In addition, there is additional exposure for vehicle purchases that require a loan, ie that can't be paid for outright.

Used vehicles can be value for money – or they can be a complete nightmare. Do bear in mind that documentation of the vehicle's full history, including maintenance history, may be missing, may never have been kept, or may not be completely truthful. If a buyer is considering a used vehicle, they may wish to purchase a vehicle from an expatriate from the West or through a reference from someone known to both parties.

Interestingly, women can purchase and thus own a motor vehicle – they just can't drive it in Saudi Arabia! This may actually be of interest to some expatriate women who do not have the benefit of a company car but wish to ensure the quality of the vehicle entrusted to their driver.

Many expatriates decide they don't want the responsibilities associated with owning a vehicle and opt for a long term lease. As with company vehicles, the responsibilities of vehicle ownership remain with the lessor. Many long term lease terms are reasonable.

Regardless of vehicle ownership, the driver should always have ownership, registration (*istimarah*) and inspection (*fahs*) papers with them at all times they are driving the vehicle.

Insurance

There are two main types of vehicle insurance (*ruksa*) in Saudi Arabia: third party insurance and comprehensive insurance

Please note that although vehicle insurance is mandatory in Saudi Arabia, not all drivers comply with this rule. Thus, it is very strongly recommended that expatriate drivers choose a comprehensive insurance policy that also protects them in case they are involved in a RTA with an uninsured driver.

Drivers should always carry proof of insurance with them whenever they are driving.

Drivers

Many Western expatriates are offered a company vehicle and a driver upon arrival in Saudi Arabia. In some cases, this arrangement is permanent; in other cases, it is temporary until the male worker gains enough confidence to drive on Saudi roads.

Professional drivers provided by most organisations employing Western expatriates are amongst the most reliable, skilled and (relatively) safe drivers. This does not mean they drive in a manner that is familiar to the Westerner back home. But it does mean they generally have significant experience on Saudi roads, which means they can often avoid the worst traffic routes and traffic jams. They are also likely to speak English well enough to communicate with their passengers. Drivers are often from the Indian subcontinent or sometimes from less affluent Arab speaking countries.

Of course, women must continue to rely on professional drivers for their entire stay in Saudi Arabia unless they are driven by a male family member. Increasingly, it is becoming more common for some expatriate business women to travel with a group of colleagues, including mixed gender groups, although this is a new and evolving practice. Having a professional driver who is trusted is paramount.

For male workers living in the Kingdom with their families with no other family member working, their driver is often sent back to their residence once the worker has been delivered to their place of employment. The driver is thus available for the rest of the family's travel requirements. This is generally a preferable option to more ad hoc arrangements.

For expatriates who do not have a driver available full time, private arrangements can be made with a driver. The driver can be hired on a per journey basis, with the rate agreed in advance. Do make sure you understand what is a fair rate. Rates include waiting time, such as for an outing to a supermarket, restaurant, or shopping mall.

Private arrangements should only be made through a personal reference by someone who can vouch for the driver's reliability, safety and any other criteria important to the passenger.

For short term visitors, drivers can be organised through 4* and 5* hotels. These drivers are generally reliable as well. Due to their high demand, it is best to ensure that arrangements for a professional driver are made well in advance of need, ideally 24 hours in advance. Services are charged by the hour and sometimes by the half hour. Most hotels will allow these services to be added to the guest's hotel bill, but it is best to check in advance.

Taxis

Taxis are generally *not* advised for Western visitors and expatriates, although they are sometimes necessary when other arrangements have fallen through, which does happen even with the best of planning. The challenges presented by general taxi drivers are less about personal safety and more about the condition of the vehicle (and sometimes the driver), a reasonable chance of a language barrier, and the passenger's ability to know the going rate to their destination and their ability to haggle well.

There are few taxi ranks in Saudi Arabia other than at the major airports and a few shopping malls in city centres. London Taxi has been established in Riyadh using black cabs familiar to Londoners and is considered the best choice. Taxis organised by top end hotels are probably safer than a random taxi, in part because someone from the hotel staff is very likely to take down the taxi's details, which the driver is aware of.

Women can expect drivers, especially taxi drivers, to move up the front passenger seat as a gesture of respect for the woman.

Many frequent visitors and residents in Saudi Arabia often collect the business cards and telephone numbers of a taxi driver they were comfortable with on a previous journey and contact them in a pinch. Some compound managers may also be able to help out.

It is important to know exactly where you are going if you must take a random taxi. Drivers are often from the Indian subcontinent and may not speak either English or Arabic well. Ensure you have the telephone numbers of someone at your destination in case you need to contact them along the way. In addition, this is not the time to start a journey with a flat battery in your mobile phone. Do ensure you are charged and able to make what could be a series of telephone calls.

Uber

Uber has arrived in Saudi Arabia, and is currently operational in Riyadh, Jeddah and Dammam, with plans to expand into other major cities such as Jubail and Yanbu. Although in its early days, appears to be successful, and is particularly popular amongst working Saudi women who out of necessity must rely on men to drive them to work.

Public transport

Local busses
Local busses are *not* recommended for Western visitors and a non-starter for women; it might even cause problems for the driver if you attempt to use a local bus as it would be considered very peculiar. Alternative transport should be arranged.

Long distance busses
Unlike the advice against using local busses in Saudi Arabia, it is possible for Western visitors to use long distance busses between cities in Saudi Arabia. The busses are modern, air conditioned and kept in reasonably good operating condition.

Whilst not recommended as a main form of transport, SAPTCO services make sense if travelling to a very remote part of the Kingdom that is not served well by a regional airport. They can also be a good way to see the Kingdom more slowly if taking a leisure trip, especially on some of the more scenic routes.

Train
At the time of publication, there are train services between Riyadh and Dammam. Although inexpensive, they are generally not popular with Western visitors as they are infrequent and relatively slow. In addition, the train is not usually a practical option due to the need for a vehicle at either end of the train route.

Future options
Saudi Arabia is making a huge investment in improving their infrastructure. This includes new public train transport in all three metropolitan areas frequented by most Western expatriates and visitors. However, it is unclear at the time of publication if decreased oil revenues will delay or otherwise impact these projects.

Projects include: the Haramain High Speed Rail project is building a system to link Jeddah, Mecca and Medina. Saudi Railways

Organization (SRO) operates the only long standing railway line from Riyadh to Dammam and has plans to interconnect all major points within Saudi Arabia. The Riyadh Metro development is now underway and will have six separate lines upon completion. Once the Jeddah Metro design plans are complete, with construction expected to begin. Mecca Metro plans have also been announced, which will compliment the Al Mashaaer Al Mugaddassah Metro system, which opened in 2010 and transports pilgrims between major holy sites. Plans have been announced in 2014 to build a Dammam Metro, linking Qatif, Dhahran and Dammam.

THINGS TO DO

Saudi Arabia is not known to be a hotbed of public social activity. Many activities taken for granted elsewhere are not available or sometimes not even legal in the Kingdom. Others may not appeal to Westerners. However, Western expatriates and visitors who come to Saudi Arabia with an open mind and an ability to find and develop their own social networks will not be bored.

It must be noted that many Western expatriates tend to develop their social life around their residential compound, work or sometimes through a sport or other hobby. Although it is possible to make friends with Saudi nationals, it can often take time and patience.

Dining out

Dining out is a major social activity for many Saudi nationals, expatriates and visitors from all over the world. Restaurants of all types of cuisines can be found in the major cities. A more limited number of options are found in more remote areas, although choices are increasing regionally as well.

Food hygiene is generally of the same high standards as found in the West, although patrons of very cheap eateries that typically cater to very low paid expatriate men, usually from the Indian subcontinent, should be approached with caution – that is, if they would serve a Westerner at all. Most of these establishments do not cater to women at all.

Many of the most upscale restaurants are found in the five star hotels. Typical cuisines found in these hotels include Lebanese, Turkish, French, Italian, American steak houses, seafood restaurants and international buffets that offer cuisines from all over the world. Excellent quality regional Indian, Chinese, Thai, and even Japanese restaurants are also popular. Attending a Friday buffet in an upscale restaurant on a Friday afternoon is a favourite pastime amongst Saudi nationals and expatriates alike.

In the major cities, there are also a wide variety of stand-alone restaurants that also cater to the upper end of the market, including many along the corniches of Jeddah and Al Khobar. Mid-range restaurants can be found throughout the Kingdom, often in upscale shopping malls. American fast food establishments are also very popular in Saudi Arabia and can be found in all major cities, both in shopping centres as well as the ubiquitous 'drive thrus'.

Saudi's love of fast food goes well beyond the usual American brands. Local and regional fast food names and other chains include the following popular establishments, which can be found throughout the Kingdom: Kudu, Java Time, al Baik, Al Tazaj, Zaatar w Zeit, Café Bateel. Most Westerners would also find these establishments appealing if they already like fast food or restaurant chains.

Saudis tend to eat later than most Westerners. Their breakfasts and lunches are relatively light meals; their main meal is usually in the evening, sometimes lasting for hours, especially if dining out with a large family group or for business.

Visitors looking for 'Saudi cuisine' might be disappointed to learn that, although there are a few popular Saudi-specific dishes, most Saudis have adapted a pan-Arab palate that draws on Levantine cuisine, especially from Lebanon and Syria. Other culinary influences come from a variety of Indian, Pakistani and Persian cuisines. Common ingredients include dates, nuts, vegetables, biryani rice, and either lamb, chicken or fish.

The dish most closely associated with Saudi Arabia is *kabsa*, a blend of biryani rice, vegetables, almonds, pine nuts, sultanas and meat – usually lamb, goat, chicken or even camel. Commonly used spices are cardamom, cinnamon, cloves, ground pepper and saffron. It is traditionally served on a large communal platter in a stewed gravy. It is eaten with the right hand or with *fatir*, a Saudi flat bread. Other countries in the region make a similar dish known as *machbous*.

Popular pan-Arab dishes found throughout the Kingdom include *mezze* dishes such as *foul medames, hummous, moutabel, tabouleh, babaganouj, and kibbeh.* Popular main courses include a mixed grill of lamb and chicken kebabs, chops, onions, peppers and lemons. *Hammour* is a popular flaky fish.

Shawarma (Levantine) and *falafel* (Egyptian), both often served with *tahini*, a sesame based sauce, are popular snacks that were once sold on the street or in the *souq*. At present, they are likely to be found as an alternative to American fast food in a shopping mall food court or similar.

Many Saudis are notorious for their sweet tooth. In fact, the Saudi population suffers from one of the highest rates both of obesity and diabetes in the world. French bakeries, Lebanese sweet shops and Western ice cream parlours all thrive. *Umm Ali*, is a particularly popular Egyptian dish made of sweetened pastry or bread pudding, cream, nuts and raisins.

Popular beverages include freshly squeezed fruit juices, *laban* – a yoghurt drink similar to Indian *lassi*, water, and American fizzy drinks, especially PepsiCola products. *Kahwa*, a strong coffee often flavoured with cardamom seeds, is popular, and is often served to guests along with dates as a traditional Saudi welcome. Some Saudis also drink very sweet tea.

Whenever you arrive at a restaurant of any description, it is important to note whether it has a family section that is still in use. Only a few years ago, it was mandatory for a single man or group of men to dine in the main or bachelor section of the restaurant, with families, groups of women, or any group that includes at least one woman to dine in the family section of the restaurant. The family section is often tucked away in the back or to one side of the main section and sometimes has a separate entrance to the main restaurant.

In recent times, many restaurants are no longer strictly enforcing family section 'rules'. This is particularly true of hotel restaurants. Instead, any group that includes a woman may request that a screen is brought to the table or booth to maintain modesty or privacy, regardless of which section of the restaurant they are sitting in.

If you are dining during a prayer time, especially in a very public place, restaurant employees are expected to close the restaurant for the duration of the prayer time and pray themselves if they are Muslim. Non-Muslims must still close up shop. The dining party has the choice of continuing to enjoy their meal or to leave and return once the prayer time has finished and the restaurant has reopened. Diners should note that if they choose to remain in the restaurant, there will be no further service until prayer time is over.

Although Saudi has not been a traditional tipping culture, in recent years, high end restaurants often expect a tip of about 10%. Tips or service charges are rarely added to the restaurant bill, although they will be included on a room service bill in a hotel. It is not necessary to leave a tip in very informal restaurants, although a couple of riyals would be appreciated.

Dining In/Home delivery

Unlike grocery shopping, restaurant home delivery services are widespread and reliable throughout all major metropolitan areas of Saudi Arabia. Websites such as

Talabat provide a wide choice of restaurants and cuisines that will deliver to your residence.

Shopping

Everyday shopping

Along with dining out, shopping is another very popular form of entertainment in Saudi Arabia. Most shopping malls are geared to children's activities and have plenty of restaurants in addition to the usual shops.

The days of shopping in atmospheric *souqs* are mostly over. Whilst a few *souqs* remain in the major cities, they are now geared mostly toward the poorest members of Saudi society. Many very poorly paid unskilled or semiskilled expatriate labourers also rely on the *souqs* to save money.

Most Saudis now prefer to shop in modern shopping malls. These may resemble anything from a typical suburban American mall to a very glitzy collection of designer shops attached to a prestigious office building or hotel. There are also a number of stand-alone shops, many of which also cater to the top end of the market.

What to expect

Western visitors and expatriates might find their first experience in a Saudi shopping mall to be very surprising. For example, many shops sell women's clothing that would normally be worn in the West and are indeed, often branches and franchises of British high street shops. Luxury brand retailers from Europe have a significant presence in the big cities.

Other shops sell very sexy women's underwear that would rival products found in Western shops like Victoria's Secret or Agent Provocateur. Of course, these garments are never seen in public anywhere in Saudi Arabia, but it does provoke curiosity as to where and when Saudi women may wear these garments.

Other items that are commonly found in most shopping malls and other popular shopping centres are children's clothing, toys and other goods, technology and gadgets, especially mobile phones, Islamic religious items from prayer beads to the Holy Qur'an, good quality carpets that are usually imported from Iran, and books, although it should be noted that Saudi Arabia continues to impose strict censorship on reading materials so choice may be limited. Al Jarir is a bookshop and supplier of notebooks, school supplies and technology accessories that is worth visiting; many branches are found all over the major cities in shopping malls as well as free standing properties.

Western visitors may also find a few other peculiarities whilst shopping in Saudi malls. Mannequins, where they exist, are displayed without heads. Promotional posters will generally exclude or pixillate the model's face. There are no dressing rooms, so items are generally purchased and then tried on back home or in the hotel. Interestingly, unwanted items are not often returned to the shop, but are given as gifts to family or friends instead.

Some shops reserve admission to 'Families only', which means that a single man or a group of men are not allowed entry, although on occasion, a blind eye is turned for men who are obviously Western. In fact, many entire shopping malls now have an admissions policy that may bar singles (bachelors) from entering other than during designated hours that are inevitably inconvenient for business people.

In many environments, including shops, hypermarkets, and government buildings, women often have separate queues, priority queues or are invited to the front of a queue, especially when they are alone. This common practice is not considered rude and often extends beyond Saudi women, with Western women often benefitting from this courtesy.

VIPs, who may be considered important for a range of reasons, are also often exempt from many queues. VIPs are not always obvious.

Opening hours

Many shopping malls operate on a split day, traditional to most other businesses in Saudi Arabia. Others may remain open throughout the day but a large number of shops within the mall remain closed. Supermarkets and hypermarkets that are integrated into a shopping mall are the exception and typically remain open throughout the day.

The most common opening times for major shopping malls are from 09.00 or 09.30 to about 12.00 or when the *dhuhr* prayer is about to start. They reopen at about 16.00 and then remain open until late at night. Some shops, especially smaller shops that cater to Saudi customers, may not open at all during the morning. This includes some *abaya* shops.

Most malls will be open until 23.00 or so during the week and as late as 01.00 on Thursday evening. Malls are closed on Friday morning; however, most are now open from 16.00 to 23.00 on Friday evening.

It should be noted that shopping malls and other shopping districts operate different opening hours during the month of Ramadan. Shops may be open for only an hour or so sometime in the morning, then will open for another short period late afternoon but close before sunset, then open again from about 21.00 until 01.00 or maybe a bit later.

Prayer times

Shoppers should take note that all shops, banks, restaurants and other businesses close during each of the prayer times. If you are shopping near a prayer time, you will hear the call to prayer that will give you a signal to complete your shopping quickly. Some shops may also announce that they are closing in x minutes.

Once the prayer time arrives, the shops will bring down their shutters and close. Shoppers in smaller shops will be asked to leave and return once prayers are over. Women and non-Muslim men may wait on a mall bench during prayer times, which can last from 20 – 30 minutes in a large shopping mall. Muslim men or men who look as though they might be Muslim could possibly be challenged by any roaming religious police, although this is much less likely than in the past, especially in Jeddah and the Eastern Province.

It is possible to be 'locked in' to larger shops, especially supermarkets, as well as restaurants. However, if you make the choice to stay, you must wait patiently in a shop and not walk around or continue shopping. It is acceptable to continue to eat your meal in a restaurant.

Shopping malls and major shopping districts

It is not possible nor is it the intention of the author to list all shopping malls and districts that can be found throughout Saudi Arabia. New malls are built. Older malls fall out of favour. Shopping districts migrate to newly trendy neighbourhoods.

The following information does, however, provide the Western expatriate or visitor with a snapshot selection of the most popular shopping destinations that are likely to appeal to their tastes and expectations.

Riyadh

Riyadh is a relatively new city and its shopping structure reflects this as well. Although there are a few traditional *souqs* situated in the old al Batha district of the city, most Riyadh shopping has evolved into an endless procession of shopping malls, strip malls and parades of often very upscale shops. The main high end shopping district is along Olaya Street, King Fahd Road, and King Abdul Aziz Road, with additional options along several of the more suburban ring roads.

The most upscale shopping malls are the Centria Mall, Panorama Mall, Al Faisaliyah Centre and the al Mamlaka (Kingdom Centre) shopping mall in the Kingdom Centre. The Kingdom Centre and Panorama Mall are noteworthy in that it has a Ladies Only top floor, where men are not allowed and women can remove their *abaya*. The ladies only floor contains self contained shops as well as the top floor of the Debenhams and Saks Fifth Avenue department stores.

Riyadh also has an assortment of shopping malls that sell a mix of luxury and high quality brands. Many Westerners are comfortable in these malls as many of the shops are a mix of British high street shops, retailers from the USA and regional variations of similar shops. Many also include a number of *abaya* shops, which female residents and many visitors will need to visit on occasion in the Kingdom. The advantage of *abaya* shops in shopping malls is the more Western style shopping experience than is found in more traditional markets, thus making the experience a bit more comfortable.

Popular malls in this category include the Akariya Mall, Centrepoint, Deira Shopping Centre Mall, Euromarche, Granada Mall, Hayat Mall, Marina Mall, Nakheel Mall, Riyadh Gallery, Royal Mall and Sahara Mall. As traffic is notoriously bad in Riyadh, especially when the malls are open, it is prudent to plan your shopping accordingly. For example, it might make sense to visit more than one shopping mall located next to each other, such as the Hayat and Sahara malls or the Granada Mall and Centrepoint.

There are several other shops along major arteries in Riyadh that don't look much different than those found in Houston or the newer cities in parts of Asia. Some hotels have a modest arcade of shops or a simple gift shop; others do not.

The days of haggling in the *souqs* for everyday goods are over in Riyadh unless you prefer to subject yourself to this method of shopping. In truth, *souqs* are used by the economically disadvantaged, older traditionalists, and those who find them a novelty. Most of the remaining Riyadh *souqs* are located in the al Batha neighbourhood and are staffed and populated mostly by people from the Indian subcontinent.

The Al Thumairi *souq*, also known as the Deira *souq*, sells furniture, local and regional artefacts from the Indian subcontinent, gold and traditional jewellery. The Princess *souq* sells second hand clothing. Those with luck and patience may find treasures, especially elaborately embroidered and decorated women's clothing. Men's and children's clothing are also sold here.

The Al Owais and Al Taiba *souqs*, also collectively known as the Kuwaiti *souq*, is located in Mohamadiyah off King Fahd Road in Olaya and sells a variety of inexpensive household items along with furniture and traditional clothing (and great place to buy cheap *abayas*) and jewellery.

Jeddah

The city of Jeddah has a long history of trade ... and shopping.

The first *souqs* were established in the old city, where a few remain. They are probably more interesting for touring or souvenir purposes than they are for practical everyday shopping. They are located in the Al Balad neighbourhood and include Souq Qabel, which sells electronics and perfumes, Souq Al Alawi, which sells home goods and spices and is in the newly named World Heritage Site famous for its distinctive coral buildings, Souq Al Jamia, which sells textiles and spices, and Souq al Nada, which sells silver and gold.

As Jeddah grew and modernised, Western style shops started to appear elsewhere in the city. Tahlia Street and its immediate surroundings remain exclusive shopping streets with shops and urban malls selling top end European goods.

Major shopping malls are found throughout Jeddah, along Tahlia Street as well as in many locations in the northern neighbourhoods of the city and near the airport. Shopping malls and centres of all sizes that are likely to appeal to Western expatriates and visitors include al Andalus Mall, al Basateen Centre, al Hayat/al Khayyat, al Salaam Mall, Aziz Mall, Haifaa Mall, Hera'a Mall, Jeddah Mall, Mall of Arabia, Red Sea Mall, Roshan Mall, Serafi Mega Mall, Thalia Roshana Centre, and the Sultan Centre. The Red Sea Mall and Mall of Arabia are amongst the largest.

Yanbu

Shopping in Yanbu is somewhat limited for the shopper with Western tastes and needs. Dana Mall is the main shopping mall, located on King Abdul Aziz Road on the outskirts of Yanbu town. Otherwise, a trip to Jeddah or beyond may be required.

KAEC

Although basic services such as a supermarket, some restaurants and the Bay La Sun hotel are open, most of KAEC's shopping facilities are not complete at the time of publication. Jeddah is approximately 100 kilometres away.

Eastern Province

The shopping experience in the Eastern Province is somewhat dependent on which city you plan to shop in. As a rule, Al Khobar is appealing to Western expatriates and visitors, as is Dhahran with the large influence of Saudi Aramco. Dammam, Jubail and smaller cities are of more limited appeal.

Al Khobar

The largest and most popular mall in al Khobar is the Al Rashid Mall and the adjacent Carrefour Rashid Mall. Other shopping malls that may hold interest include the Al Khobar Mall, Rahmania and Venicia. There are also some shops along the Corniche and near the major hotels as well.

Dhahran

The other large, shopping mall popular with Western expatriates and visitors in the region is the Mall of Dhahran.

Dammam

Shopping in Dammam tends to cater to the tastes of Saudi nationals. Noteworthy malls and shopping centres include Al Bilad, Al Shatea, Marina and Oithman Malls.

Jubail

Jubail shopping is somewhat limited and, counter intuitively located in the Jubail Industrial Zone area of the city and not the city centre. Most Westerners rely on the Fanateer Mall or Al Huwaylath commercial centre. At the time of publication, Jubail was in the midst of a building boom that included the construction of new retail shops, including the Galleria Centre near the Fanateer Mall. However, many Westerners may prefer to make the journey to Dammam, Dhahran or Al Khobar, where the selection is much greater and often more appealing to Western tastes.

Souvenirs

Since Saudi Arabia does not promote general tourism, it should come as no surprise that tourist mementos and souvenirs that might appeal to Western visitors are not easy to find. Even t-shirts with a Saudi Arabian reference are thin on the ground, although they do exist. You may need to ask the clerk, who may be keeping a small selection behind the counter as they may contain an image that could draw the attention of the religious police. Some t-shirts can be found within shops of a different context, such as a scuba diving shop or even Harley Davidson. Starbucks also do a range of mugs and other items that include Saudi city names.

Western visitors might wish to look around their hotel gift shop, although not all upscale hotels have a selection of touristy items. It must also be pointed out that many items are actually imported from India and Kashmir, so buyer beware.

For more authentic Saudi artefacts, shoppers may wish to visit Lamsa, a series of Saudi owned shops that are found in major cities throughout the Kingdom. Some Westerners have found suitable items in the Granada Mall in Riyadh, the Red Sea Mall in Jeddah and the al Rashid Mall in al Khobar.

For those shoppers who are looking for Saudi gift ideas, here are some items that may appeal: Scents for the room: incense, frankincense and myrrh. Perfume scents, especially *oud*, a wood based perfume. *Oud*, the musical instrument of the same name, is a more elaborate gift idea. Beauty items such as henna to decorate hands and feet, or kohl, which is used to outline the eyes, may appeal.

Traditional Saudi clothing makes an interesting gift, including the *thobe, shemagh* or *ghutra, agal* and *bisht,* all of which are part of men's national dress. The *abaya, shayla* and *niqab* are memorable garments that are part of women's national dress. Women's elaborately designed dresses, traditionally worn under the *abaya,* are another option and can be very pretty. All of these garments are described in fuller detail later in this Section.

Saudi coffee pots known as *dallah* are a good souvenir. The *dallah* is usually part of a set of six cups and a tray. Dates and honey can be good buys and are delicious.

Water pipes, known as a *hookah, nargila, shisha* or hubbly bubbly are popular. Although their origins are in the Levant and Iran, they are smoked in many coffee shops and restaurants in Saudi Arabia and might bring back fond memories for some smokers.

Finally, elaborate craftwork in silver or gold can be found in Saudi Arabia. Silver works can be beautiful and may be reasonably priced for the amount of effort that has gone into the item. Gold shops and *souqs* exist in Saudi Arabia, but many regional travellers may prefer to wait and make their gold purchases whilst in Dubai.

Shopping and transport

Shopping malls have a wide range of parking options. Some have underground parking. Others have big American style car parks, often but not always covered to provide a bit of shade. However, most parking is very crowded, with many Saudis in particular hovering for a near-to-the-door parking space, thus blocking other drivers' progress. Many drivers often take their time dropping off their passengers near the door regardless of others' inconvenience. Many upscale shopping centres have VIP or valet parking as well.

Women who rely on drivers will generally be dropped off at a gate or door that is conventionally used by drivers. It is very important that the woman takes note of the door or gate number, which will be prominently displayed. This is normally where her driver will return to collect her once she is finished shopping.

Although some women may know exactly how long it will take for them to shop and thus are ready to be collected by their drivers at a precise time, most do not. Thus, it is an excellent idea to store your driver's mobile number and even test it by ringing him whilst still in the vehicle to make sure it works and his battery is charged.

When the woman is ready to leave the mall, she should ring her driver a couple of minutes before reaching the gate or door. Women who are visiting Saudi Arabia should ensure they have a local Saudi mobile number as drivers can rarely afford to make a call abroad as the roaming charges are prohibitive on their wages. Some may not even be able to afford receiving a call from a Saudi mobile number supplied by a different service provider. In this situation, the driver may ask you to send him a 'missed call' when you are ready to be collected.

Although a few of the biggest shopping malls on Olaya Street do have taxi ranks, many others do not. For those women who cannot organise their own transport or if their transport has fallen through, it is better to find the taxi dispatcher than to randomly accept a ride from a taxi tout.

Sport

Although Saudis are not known for their sporting prowess, there are a number of sporting facilities in the Kingdom. Sporting activities are gender segregated. Many are generally male only, including most spectator sports.

Outside the expatriate compounds, these include fitness centres and gyms, with accommodation for a variety of racket sports. Fitness centres and gyms exist in freestanding buildings as well as in most upscale hotels, where there are also some facilities available for women, such as women's workout centres.

Further sporting activities include a wide range of equestrian activities. Football is also very popular.

There are a few golf courses, mostly located in the Eastern Province or around Riyadh; most are sand courses as opposed to grass. Some have a family membership policy, such as the Dirab Golf and Country Club in Riyadh, thus allowing women access. Arizona Country Club, also in Riyadh, is within the expatriate compound of the same name.

Of course, sporting facilities abound on expatriate compounds and are often orientated to reflect the nationalities and sporting interests of the dominant nationalities living on the compounds. Thus, it is possible to find cricket, baseball, basketball and hockey within certain compounds.

For expatriate residents and visitors to the Eastern Province and especially to Jeddah and the Red Sea coast, there is a terrific selection of water sports. This includes boating, jet skiing and other motorised water sports, and snorkelling.

Scuba divers will be delighted to learn that the Red Sea near Jeddah offers some of the world's best scuba diving, especially for those divers prepared to take a boat ride out to some of the shallow reefs found about an hour away. Most diving in Jeddah starts from the beach clubs found in North Obhur and can be organised through affiliated hotels or scuba shops. Jeddah has many PADI, NAUI and BSAC certified dive centres with properly qualified dive masters. Scuba enthusiasts will be pleased to know that diving can also be organised if working in KAUST, KAEC or Yanbu, all north of Jeddah. Divers looking for an unspoilt diving experience may wish to dive in the Farasan islands in the southeast of the country.

Expatriates and visitors who enjoy more leisurely activities in the sun and sea may wish to take out a membership at a private beach in the Eastern Province or around Jeddah. Private beaches have the advantage of allowing Western dress, including swimming costumes, and are open to women. Many also have swimming pools, restaurants, and a children's play area.

Since 2013, women are now allowed to ride bicycles and motorbikes, but for recreational purposes only, such as in designated parks. As she is in public, she must do so whilst wearing an *abaya*.

Exploring Saudi Arabia

Many expatriates settle into a routine once they arrive in Saudi Arabia and never find the time or take an interest in exploring their surroundings. Others may be fearful, especially if they do not take the time to learn about the realities on the ground in the Kingdom. Whilst there are no-go areas for Westerners (and others), most of Saudi Arabia is very safe to explore. Your main concerns are the ever dangerous poor driving standards and becoming isolated, whether on a desolate road or especially if going off road into the desert.

This book is not intended to be a tourist guide. However, it is worth highlighting some of the most popular activities and sites that would be interesting to the average tourist ... if average tourists were allowed to visit Saudi Arabia.

It must also be noted that this Section does not explore Mecca and Medina, which are off limits to all non-Muslims regardless of nationality.

In and around Riyadh

In addition to shopping and eating out, Riyadh does offer a few other leisure activities. There are a number of family friendly parks that may give some expatriates an opportunity to break out of their bubble and mix with Saudi nationals and others – children are a great ice-breaker to conversation.

The Masmak Fort was used by the al Saud family during the expansion years of the Saudi Kingdom, and has been turned into a historical museum. The King Abdul Aziz Historical Centre contains the Murabba

Palace, the de facto replacement of the Masmak Fort, and the National Museum. Both are relatively near to the Deira *souq*, which could all be visited comfortably in a day, weather permitting.

To the east of Riyadh is the Camel Market, which makes an interesting excursion for many Westerners.

In and around Jeddah

Jeddah – Jeddah's old city is in the al Balad neighbourhood. It is worth visiting the Naseef House, which contains a museum and cultural centre. You might need to ask someone nearby to find someone who will let you into the building.

Otherwise, Jeddah's corniche is a great place to stroll and people watch, especially during the evening, when Saudi families do the same.

Jeddah is also known for a series of unusual sculptures in the centre of many of its roundabouts. As there are constant threats that urban expansion may put some of these landmarks in jeopardy, you might want to see if you can find the globe, bicycle, cars, coffee pots, engineering, camel, airplane, astronomy, wave, boat, pots (hanging vessels), sea shells, flying carpet and others before it is too late and they are removed.

Around the Eastern province

Most people in the Eastern Province find their way to the parks and the Al Khobar and Jubail corniches, where they can enjoy the relatively relaxed outdoor environment. Due to its proximity, many Western expatriates with a valid exit visa and visitors with a multiple entry Saudi visa also take advantage of the King Fahd Causeway and make their way to Bahrain for a short break from the Kingdom. The Causeway can be very busy during the weekends.

Further afield

In addition to enjoying the natural beauty of the Red Sea, both above and beneath the water, Saudi Arabia has other places of natural beauty that might be of interest to curious Western expatriates and to visitors who may have some spare time in the Kingdom.

Many Western expatriates find it fun and even liberating to make an excursion into the dessert. This may be a simple trip just a few hundred metres off a main road or it may be a big adventure that includes camping, *wadi* bashing (driving along dry river beds) or simply enjoying an evening picnic under the stars. In either case, never venture out into the desert alone, which includes only one vehicle. It's best to make your desert adventure a group affair, and it's a great way to bond with your friends and neighbours.

Very intrepid desert explorers might be interested in exploring Saudi Arabia's rock art, which dates back to the Neolithic period of history from up to 10,000 years ago. Jubbah and Shuwaymas in the Ha'il region of Najd province contain many examples, as does Sakaka and other locations further north and west of Ha'il. Slightly younger rock art can be found at Bir Hima in the of Najran province, and in other areas of the Kingdom.

Also in the northwest of the Kingdom is the remainder of the old Hejaz railway, built in the dying days of the Ottoman Empire in the early 20th Century. Meant to run from Damascus to Mecca to serve Hajj pilgrims, it was never built beyond Medina. Some stations and track still exist today.

The most famous of Saudi Arabia's national parks is Asir National Park, a popular destination year round in the southwest of the Kingdom. Many people visit for hill walking, to escape the worst of the summer heat or simply to enjoy a relatively green part of the country. Al-Khunfah is the Kingdom's largest wildlife reserve, found in the north central region of the Kingdom. Lucky visitors might spot the Arabian oryx or a variety of birds of prey.

The Farasan Islands, also located in the southwest, are an unspoilt archipelago of dozens of islands that would entertain those with an interest in marine or bird life as well as those with an interest in Ottoman architecture that has been left to age gracefully.

Smaller parks and sanctuaries are dotted elsewhere in the Kingdom; some require tickets or permits. Specific information may be difficult to find, so allow some time to ask what is required near the location.

UNESCO *World Heritage Sites*
Saudi Arabia is also home to three UNESCO World Heritage Sites. The At-Turaif District in Diriyah, just outside Riyadh, was the first capital and stronghold of the al Saud dynasty that rules Saudi Arabia to this day. Historic Jeddah was added to the list in 2014, and contains

architecturally distinct coral buildings and tower buildings found in the oldest part of this port city. Finally, for those who are able to make a longer excursion from the major cities might find the more remote site of Mada'in Saleh worth a visit. Mada'in Saleh, located just outside the isolated northwest town of al-Ula, is the sister city to Petra in Jordan. The site contains a large number of Nabataean tombs and other archaeological remnants of Nabataean culture that date back to pre-Islamic and pre-Christian times.

As always, geopolitical events can make some destinations within the Kingdom less safe than others. It is always best to seek advice from local contacts who are knowledgeable and trustworthy. Many Western expatriates and visitors may also wish to check the official advice from their country's embassy.

What you will not find in Saudi Arabia

Although most expatriate residents and guests find a way to socialise, they must be prepared to accept that many forms of entertainment are absent from Saudi Arabia, other than perhaps informally and not always entirely legally on some compounds.

Entertainment activities not found in public in Saudi Arabia include cinemas, concerts or other live music, theatre, opera, ballet, any other live dance, bowling alleys, circus related activities (other than children's face painting) and of course bars, pubs, and nightclubs.

SAFETY AND SECURITY

Assessing your personal safety and security requirements

Nowhere is 100% safe. This includes Western countries as well as Saudi Arabia. However, it is important to put safety issues into perspective as they relate to working and living in Saudi Arabia.

It is also important to point out that things can change within the country, sometimes quickly and with little notice. Other changes are a bit more predictable. It is also important to acknowledge that different people have different attitudes toward safety and security for any number of reasons. Only the reader and their family can decide if they feel safe working and living in the Kingdom.

The following information and advice is given from the perspective of many years' experience in Saudi Arabia. It should only be taken as one person's informed perspective, with professional advice from a number of sources taken in to consideration. Many people will do their own research, often starting with their own country's official government travel advice. A list of prominent English speaking Western countries' websites is provided at the end of this book.

Issues most people worry about

Although safety and security is a personal matter, there are recurrent themes regarding safety that should be taken into account by anyone planning to travel to or live in Saudi Arabia.

Political crime

Threat of terrorism

For the purposes of this topic, the author regards terrorism as it is defined in the Oxford English Dictionary: 'The unofficial or unauthorised use of violence and intimidation in the pursuit of political aims'.

Saudi Arabia is not immune from terrorism. From a Saudi perspective, the worst act of terrorism in modern times took place on home soil in 1979, when a group of Saudi national extremists seized the Grand Mosque and surrounding area of Mecca. Several people were killed; the perpetrators were swiftly executed. This led directly to a much stricter interpretation of Islamic behaviour in the Kingdom that is only now beginning to relax over the past few years.

From a Western perspective, the terrorist bombings of several Western compounds within Saudi Arabia in the early 2000s caused several Western expatriates to reassess their comfort levels working and living in the Kingdom. At the time of publication, the last of these occurred in 2004. On the other hand, since 2004, individual Westerners have encountered difficulties around road rage, labour disputes, illegal trade in alcohol and other banned substances, crimes of passion, and other mostly avoidable offences.

There has been an escalation of bombings in 2015, which have taken place mostly outside Shi'a mosques in either the Eastern Province or near the Yemen border.

US Americans in particular are also well aware that 15 of the 19 people directly involved in the collection of terror attacks in the US known as the events of September 11th were Saudi nationals. Whilst this did not occur on Saudi soil, it does have an impact on many Westerners' decision as to whether to work or live in the Kingdom.

Of course, if a quick search of terrorist activities is undertaken over the past 15 years elsewhere, results are returned for several Western countries (and plenty of others), including but not limited to Australia, Belgium, Canada, France, Germany, the Netherlands, Norway, Russia, Spain, Turkey, the United Kingdom and the United States.

The Saudi government takes domestic terrorism very seriously and has stepped up activities to prevent incidents from happening within its borders. Although no guarantee, security measures are in place in high profile locations, including most high end hotels, offices, and of course compounds where Western expatriates live.

War and military conflict

In modern times, Saudi Arabia was a participant in the Arab Israeli war of the late 1940s. As this military conflict was never formally resolved, Saudi Arabia remains in a technical state of war with Israel although there has been no formal military conflict for decades. However, it is a main reason why travellers to Saudi Arabia cannot be admitted to the Kingdom if evidence of travel to Israel is discovered. This practice is unilateral.

Saudi Arabia was engaged in the Gulf War of 1990-1991, allied alongside a number of Western and other Middle East countries, supporting Kuwait against Iraq.

Saudi Arabia has a history of engagement with civil wars and other unrest in Yemen. At the time of publication, Saudi Arabia is engaged in another military conflict in Yemen against rebels who have been impeding the current Yemeni President from fully taking power. Travel to the region of Saudi Arabia that borders Yemen is currently considered off limits to most Westerners as advised by their respective governments.

Many analysts would also say that Saudi Arabia is engaged in a proxy war with Iran, where it is being played out in Iraq, Syria and Yemen.

At the time of publication, most Western countries continue to support and supply Saudi Arabia's military to varying degrees.

General political stability

Saudi Arabia has enjoyed a good level of political stability since independence in 1932. However, it is also fair to note that there is some political dissatisfaction within the Kingdom, countered by a robust government response to quell the conflict, often brutally.

At the time of publication, there is an increased level of unrest in the Eastern Province, where the majority of the Kingdom's Shi'a population live. Many Shi'a believe they have been marginalised or worse; some have protested or preached for reform. Most of these activities have been declared illegal by the Saudi authorities, with consequences that have included both corporal and capital punishment of the accused.

Longer term, there are many sensitive questions over the succession of the current King to what strongly appears to be the beginning of the next generation of the House of Saud. This is new territory for the Kingdom and indeed the world. King Salman has indicated his preferences by naming a nephew as Crown Prince and one of his sons as Deputy Crown Prince, both of whom are descendent from the Sudairi Seven, a powerful coalition of full brothers and sons of the first king, King Abdul Aziz ibn Saud. The Crown Prince and Deputy Crown Prince, although technically of the same generation, have an age gap of about one generation.

What you can do

As always, geopolitical events can make some destinations within the Kingdom less safe than others. It is always best to seek advice from local contacts who are knowledgeable and trustworthy. Many Western expatriates and visitors may also wish to check the official advice from their country's embassy at the time they are considering travel.

It is also a good idea for expatriate residents and long term business visitors to officially register their presence in the Kingdom with their embassy should the need to leave the country quickly or to be evacuated ever becomes necessary.

Other crime

Violent crime

Although not completely absent in Saudi Arabia, the rate of violent crime in the Kingdom is significantly lower than in most of the Western world. Although it would be naïve to suggest that all violent crime is reported in Saudi Arabia, especially rape and honour crimes, crime can be underreported in the West as well.

As an example, the homicide rate in the US is more than five times greater than that of Saudi Arabia. In absolute numbers, that translates to 14,748 vs 265 with the Saudi population approximately 10% the size of the US population.

Personal safety issues

Saudi Arabia is generally safe when it comes to personal safety matters. According to most Western embassies, pickpockets, assaults and theft are much lower than in most Western countries, although crimes related to sexual harassment are unlikely to be truly represented in any official figures.

Although it is not recommended to test this unnecessarily, it is still possible to mistakenly lose or leave a valuable item behind somewhere in public and it will most probably still be there or put in safekeeping for when the rightful owner returns to claim it.

Corporal and capital punishment

Saudi Arabia is amongst the top five countries that practice capital punishment, along with China, Iran, Iraq and the United States.

As a reminder, the following behaviour can attract the death penalty in Saudi Arabia: murder, rape, apostasy, blasphemy, armed robbery, illegal drug smuggling, repeated drug use, adultery, sodomy, homosexual sexual activity, witchcraft, sorcery and terrorism.

The Kingdom also practices corporal punishment, which usually involves flogging with a set number of lashes, or amputation of a hand or foot in some instances.

It is imperative for Westerners to understand that they are not exempt from these punishments if found guilty of violating Saudi law. Further details about corporal and capital punishment can be found in the Islam section of this book.

Coming from a Western country/Western culture

Saudis have a wide range of attitudes toward Westerners. Some embrace them wholeheartedly. Others embrace some of their values, such as advancements in science, education, technology and business, but not others, such as social practices or ethics. It is also true that a number of Saudis have a neutral or even negative opinion about Westerners. The vast majority of the former tolerate their presence in the Kingdom; many of the latter simply avoid them.

Your experience in Saudi Arabia as a Westerner will depend on your own attitude and your ability to adapt to the Saudi way of life, even if you don't agree with some aspects of it. It is also worth choosing your battles about very difficult issues, keeping in mind that, as Westerners, we are only guests in a foreign country.

Data protection

Data protection concerns are growing around the world, including in Saudi Arabia. Whilst the Kingdom is nowhere nearly as restrictive as it is in countries such as China, care should be taken by anyone who is managing sensitive information, whether for commercial or personal reasons.

It is best to have an attitude that, although the authorities' behaviour may not default to actively monitoring your every keystroke or voice call, it is almost certainly possible they could produce copies of them if there is a motivation to do so.

For anyone who requires robust data protection, it is recommended that they seek professional advice prior to travelling to Saudi Arabia. There have also been instances in the past where data protection techniques such as encryption have been deemed illegal or, in the case of the use of BlackBerry devices a few years ago, threatened with banning.

What you can do

Managing your personal safety and security is ultimately up to you. Only you and your family can determine the boundaries of your own comfort and what you should do if they are breeched. Other ideas that many Western expatriates find effective:

- Show respect for Saudi culture
- Don't be alone with just one other person
- Do not send the wrong signal to another Saudi that could be interpreted as sexual availability
- Don't be too casual about protecting your personal possessions, especially by leaving them unattended in public or in plain view in a vehicle
- Encrypt or otherwise protect your computer and other technology. Even so, have a healthy suspicion that the Saudi authorities could trace your electronic footprint if motivated to do so
- Trust your instincts

Issues to take into consideration

There are a host of safety and security measures that should be taken into consideration when travelling to or living in Saudi Arabia, some of which many Westerners give little thought so.

The effects of the sun

Don't ignore the fact that it is very easy to become sunburnt in Saudi Arabia, even if you are outside for only a short period of time. Be particularly careful if you are in an environment such as on a Western orientated compound or anywhere else where the dress code is relaxed.

It is a good idea to import plenty of high factor sunscreen as it is very difficult to find in Saudi Arabia. Although much easier to find, you may also wish to purchase several sets of sunglasses with good UV protection.

The effects of temperatures reaching up to 50C

Many people are unaware of how easy it is to become dehydrated, especially when the temperatures soar, especially in the relatively dry climates of Riyadh and other areas away from the coasts.

Drink plenty of water and make sure you have a sufficient supply of water with you whenever you are travelling by road. Still water is advised; sparkling water and other fizzy drinks can become problematic if stored in a hot vehicle for any length of time. As a reminder, this will be a difficult challenge to manage during Ramadan, when drinking in public, including water, is not allowed during daylight hours.

Road traffic

By far, the most dangerous part of working and living in Saudi Arabia is related to road traffic, as has been detailed in several other sections of this book.

As much as many Westerners' sense of fair play may be offended, it is strongly advised that all drivers and concerned passengers keep the following in mind.

For drivers, consider traffic to be Darwinian. If it's bigger than you, it wins. If you are bigger than it, you win. That's for a start. It's also important to acknowledge that this principal also applies to the hierarchy of nationalities, beginning with whether or not a Saudi driver has also been involved. Thus, it is important to try to work out who is driving as well.

The second consideration is where your vehicle is in relation to another vehicle. If they are in front of you, then you need to be aware and react accordingly. This includes when drivers cut out in front of you, decide to turn left from the extreme right lane, etc. or anything else unknown in the equivalent of the Highway Code.

However, most drivers give little thought to vehicles behind them, other than on the occasions when a vehicle is flashing, hooting and being driven on the shoulder of the motorway trying to get past you. In this situation, it is best to simply yield and let this very dangerous driver overtake you.

Do keep in mind that the majority of drivers are not Saudi but are from countries where it is customary to drive on the left side of the road. This, coupled with the likelihood that many drivers have had a less than robust set of driving lessons and may be unfamiliar with high speed driving prior to coming to the Kingdom also make driving in the Kingdom even more challenging. Some drivers are also not familiar with dual carriageways, motorway junctions etc that simply do not exist back home.

Although pedestrian traffic is rare in most of Saudi Arabia, do take extra precautions if you are on foot and attempting to cross the road. Never trust traffic to stop for you, even if it is supposed to do so.

Zero tolerance for alcohol

Westerners are not exempt from punishment if they are found in possession of alcohol, including home brewed alcohol that can be found on some expatriate compounds.

It is also worth noting that it is an offence to arrive at the airport or over the causeway from Bahrain intoxicated, although airlines that are not dry generally do serve alcohol on flights to Saudi Arabia until they are in Saudi air space.

Zero tolerance for drug abuse

Never take the chance of possessing or consuming any drug that is forbidden in Saudi Arabia. Visitors and residents who are taking prescription drugs should check with the Saudi Embassy in their home country or through another official channel if they are unsure their medication will be allowed into the Kingdom. People who choose to travel to Saudi Arabia with prescription drugs should do so with the prescription and ideally with the items in their original packaging.

Becoming involved in illegal drug use or trade is a very bad idea indeed as it can attract the death penalty.

Sexuality issues

It is worth repeating that the only legal sexual relationships in Saudi Arabia are between a heterosexual married couple. Extramarital heterosexual affairs are highly illegal and in theory could attract the death penalty for either partner who is married to someone else. Any unmarried participant could suffer corporal punishment. All homosexual activity is illegal and is theoretically also a capital offence.

Of course, people are people and relationships do happen. Many people are never officially found out and thus 'get away with it'. But all it takes is one disgruntled person to bring the illicit relationship to the attention of the authorities – or an employer, who is unlikely to take the risk of keeping a problem employee that could compromise the organisation's standing in the Kingdom. Those involved who have been found out may be in a very different and unpleasant situation.

Expatriates with children who have reached puberty are strongly advised to have a thorough conversation with their sons and daughters about sexuality in Saudi Arabia and what behaviour, as parents, you expect of them. A reminder that their mum or dad could also lose their job and the family deported can also be effective.

Dealing with uncomfortable public behaviour

Whilst not particularly dangerous, some public behaviour commonly found in Saudi Arabia can make others very uncomfortable. Whilst there is not always one way to deal with these issues, they are important to recognise. They include:

- *Rude or obscene comments and gestures* – These are usually made toward women when they are momentarily alone with one man and are not unknown throughout the world. Other places where they can commonly occur are on the road, similar to road rage.

- *Queue jumping* – The concept of a queue in Saudi Arabia is tenuous at best. Do not be surprised if there is no queue in many public situations where one would be expected. For example, parcels from other shops cannot be brought into supermarkets but must be checked. At the check-in desk, there will almost certainly be no queue but a free for all. You will need to attract the attendant's attention and standing around demurely waiting your turn will not work.

- *Smoking* – It is estimated that approximately 40% of the male Saudi population smokes. From a non-smoker's perspective, smoking has thankfully been banned in most public places since 2012, including government offices, airports, restaurants, coffee shops, supermarkets and shopping centres. This includes cigarettes and water pipes and presumably cigars as well. Non-smokers will find that the antismoking rules are generally adhered to, although cigarette smoke can sometimes be smelt behind closed doors in some places. It should also be noted that it is strongly frowned upon for women to be seen smoking in public, including expatriate women.

WOMEN'S DAILY LIVING ISSUES IN SAUDI ARABIA

The dress code – realities and practicalities

All women and girls who have visibly reached puberty must be modestly dressed in Saudi Arabia. This includes all expatriate women regardless of their nationality, religion, or any other factor.

At one point in time, some expatriate women were comfortably able to wear Western style clothing that was adapted to ensure all of their body was covered other than their feet, hands and face. However, this changed in the 1980s, after the 1979 terrorist attack in Mecca when the religious authorities were able to enact many strict behaviour expectations.

Since the 1980s, women now wear the *abaya*, the long black dressing gown-like garment that covers the female form from the shoulders to the floor, and until recently, were generally expected to wear the headscarf as well in most situations in public. Women who opt for Western modest clothing such as a floor length skirt and long blouse do not gain respect and would be considered unsuitably dressed as a business woman. She may also attract unwanted attention, including unpleasant comments and staring.

The expatriate women's dress code was further modified in the recent years and has relaxed, but just a tiny bit. At the present time, many expatriate women are no longer wearing the headscarf, although they should always carry one with them or wear one around their neck as some situations still require their use. It is also possible that the religious police might request the headscarf to be worn if the woman is in a particularly conservative area of the Kingdom, although this is no longer routine.

Ideally, a woman should enter Saudi Arabia wearing an *abaya* and should have her headscarf with her in her hand luggage. It is possible to see some Western women and an increasing number of women from some Far East Asian countries wearing loose Western clothing, especially if they are accompanied by other family members. Although the immigration authorities are currently unlikely to directly challenge these women, they could do so.

For businesswomen, it leaves a very bad impression if you are meeting your sponsor or sponsor's representative in the arrivals hall. It is especially advisable for women travelling alone to wear the *abaya*.

Women who are travelling to Saudi Arabia for the first time should purchase an *abaya* prior to boarding their flight. Most major Western cities will have at least one neighbourhood where they can be purchased. Women who are travelling to another Gulf country prior to Saudi Arabia can easily purchase an *abaya* there. Women who do not have these options can purchase an *abaya* on line. Please refer to the 'Preparing to Travel Short Term to Saudi Arabia' for further information about how to buy the correct *abaya* that will suit the wearer.

Women's clothing terms

There continues to be some confusion surrounding Islamic clothing terms, particularly in the West. Although there are regional differences within the Middle East, the following terms are commonly used in Saudi Arabia.

Hijab

Hijab simply means modest dress. It does not specifically refer to a headscarf, although many Muslims would agree that wearing a headscarf is a part of a woman's modest dress code.

In Saudi Arabia, modest dress for a woman means covering her body so that everything other than her feet, hands and face are not exposed and that she is covered in a manner to conceal her body shape. As just discussed, this almost always means wearing the *abaya*.

Abaya

The *abaya* is the black, cloak-like garment that covers a woman's body from her shoulders to the floor as well as fully covering her arms and concealing her body shape, especially her waist. The fabric can be of varying weight, which is useful for adapting to the summer and winter climates. Further details about *abaya* styles can be found in the 'Preparing to Travel Short Term to Saudi Arabia' section.

Women's headscarves – tarha, boshya

The choice a woman makes about her headscarf is very individual and varies widely throughout the Muslim world as well as regionally. For the purposes of this book, we will stay with choices made by most Saudi women and what is generally expected of Western women when required.

The Arabic word name for a headscarf in Saudi Arabia is either a *tarha* or a *boshya*. They are broadly equivalent terms to the term *shayla*, which is often heard elsewhere in some other Gulf countries.

In Saudi Arabia, most *abaya* purchases will include a matching headscarf. It is important to enquire whether the price of the *abaya* includes the headscarf or if it is priced separately. Both are common.

It is also very common to buy headscarves separately. Many Western women find headscarves both attractive and useful both inside and outside the Kingdom.

Niqab

The *niqab* is a face veil that many Saudi women wear in public, especially in very conservative areas of the Kingdom. *Niqab* styles vary, from a cleverly constructed garment that is secured around the head containing two rectangles of fabric that provides a slit for the eyes. This style *niqab* is secured either by tying it around the head or fastening it with Velcro incorporated into the garment. In some instances, there is a string between the eyes to ensure the slit or gap is not too wide.

Other *niqab* styles are full face veils, where the woman's eyes are covered by a sheer piece of fabric.

It is important to understand that wearing the *niqab* is considered by most Muslims worldwide to be a tradition and not specifically a part of the Islamic dress code. Western women are never expected to wear the *niqab*.

Buying an *abaya* and headscarf in Saudi Arabia

Do be aware that *abaya* styles fall in and out of fashion. Very trendy *abayas* in one season can quickly look dated in a year or two. There are also styles that are clearly more suitable to certain age groups. It is also important to recognise that, although some *abaya* styles are very 'bling-y', these are not always appropriate to wear in the presence of either very conservative Saudi nationals nor are some designs considered to be business appropriate.

It is also important to be aware in particular about sleeve styles. In a business environment, sleeves that are too loose can be very awkward when presenting in front of an audience or similar, as the sleeve could easily ride up a raised arm at a very inconvenient time.

Please note that very tall or very large women may require the services of a tailor, who can create a bespoke *abaya* that will suit their requirements. All good *abaya* shops can offer this service, although the shopper may need to return after a day or two to collect the item.

With a quick bit of research or a friendly word at an *abaya* shop, it is not difficult to work out styles and trends that are suitable for the wearer's use.

Saudis can quickly tell the quality of an *abaya* and will often judge the wearer on their choice of garment. If you are unsure, it is possible to get advice from a sales clerk at a good quality *abaya* shop. Fabrics that breathe are particularly important in the warmer months. For an *abaya* that is suitable for business, the author recommends a budget of at least £100 or equivalent as these will generally be of sufficiently good quality to wear at work. It is possible but unnecessary to spend thousands on bespoke, jewel encrusted *abayas*.

Where to buy an abaya in Saudi Arabia

Most women will buy good quality *abayas* in a high end shopping mall or in a standalone shop in an upscale shopping district such as around Olaya Street in Riyadh or Tahlia Street in Jeddah. The following shops are good places to look for good quality *abayas*. This is not an exhaustive list; you may find another suitable shop that is not mentioned.

Alwan
Bidoon Essm
Bukanan
Fashion Line
First Choice
Gulf Lady
Lamsa
Maghateer
Al Mutahajiba
My Fair Lady
Riyadh Lady

Many women also wear off-duty or weekend *abayas*, ie *abayas* that may be less expensive or will be worn when involved in activities that could soil the garment. For example, the author has worn this type of *abaya* travelling to and from scuba diving. Women who are simply walking outside for exercise in public on a moderately warm day, or women going into the desert might be other examples.

For women looking for a more functional *abaya* that may see a bit more wear and tear, and may also cost significantly less, it is possible to purchase a more modestly priced *abaya* in *abaya* souqs that still exist, although in dwindling numbers, throughout the Kingdom. In Riyadh, al al-Uwais souq, popularly known as the Kuwaiti souq between King Fahd Road and Olaya Street is popular, as it Souq al Bawadi in al Balad, Jeddah.

Wearing the *abaya* and headscarf

Abaya styles

As previously discussed, there are two main styles of *abaya*: closed or open. A closed *abaya* is put on over the head; an open *abaya* is fastened in front, usually with snaps. These style choices are mostly a matter of personal preference. However, women choosing to wear the open *abaya* will need to be a bit more cautious about what else she wears on her lower body as open *abayas* often gap, especially when walking or sitting down as the fasteners rarely go below the knee.

198

Under the *abaya*

For most women, the *abaya* is worn over normal, Western clothing. However, when wearing an open *abaya*, women generally choose to wear black or other dark ankle length trousers, or alternatively an ankle length skirt. Wearing a closed *abaya* gives the woman more freedom about what to wear beneath her *abaya* as a properly fitted closed *abaya* will continue to cover the woman's body when she is walking or sitting as well.

Weather considerations

Woman should take the weather into account when wearing an *abaya*. It is not always hot throughout Saudi Arabia. Although Jeddah and the Eastern Province experience either warm or hot and humid weather year round, Riyadh can be somewhat cold in the evenings during the short winter months. Mountainous areas in the north and southwest of the country can be downright cold. It can even snow some years.

Women should dress appropriately for the weather under her *abaya*. This may mean accommodating a jumper or even a heavier coat. Layers are often a good solution, especially if she is outside for much of the day, when afternoon temperatures may become more mild.

Women living in or travelling to Riyadh and other locations with cooler winter weather should also consider purchasing an *abaya* at least one size bigger than their usual *abaya* size to accommodate layered clothing, a jumper or jacket worn underneath.

Businesswomen and the abaya

Businesswomen should wear a very conservative business suit under her *abaya*. This is because in some offices, she may actually be invited to remove it once she is situated in a very private part of the office where the public cannot randomly see her. This happens more often than one might think. The invitation can come from Saudi nationals as well as other employees who know their Saudi sponsor advocates this position. If the woman has made a different dress choice under her *abaya* and feels she must decline the offer of removing her *abaya*, it can lead to unwanted speculation as to what she might (or might not) be wearing underneath.

Businesswomen should always be aware of the need to wear a headscarf in some situations. This includes meeting with very conservative clients, most government officials, and in most regions outside the big cities. If a woman wears a headscarf, it should be folded and secured in a way that no hair is revealed, although sometimes women may push a bit and show a little fringe.

Women should note that dress becomes more conservative during Ramadan, including in Saudi Arabia. In general, it is advised that women wear plain *abayas*, with minimal, non-contrasting decoration. It is not unreasonable to expect to wear a headscarf more often in public as well.

Headscarves

Headscarves are folded in a variety of styles, which change with fashion, although very religious women may stick to a particular style. Western women might wish to ask for help from another woman if she is having difficulty wearing her headscarf in a manner she thinks looks good. It is also a good idea to have some safety pins that can subtly secure the headscarf.

Readers should also be aware that in late 2015, some offices now have a headscarf policy, including in some mixed gender environments which can include some multinational organisations.

Businesswomen who are in a relaxed environment and women generally in public who choose not to wear a headscarf might wish to tie back their hair if it is long enough to do so.

Footwear

Women can wear any footwear that would be considered appropriate for their environment, although the likes of red stilettos would be frowned upon.

Tattoos and piercings

Women (and men) should note that tattoos are considered forbidden in Islam. However, most Saudis, whilst not enamoured with visible tattoos, but unlike with men, are unlikely to tolerate visible tattoos on women. Women should take care to cover all tattoos that could be exposed whilst wearing the *abaya*, including on their hands or feet. Temporary henna tattoos, on the other hand (pun intended), are perfectly acceptable.

Ear piercings are fine for a woman, although it is not advised to wear large earrings when not wearing a headscarf. Large earrings are also impractical when a woman does wear a headscarf. Nose piercings are acceptable, although somewhat culturally confusing if worn by a Western woman as they are more closely associated with women from the Indian subcontinent. Other visible face piercings are unlikely to be accepted by the general Saudi population.

Places where wearing an *abaya* is not necessary

There are a few places where women, as an exception, do not need to wear an *abaya*. This includes her home or hotel room, on residential compounds that accommodate a Western lifestyle, if visiting Saudi Aramco, KAUST, Riyadh's Diplomatic Quarter, beyond the security gates of Western and some other embassies or consulates, and privately owned clubs such as beach clubs north of Jeddah. She does not need to wear an *abaya* in some sporting situations, such as gender segregated gyms and sometimes golf courses, perhaps during the old fashioned 'ladies' days'. Assuming the host has no objections, women who are far enough off shore on a boat may also dispense with their *abaya* once she is out of eyesight of the general public as well.

Male guardian - *mahram*

Definition
In Saudi Arabia, women are supposed to have a male guardian, known in Arabic as a *mahram*, who looks after her well being. From a Western perspective, it's infantilising as of course women have been emancipated, making their own decisions and accepting their own responsibilities, although not for as many generations as some people may think.

Within the Saudi family, a *mahram* is a male relative of the woman whose relationship precludes marriage. This means her father, husband, or in their absence, a brother or even a son. Cousins and uncles are not eligible, although a grandfather or grandson are.

For expatriate women, her *mahram* will depend on her status in the Kingdom. For women who are dependent on their husband's *iqama*, her husband is her *mahram*. Daughters' fathers are typically their *mahram*. For women who are in the Kingdom on single status, whether resident, on a business visit or work visa, her sponsor is her *mahram*.

In public

Historically, women have been expected to have a *mahram* with them whenever they are out in public, including Western expatriate women. For women in the Kingdom as a part of a family, this would be a family member. For businesswomen, this would be their sponsor or their sponsor's representative. Drivers are also considered de facto *mahram*.

Until a few years ago, if women who were out in public without a male accompanying them, especially if they were alone, the religious police or other authority could challenge them as to where their *mahram* was. This also applied to women arriving at the airport, although this is no longer routinely the case for Western women, even in Riyadh. Although this is still technically possible, in practice, this has relaxed significantly.

It is now possible to commonly see a woman or groups of women shopping, in restaurants and coffee shops on their own. Businesswomen who are moving around the major cities are generally unhindered by the lack of presence of a *mahram*, although they are still reliant on their driver. As previously mentioned, women are even travelling in taxis and through Uber on their own. However, it remains wise to be able to contact your *mahram* by mobile phone if circumstances arise where a woman is uncomfortable, especially if approached by less than friendly religious police.

THE DRESS CODE FOR MEN

The dress code – where men begin

For many men, the Saudi dress code may not be something they have given much thought to. However, like women, all men and boys who have visibly reached puberty must be modestly dressed in Saudi Arabia. This includes all expatriate men regardless of their nationality, religion, or any other factor.

Men's clothing terms

Hijab
Hijab simply means modest dress. It does not specifically refer to a headscarf, although in the context of women's modest dress, many Muslims would agree that wearing a headscarf is a part of a woman's modest dress code.

In Saudi Arabia, modest dress for a man means covering his body from his shoulders and top of his arms to and including his knees. Body hair should also be concealed from the same parts of the body to be covered, although facial fair and showing leg hair below the knees is ok. Men should also take care not to wear clothing that is too tight or otherwise reveals the contours of their body.

Traditional Saudi men's clothing

It is worth a quick look at traditional male clothing as found in Saudi Arabia. Do note that Saudi men generally wear traditional clothing at work unless their work involves the wearing of a uniform or other specific dress code. It is considered formal dress. Saudi men may choose to wear informal Saudi dress when not working, especially at the weekend. Saudi men and especially boys also can be commonly seen wearing Western clothing at the weekend as well.

It should be noted that Saudi men can be very fashionable. What accessories they wear, how they fold their *keffiyah*, and even the *angle* of their *agal* can all indicate the latest fashion.

Thobe/thawb

Most Saudi men wear the *thobe*, which is a garment that covers the man from the shoulders to the ankles and wrists. Many Saudi boys also wear the *thobe*, especially when at school or on occasions when smart dress is required.

The *thobe* is generally made from very fine fabric if the man can afford it although silk is avoided. There are many versions of *thobe* that vary in their finish. The typical Saudi style *thobe* includes a two button collar and a finish at the wrists that requires cufflinks. It also contains deep pockets at the sides that hold anything from a wallet to multiple mobile phones. They do not always have a pocket at the breast.

Although most Saudi *thobe*s are white, some Saudi men wear dull colour *thobe*s in the winter. Informal *thobe*s may even be of a darker colour.

It should be noted some that very religious Saudi men wear the *thobe* much shorter than the general population, often ending mid-to-lower shin rather than at the ankle. Socks can often be seen. This generally applies to the *muttawa* as well.

Keffiyah/shemagh

Most Saudi men wear a fabric head covering called a *keffiyah* or sometimes a *shemagh*. This is the red and white check design – with subtle differences in the pattern that is driven by fashion. Some *keffiyah*s are made of very fine fabric; others are made of more sturdy fabric. Saudi men are highly unlikely to wear the black and white version as this garment is closely associated with Palestinian and some Iraqi men. Fewer boys wear the *keffiyah*, *ghutra* or *agal*, although a few may wear the *taqiyah*.

Ghutra

Some Saudi men wear a fabric head covering called a *ghutra*. Although the term is sometimes used interchangeably with the terms *keffiyah* or *shemagh*, the *ghutra* is more commonly associated with the all white version of the head covering. It is also usually made from a finer and lighter fabric, but not always.

Agal

Most Saudi men will also wear an *agal*, which goes over the *keffiyah* or *ghutra* and is usually a double strand of black rope like cord. The *agal* also positions the fabric more securely.

It should be noted some that very religious Saudi men choose not to wear the *agal*. This generally applies to the *muttawa* as well.

Taqiyah

Saudi men typically wear a *taqiyah* under their *keffiyah* or *ghutra*. This is a religious skullcap. It is usually white and knitted or crocheted as worn by most Saudi men and boys.

Bisht

The *bisht* is an outer robe, usually black with gold trim, and is generally worn in Saudi Arabia only by very elite men and royalty.

Western men and traditional Saudi clothing

Unlike Western women, Western men are not expected to wear Saudi national dress whilst in the Kingdom. In fact, it is strongly recommended that they do not wear national dress in public at all, perhaps unless they are also Muslim and then generally only when in a mosque. Saudis are very likely to react to a Western man wearing national dress as someone who is mocking their culture.

Buying male Islamic clothing in Saudi Arabia

Having advised against Western men wearing Saudi national dress, it is not specifically illegal and many men report that it is comfortable attire, especially during the hot summer months. Thus, a Western man who wishes to wear a *thobe* in the privacy of their own home or hotel room would not be prevented from doing so.

Men can purchase high end *thobes* and other items of national dress in high end shopping malls if they are prepared to pay upscale prices. As with women's *abayas*, men can also find more modestly priced *thobes* etc in traditional *souqs*, often adjacent to where women can purchase *abayas*.

Please note that very tall or very large men may require the services of a tailor, who can create a bespoke *thobe* that will suit their requirements. All good *thobe* shops can offer this service, although the shopper may need to return after a day or two to collect the item.

Realistic clothing choices for Western men

At work

Most Western men, especially those who are working in offices or who are calling on other professionals should wear a good quality, well tailored business suit with a minimum of accessories, especially jewellery. A watch and a wedding ring are fine.

If the man is working in an industry that requires him to wear a uniform, then the issue of clothing selection is removed. Casual dress in a business environment should generally be limited to going on site where clothing could be soiled or where some physical labour might occur. Otherwise, most Saudis consider casual clothing a bit disrespectful in most business environments.

At leisure

Within reason, Western men can wear what they wish whilst at leisure if they are modestly dressed although they should keep in mind that good grooming gives a good impression, even when wearing casual clothing.

Clothing and exercise

The modest dress code also applies to men who are exercising or are participating in sport. In general, the rule remains to cover the knees, shoulders and upper arms. Never change into sport clothing at home before travelling to a sporting venue. Never change in your hotel room where you must then take a lift or walk though public areas of the hotel, especially the lobby or restaurant. In both instances, change in the changing area adjacent to the sporting facilities and go directly there.

Additionally, men should never walk around naked in a changing facility, including immediately after taking a shower, and even if they are comfortable doing so elsewhere in the world. For some Saudis, this is coded behaviour for a very illicit homosexual encounter.

Footwear

Men can wear any footwear that would be considered appropriate for their environment.

Weather considerations

Although the weather can be very hot in Saudi for most of the year, this does not excuse the Western man from being properly dressed, even in a business suit and even when the temperature exceeds 40C (or even 50C). Instead, the man should carefully select lightweight fabrics that can breathe. Loosely fitted clothing also helps. Men should also keep in mind that they will usually be in buildings that are heavily air conditioned.

What men should avoid wearing

Most Muslims believe that men should not wear any item that is considered feminine. This includes items made of silk, gold or diamonds. Although it is possible to see some Muslim men wear these items, others do not approve.

Saudis do understand that non-Muslim men have different traditions, and are likely to tolerate gold jewellery, especially wedding bands and usually watches. But it is also advisable for Western men to avoid wearing additional gold jewellery or most other jewellery that contains diamonds. Silk clothing should generally be avoided as there are reasonable alternatives that most men would also routinely wear.

All men, including Western men, must _not_ wear shorts in public that expose the knee. Cropped trousers are generally accepted in the Eastern Province, Jeddah and even parts of Riyadh, although this may not be the case in more remote regions.

Men can now wear short sleeved shirts including dress shirts in the big cities, although this is not advised in more remote locations or in the presence of a very religious man.

Men can wear conventional T-shirts in the same major cities if they are not too tight and they do not expose more than a small amount of body hair at the neckline.

Men should avoid wearing any article of clothing that could be perceived to be military, including camouflage designs, and should never wear any T-shirt containing military content or anything politically or socially contentious.

There are no specific colours to avoid wearing in Saudi Arabia, although an all pink ensemble might attract unwanted attention.

Male dress code during Ramadan

During Ramadan, the male dress code also becomes stricter. Men must cover to the ankles and to the wrists, both at work and at leisure.

Tattoos and piercings

Men (and women) should note that tattoos are considered forbidden in Islam. However, most Saudis, whilst not enamoured with visible tattoos, will tolerate non-controversial tattoos on men. Any man who has a tattoo could be seen as controversial should cover it. This is especially true if the tattoo has any reference to any religion, is a depiction of a human or animal, or represents a controversial topic. Arabic script is generally not tolerated due to its close association with the Qur'an as it is considered a holy language.

Places where the male dress code is relaxed

Similar to women, there are a few places in Saudi Arabia where the male dress code is also more relaxed. This includes his home or hotel room, on residential compounds that accommodate a Western lifestyle, if visiting Saudi Aramco, KAUST, Riyadh's Diplomatic Quarter, beyond the security gates of Western and some other embassies or consulates, and privately owned clubs such as beach clubs north of Jeddah. Assuming the host has no objections, men who are far enough off shore on a boat may also relax their dress code once out of eyesight of the general public as well.

MIXED GENDERS AND
PRACTICAL ETIQUETTE

Gender and etiquette

Although most Muslims believe that modest behaviour is a virtue across the gender barrier, how it is interpreted varies throughout out the world. As with many other social issues, Saudi Arabia has a strict interpretation of what is considered correct behaviour and what is not. Furthermore, much of this behaviour has been enforced to varying degrees by the *muttawa* or religious police.

Although times are changing and many practices that would have been out of the question just a few years ago are becoming normalised, at least in the big cities, it remains prudent to recognise that acceptable public behaviour can become more stringent as well as more relaxed.

Gender segregation

In general, Saudi society traditionally operates in a gender segregated manner, where gender mixing in some circumstances is discouraged or even illegal. For most Western expatriates, gender segregation issues arise in several predictable situations. They generally include the work environment and out in public, including transport, shopping, restaurants, sport and other leisure activities, and other people's homes.

The work environment
Traditionally, if an office or other work environment employed women, they were expected to work in a separate room to male employees. This could include separate entrances to the building where relevant.

Women who needed to speak with men would generally do so without being seen. Reasons requiring communication with men could range from male management to accepting a courier delivery to organising transport. In modern times, that often meant the use of a speaker system, or if the women were wearing *abayas*, through video link.

At the present time, there are some office environments where men and women are working together more closely, perhaps utilising private offices or the strategic placement of screens and other temporary separation devices. Although this practice is on the increase, there is a grey area as to what would no longer be tolerated, including by the women themselves.

On the other hand, there are many working environments where gender segregation practices are much more relaxed. This can include many in the medical profession, some banking, education, multinational businesses, and organisations set up in certain zones such as the Diplomatic Quarter.

For Western businesswomen who are working or visiting Saudi offices, some exceptions are made. Many mixed gender meetings are conducted in the usual manner, albeit in private meeting areas within the offices. Western businesswomen are generally at a distinct *advantage* in more traditionally configured gender segregated offices as we are often regarded as if we are a third gender, i.e. women whose gender behaviour expectations are suspended and thus exempt from some of the negative repercussions of gender mixing for the purposes of business. Thus, working separately with both male colleagues and female colleagues is acceptable, unlike for her Western male counterparts.

Women who are meeting in a very public venue, such as a business centre in a hotel, should check with the hotel to understand their mixed gender policy. For example, many top end hotels will allow or turn a blind eye to meetings held wholly amongst other Westerners, especially in a low traffic location.

Others will be more reluctant to permit this without permission or sometimes a very influential Saudi national. Others will require an additional Imarah permit, especially if a woman is leading a meeting or training session that will be attended by both genders, and especially if the meeting includes Saudis and other mixed Muslim nationalities. This is especially true if the event if being held at a public venue such as a hotel.

Out in public

- Transport

  In Saudi Arabia, women are not allowed to travel in a vehicle with an unrelated man unless the man is her driver. In theory, this would apply to a mixed gender group of professionals sharing public transport or even if a man was driving a mixed gender group or a single woman in his own vehicle.

  At the time of publication, this rule has been effectively ignored unless the vehicle draws the attention of the authorities for another reason, such as a traffic infraction or a violation of the dress code.

- Shopping

  In Saudi Arabia, the shopping mall is currently a female dominated environment. Many shops advertise that they only allow 'families' to enter all of part of their shop. In this context, 'families' generally mean no single men or male only groups. Some shopping malls also have a female only floor, usually the top floor, where men are not allowed at all regardless of who else they may be with.

  Additionally, there are some shopping malls that do not allow access to the entire mall to a single man or group of men, although this rule is often ignored by non-Western, non-Saudi security guards if the man has an obviously Western appearance and if he is alone or perhaps with only one other man.

  It is very common to see groups of women or even single women alone in a shopping mall, sometimes not even shopping but dining or simply meeting other female friends in a relaxed environment such as a coffee shop. This is especially the case in some of the more upscale malls, especially those with favouring shops selling goods and services that appeal to Westerners.

- Restaurants

  The first time a new arrival enters a Saudi restaurant can be disorientating. This is because restaurants in the Kingdom have traditionally been gender segregated. As previously mentioned in the earlier Things to Do, Dining Out section, most restaurants have had a main, singles or bachelor area, where single men or groups of men are allowed to dine. Restaurants usually but not always also have a family section, which must be used anytime a woman or small child is present. If there is no family section and gender segregation is being enforced, then women are not allowed to dine at that particular establishment. In reality, these would not be likely venues that would interest most Westerners of either gender. Sometimes the family section is accessed via a separate door or entrance; others are a room situated through the main section either to one side or at the back. Mixed gender groups of adults must also use the family section.

At the time of publication, enforcement of gender segregation in restaurants is in transition. Thus, it is important to observe whether the restaurant you choose to dine in allows diners to sit wherever they like or if they must comply with traditional rules. If the dining party inadvertently sits in the wrong area, the host will politely ask them to move to the correct section. Fast food courts in shopping malls may also practice gender segregation, although in practice, it is more common to see the signs at the ordering counter, but the clerks then inviting the other sex to use an empty queue. Finding seating in the food court after placing an order may also involve identifying which area is designated singles and which is family.

Please note that most upscale hotels no longer enforce gender segregation in their restaurants, although they will provide a screen or similar private area for women or families who want to be segregated from the general population. The screen technique is also used as an option for make dining booths or tables more private in a mixed public restaurant environment.

- Sport and other leisure activities
Perhaps not unsurprisingly, Saudi Arabia does not encourage women to become involved in most sporting activities. However, in recent years, it does recognise that many women who work or live in the Kingdom have an interest in personal fitness. The number of women only gyms are beginning to grow in the Kingdom, often tucked away in restricted access

venues such as the fitness centre located on the Ladies only floor of the Panorama Mall in Riyadh, or at the women only Luthan Hotel.

Women will not be able to jog in public, although a brisk walk will generally be tolerated, at least during the winter months. Women located in the Eastern Province or in Jeddah can take advantage of the various corniches for this purpose.

Happily, the number of separate fitness areas for women are increasing in the top end hotels in Saudi Arabia. They are usually former guest rooms cobbled together far away from the main fitness facility and are clearly an afterthought in most places. However, as the main gym and work out facilities, including the swimming pools are off limits to women, they are an improvement from the recent past, where no facilities were available at all.

Women who consider keeping fit a high priority might also wish to make a connection with Western compounds, where the usual facilities may be available for use, especially if invited by a resident or if the woman chooses to incorporate a short stay on the compound during her visit to the Kingdom.

- Other people's homes

For Westerners who are fortunate enough to be invited to a Saudi home, it is not always easy to know exactly what to expect. Firstly, invitations to a Saudi home are generally meant for the person or people directly receiving the invitation and not other family members unless explicitly invited as well. Some Saudis live in an outwardly Western manner, and may freely mix in their homes.

Other Saudis live in a traditional manner, where male guests are only invited to the *diwan*, effectively a meeting room similar to a living room or drawing room in the West. The *diwan* is generally for men only; there may be another *diwan* used by female members of the family. On the surface, this could present a problem for the Western businesswoman who is invited to a traditional home as it may be unclear where she is or may not be welcome.

However, it is the author's experience that women who are invited to a traditional Saudi home because of her work is generally treated as an 'honorary man' and thus able to join the others in the male *diwan*. This may not be the case for a married couple who have accepted a purely social invitation.

If a woman is a guest in a Saudi home, she should ask about the dress code if she is unsure. In some instances, she will be invited to remove her *abaya*. In other situations, she may expect to wear it for the length of the visit, at least whilst she is in mixed company.

Etiquette between men and women

In spite of the discouragement of gender mixing in Saudi Arabia, it does happen, even in the most benign of circumstances. Hotels, supermarkets, and everyday life present opportunities, even for people who are unlikely to work with anyone of the opposite sex at work. When these events occur, there is often correct etiquette on how to behave. Examples of the more common situations likely to be encountered by Western expatriates and business travellers, both men and women, follow.

Offices and closed doors

It is relatively rare for meetings to take place in Saudi Arabia between only two people, even if they are both the same gender. However, if you find yourself in a situation where you are meeting with only one other person and they are of the opposite sex to you, it is best to ensure that you follow a couple of basic rules.

Do make sure the two parties never meet alone in a closed environment such as a private office with the door closed, especially an office with opaque walls. If you must meet, then open the door or, if the office has a glass window, then ensure the blinds or any other obscuring object is removed from the window and it is easy to see in.

If neither of these options are possible, then a third person should be invited to sit in on the meeting, even if they have no involvement. They are acting as a chaperone. This also serves as protecting the reputation and even honour of both the woman and the man.

Back seat of taxis/vehicles with professional drivers

Women should never ride in the front seat of a vehicle that is being driven by a professional driver. This includes drivers organised by your sponsor or hotel who you may use frequently and thus get to know. It also includes taxis.

If a woman is otherwise willing to accept a ride from an unrelated man who she knows in either a professional or social capacity, then there is no specific need to sit in the back seat in this situation; in fact, it would look awkward to most observers.

Of course, women can sit anywhere they like other than in the driver's seat in a vehicle driven by a male family member.

Lift etiquette

Lifts are by definition a small space. Many Saudis do not wish to be in the presence unrelated people of the opposite sex in such a small space. No matter how little exposure you may otherwise have with the opposite sex, anyone staying in a top end hotel or working in a high rise office building is almost certain to encounter women at some point, at least in the big cities. On the other hand, in a high rise building, nearly everyone will be taking the lift. In fact, most Saudi buildings are not designed for people to use the stairs other than for emergency purposes.

For Saudi nationals, few situations cause more etiquette challenges than the use of a lift/elevator and gender mixing, especially for women and often their families. Thus, men should always assess the people in a lift when it arrives. If only women are on the lift, then ask permission to board it. If the women are not responsive or say no, either verbally or through their body language, then wait for another lift. This also applies to a man and a woman on the lift; in this instance, look to the man and work out whether it's ok to board from his response. Women can get on the lift in either of these situations.

However, Saudi men may also be uncomfortable sharing a lift with an unrelated woman. In the instance of a Western woman about to take a lift, she should also ask permission to board if it is already occupied by a man or group of men. Although it is probable that more Saudi men won't mind, there are others who would. In the latter situation, the woman should wait for another lift. Of course, women should only ever board a lift with another man or men if she is comfortable doing so regardless of where she is in the world.

215

Right of way

In much of the West, it has been conventional to let a woman go through a narrow passageway such as a door ahead of a man who may have arrived there at about the same time. Although this may seem to be old fashioned behaviour amongst some Westerners, others continue to follow this practice.

In Saudi Arabia, the convention is for the person to the right to enter the narrow area first, regardless of gender. In many business and social settings, Saudi and indeed people from elsewhere in the Middle East have a knack of ensuring a guest is to their right so they can extend this courtesy.

Eye contact

Traditionally, eye contact between unrelated men and women was to be avoided as it violates the perception of modesty. Although some people, especially very traditional or very religious people may continue to look away when they are speaking to a member of the opposite sex, this is also changing.

In many business environments, direct but not overly steady eye contact can now be expected across the gender divide. The best advice for others is to match the behaviour of your Saudi counterpart. This behaviour can also be seen amongst people from elsewhere in the Middle East as well as people from much of the Indian subcontinent.

Touch

Do not touch someone from the opposite sex in Saudi Arabia other than if a handshake is extended. Of course, it will become obvious that people of the same sex can be very tactile with one another beyond what is conventional in most of the West.

In the event of an emergency situation, such as helping someone of the opposite sex who has fallen or who has other mobility difficulties, it is conventional to offer a forearm rather than a hand in most situations.

Personal space

Although many Saudis who become comfortable with another person can close the personal space gap to a very narrow distance, this will only happen between members of the same sex. People of the opposite sex should maintain a respectful distance between them, usually at least a full arm's length away.

Level of friendliness

Some Westerners are naturally friendly. Many Saudis are excellent hosts and can make guests feel very welcome in their country. On a professional level, this can be one of the greatest joys working and living in Saudi Arabia.

However, the level of friendliness must be appropriate, especially when interacting with the opposite sex. Being personally very friendly is not the same as being professionally warm and comfortable to be around.

What can be innocent behaviour from a Westerner, especially but not exclusively from a woman, can be misinterpreted by their Saudi counterpart. This may be especially true when dealing with Saudi nationals with either limited exposure to the West or who take their cultural cues from distorted Western media.

Women should be very careful about how and when they smile as it can be seen as an invitation that could cause a very unwanted response if misinterpreted. Whilst smiles are very welcome in the Kingdom, do ensure they are professional by your body language as well as in the context of your conversation.

Western men who have an increasing opportunity to work with Saudi women should be particularly careful in their behaviour. In addition to friendliness or familiarity challenges, other behaviours that could be easily misinterpreted include banter, humour and anything too personal, including a well intentioned compliment. It is imperative to keep in mind that not only is the woman's honour at risk, but so is the reputation of her entire family.

SECTION 6

COMMUNICATION AND LANGUAGE IN SAUDI ARABIA

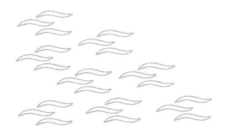

LANGUAGE

Communication in Saudi Arabia goes much further than learning a few words of Arabic. Communication is not only what language you speak, but how you use language in terms of content, context, directness, situation and style. Communication is both verbal and non-verbal.

In Saudi Arabia, although English is the language of multinational organisations and an increasing number of diverse Saudi owned businesses, Arabic remains the language of the Saudi government.

Arabic and English are the main languages of everyday life in the Kingdom, depending on location within the Kingdom and who you are speaking with. Of course, there are a wide range of other expatriate languages spoken in Saudi Arabia within these communities as well, especially from the Indian subcontinent.

The English language

English language proficiency is generally less robust than it is in all other GCC countries and indeed almost anywhere else in the Middle East, with the possible exception of Yemen and rural Egypt. It is also one of the main challenges being addressed in the Kingdom, where an improvement of English language skills amongst more young Saudis can be seen as the years go by.

English and Arabic are the languages of business and a fair bit of everyday life.

Some but not all Saudis working in a business that is likely to interface with Westerners have been educated to a high standard of English. This continues to improve as time passes.

In general, young Saudis are more likely to speak English than older Saudis. Men are more likely than women; people from the big cities more so than from rural or remote areas; those educated abroad more than those wholly educated in the Kingdom. As a rule, Saudis and indeed many other Arab nationals might be better at speaking and listening to English than they are at reading and especially writing it.

For most Western expatriates, English will be spoken at work, including by other educated expatriates who may speak a different mother tongue. It will also be spoken in your compound and in many other locations that cater to Westerners, including many upscale restaurants and shops. Other public venues that cater to a wider audience may not always have staff with English language skills. Some signs may only be in Arabic in these locations.

The English language skills of your driver can vary. Taxi drivers may not speak much English (and sometimes not much Arabic either) at all.

Do not be surprised if you hear many different English accents, dialects, slang, and other variations of the language. In Saudi Arabia, common English language influences are heard from the Indian subcontinent and the Philippines at least as often as they are from British, North American, Antipodean, or Southern African English speakers.

The Arabic language

For most Westerners, Arabic is a difficult language to learn, especially for adults. Not many Western expatriates progress beyond the basics, if they even achieve that much. This would not generally be a problem for people living in the other Gulf States; however, there may be occasions in Saudi Arabia where a little bit of Arabic makes life a lot easier.

Do not be surprised if some everyday information is only written in Arabic. Although this doesn't always impact Westerners, it may come as a surprise to find many websites published only in Arabic. Others may contain an English language tab that doesn't work or that simply generates a 'website under construction' message.

The following information is not intended to be a robust language lesson. However, it does provide some basic practicalities for Westerners who may find themselves in a situation where no English speakers are present.

Use

Modern Standard Arabic (MSA) is derived from the Qur'an. It is widely taught and is thus the basis of what an educated person would speak in a formal setting. However, it sounds artificially stiff when spoken in everyday life. The equivalent in English would be someone officially reading the news or the Queen giving a speech.

Arabic is the official language of Saudi Arabia. There are multiple dialects of everyday Arabic, which can be described as the spoken language of a population. Although there are a variety of dialects within Saudi Arabia, people can easily understand one another.

Spoken Arabic varies significantly from MSA and also varies significantly from the Gulf, Levant and Maghreb, especially as the languages become more distant from a geographical perspective. For example, a Saudi Arabic speaker would easily understand a Kuwaiti or other Gulf national. They would also understand a Lebanese or Palestinian Arabic speaker, although in this instance, some slang, words, etc would be notably different.

Egyptian Arabic is effectively its own dialect. Fortunately, it is widely understood by nearly all Arabic speakers due to its influence in mass media and popular culture. However, a Saudi Arabic speaker might find an Arabic speaker from Morocco or Algeria barely understandable.

Basic characteristics

There are 28 characters in the Arabic language, with only three long vowel sounds. Short vowel sounds are not generally written but are gleaned from context.

Arabic letters are written from right to left. They change in context, depending on whether they are found at the beginning, middle or end of a word. There is an additional distinction if they stand alone, such as in a list. However, numbers are written from left to right, as in English.

Arabic is a consonantic language. This means that words have tri-literal roots with cluster meanings. For example, the letters: k t b are the root consonants for the words *kitāb* 'book', *kātib* 'writer', *maktūb* 'letter', *maktab* 'desk', *maktaba* 'library'. Dictionaries are organised by tri-literal clusters.

The Arabic language contains some sounds not used in English, making it difficult to pronounce some letters and words. Additionally, the Arabic language does not contain the commonly used sounds of p, g, and v in English (although some dialectal Arabic uses the hard g, such as Egyptian but not Saudi Arabic). This creates a range of transliteration difficulties.

The Arabic language has no upper and lower case distinctions.

Sentence structure, syntax and grammar all vary widely from English. This includes but is not limited to verb-subject-object sequencing, use of gender words, and different rules for pronouns and plurals.

Most expats and visitors do not learn it to working level proficiency. Those who do are much more likely to be conversant than literate.

The Arabic alphabet and numbers

Here are the isolated characters of the Arabic alphabet.

ر	ذ	د	خ	ح	ج	ث	ت	ب	ا
Raa'	Thaal	Daal	Khaa'	Haa'	Jiim	Thaa'	Taa'	Baa'	'Alf
r	d	d	kh	h	j	t	t	b	a

ف	غ	ع	ظ	ط	ض	ص	ش	س	ز
Faa'	Ghayn	'Ayn	Thaa'	Taa'	Caad	Saad	Shiin	Siin	Zaay
f	g	z	t	d	d	s	sh	s	z

ي	و	ه	ن	م	ل	ك	ق
Yaa'	Waaw	Haa'	Nuun	Miin	Laam	Kaaf	Qaaf
y	w	h	n	m	l	k	q

Here is the full set of contextual characters of the Arabic alphabet.

IPA	Value	Name	Final	Medial	Initial	Isolated	IPA	Value	Name	Final	Medial	Initial	Isolated
[d̪]	ḍ	ḍād	ض	ض	ض	ض	[ʔ]	'(a)	alif	ا	‒	‒	ا
[t̪]	ṭ	ṭā'	ط	ط	ط	ط	[b]	b	bā'	ب	ب	ب	ب
[ɛ]	ẓ	ẓā'	ظ	ظ	ظ	ظ	[t]	t	tā'	ت	ت	ت	ت
[ʕ]	'	'ayn	ع	ع	ع	ع	[θ]	th	thā'	ث	ث	ث	ث
[ɣ]	gh	ghayn	غ	غ	غ	غ	[ʒ]	j	jīm	ج	ج	ج	ج
[f]	f	fā'	ف	ف	ف	ف	[h]	h	ḥā'	ح	ح	ح	ح
[q]	q	qāf	ق	ق	ق	ق	[x]	kh	khā'	خ	خ	خ	خ
[k]	k	kāf	ك	ك	ك	ك	[d]	d	dāl	د	‒	‒	د
[l]	l	lām	ل	ل	ل	ل	[ð]	dh	dhāl	ذ	‒	‒	ذ
[m]	m	mīm	م	م	م	م	[r]	r	rā'	ر	‒	‒	ر
[n]	n	nūn	ن	ن	ن	ن	[z]	z	zāy	ز	‒	‒	ز
[h]	h	hā'	ه	ه	ه	ه	[s]	s	sīn	س	س	س	س
[w]	w	wāw	و	‒	‒	و	[ʃ]	sh	shīn	ش	ش	ش	ش
[j]	y	yā'	ي	ي	ي	ي	[s]	s	ṣād	ص	ص	ص	ص

Here are the digits used in Saudi Arabia. They do not change in context and they are read from left to right, thus changing direction from the body of text they may be found in. In Saudi Arabia, a mix of Arabic digits and digits used in the West are both commonly found, even in text otherwise written entirely in Arabic. Note that other countries who have adopted Arabic script for their languages, notably Iran and Pakistan, use slightly different characters for some digits.

0	٠	5	٥
1	١	6	٦
2	٢	7	٧
3	٣	8	٨
4	٤	9	٩

Advice

- At a minimum, it is good form to learn the basic courtesies. This is simply being a good guest in another country and shows respect.

- From a practical point of view, try to learn basic practicalities, including travel and food vocabulary.
- Don't be shy to try out your Arabic with any willing Arabic speaker in a casual environment. Be aware that you might be learning a variety of spoken dialects – sometimes in the same sentence!
- However, it is not a good idea to try out your broken Arabic in a formal work environment. Not only is it painful for the Arabic speaker, it can also imply that you think their spoken English is not very good and can cause an unintended insult.

Some survival Arabic

Here are some basic survival words and phrases that would be appreciated by most Saudis and other Arabic speakers. Do not be surprised if you encounter some dialectal differences.

ENGLISH	ARABIC
Hello	*as salaam aleikum* – formal *marhaba* – informal
Welcome	*ahlan wa salan* – formal *marhaba* – gulf countries
My name is	*ismi*
How are you	*kaif ħālak (m)* *kaif ħālik (f)*
I'm fine (response to above)	*bekhair, al-hamdu lillah*
Thank you (very much)	*shukhran (jazeelan)*
You're welcome	*afwan*
Excuse me (interruption, mistake)	*al madirah, ismahli*
Excuse me (attention)	*law samaht*
Please (pleading more than politeness)	*min fadlak (m)/ min fadlik (f)*
Sorry	*asif*
Yes	*aywa/naam*
Maybe	*mumkin*
No, no problem	*la*
No problem	*mafi mushkila*
Good, bad	*jayyid, sayyia*

ENGLISH	ARABIC
How much	*kam thamam, kam si'r*
OK	*tayyib, tammam*
I don't speak Arabic	*la atakallam arabi*
I don't understand	*lā afham*
Do you speak English	*hal tatakallam al-ingliziyya*
Please speak slower	*takallam bibuṭ' min fadlak (m)* *takallam bibuṭ' min fadlik (f)*
Goodbye/response	*ma'a salaama/allah yasalmak*

Here are some basic survival words and phrases for everyday life situations that might come in handy:

Out and about

ENGLISH	ARABIC
Left	*yasaar*
Right	*yameen*
Straight ahead	*ilaa al'a-maam, sida*
Reverse/behind	*waraa*
Slowly	*bibot*
There	*hunaak*
Now	*al aan*
Stop	*waqafa*
Wait	*intazara*
Go	*zahaebae, y'aleh*
Air conditioning	*taekyif haewae*
Open	*maftooh*
Closed	*mughlak*
Entrance	*madkhal*
Exit	*makhraj*
Today	*al yom*
Tomorrow	*gaedaen*
Yesterday	*aems*
xx Minutes	*xx daqiqa*

ENGLISH	ARABIC
xx Hours	*xx sae'ae*
All day	*yom kaemil*
Shopping mall	*markaz*
Hotel	*funduq*
Airport	*matar*
Office	*maktab*
Restaurant	*matam*

Eating out

ENGLISH	ARABIC
Menu	*qa'emat ta'am*
Waiter/waitress	*naadil/naadila*
Pork	*lahm al khanzeer*
Non smoking	*mamnooa tadkheen*
Alcohol	*alkoohl*
Coffee	*qahwa*
Chicken	*dajāj*
Lamb	*hamal*
Beef	*baqari*
Fish	*samak*
Vegetarian	*nabaatee*
Bread	*khubz*
Butter	*zubda*
Rice	*aruuz*
Tea	*chai*
Milk	*haleeb*
Sugar	*sukkar*
Juice	*'asiir*
Water	*ma'a*
Salt	*malh*
Pepper (black)	*filfil'(áswad)*
Sweets	*halwayaat*
The bill	*faatuura*

STYLE

Directness

Many but not all Westerners can be very direct when communicating. This is especially true of most Scandinavian, Germanic, Slavic and many English speakers. Most people from the Middle East use indirect language, as do most people from much of Asia. Westerners from Mediterranean backgrounds and many Latin Americans tend to fall somewhere in between.

Being very direct has the advantage of people knowing where the speaker stands on their topic of conversation. However, it can also come across as too simplistic, blunt, rude and inappropriate, especially if it is also confrontational. Very direct communicators can be perceived as people who can dangerously present a situation where a loss of face is possible.

Content and context

Most direct communicators focus on content. Most other speakers take context into greater consideration. This can impact anything from what someone says to how they say it. It can also mean leaving things unsaid so that the message must be gleaned from reading between the lines. This can be a real challenge for direct communicators who are not used to picking up on coded or non-verbal context or reading between the lines but who say what they mean and mean what they say. They can miss the entire point of some conversations.

'Yes culture'

One of the most frustrating aspects of communication in Saudi Arabia is the use of the word 'yes'. This can be used for anything from explicit commitment to a request to a subordinate attempting to show you respect even when they don't understand you. 'Yes culture' can be found in most Asian cultures as well as in the Middle East. Although it is very situational behaviour, the best advice is to interpret 'yes' as an intention rather than a literal acknowledgement or commitment to a request.

It is possible to avoid most frustrations with 'yes culture' challenges by rephrasing your questions so that a 'yes' response becomes nonsensical. Open questions starting with who, what, when, why, how, and requests to describe or explain something tend to work much more effectively.

Not saying 'no'

In tandem with 'yes culture', most people will also avoid saying 'no' directly. Instead, they often use tactics such as indirect phrases 'it might be a problem', 'that could take some time', 'let me check', 'because …', etc. It is good practice to use open questions to manage these communication challenges as well.

Silence

Although most people from the Middle East are not known for their silence, many other expatriates from outside the West may remain silent in a number of situations, including some that might be frustrating to some Westerners. Silence can be interpreted as meaning anything from 'no' to showing respect to an authority figure. It can also be another way to avoid causing a loss of face in a group environment.

If you expect everyone to verbally participate in a meeting, training or similar event and are working with people from face cultures, especially from Asia, it might be a good idea to set this expectation well in advance of the session. The more detail you can provide in terms of expectations, the more comfortable they may be in giving input or feedback.

Speaking and listening

Some cultures are good at speaking. Other cultures are good at listening. Saudis and people from the Middle East in general are good at both (as are some Mediterranean cultures). Do not be surprised if your Middle East counterparts hold multiple conversations and are genuinely able to keep track of the content of each conversation and respond to them accordingly.

It is also common practice for many people from the Middle East (and the Med) to talk over one another and is not generally considered to be rude. Western expatriates may sometimes find themselves in a situation where they may need to jump into the middle of a conversation or risk not being heard at all.

Do not be surprised if some Saudis and other Arabic speakers speak in an animated tone and with a lot of emotion. This is not generally meant to be argumentative, disrespectful or rude but rather interested and engaged. However, be careful not to be very animated with many people from most of East Asia in particular as this can come across as aggressive.

Humour

Saudis do have a good sense of humour and appreciate humour in the right place at the right time. However, their sense of humour may not always align with yours.

The biggest challenge for most Western expatriates who like a laugh is to determine what could cause offence and hopefully avoid it. Situations that put a Saudi in a position of embarrassment or feeling ashamed are not a good idea as they cause a loss of face. Remember that Saudis can easily personalise the feeling of a loss of face not only for themselves and their family but also their wider community, whether it is national, ethnic, religious or corporate.

In general, word play and recognition of benign absurdities can work well. Irony tends not to translate much beyond the UK; nor does self-deprecation. Sarcasm and teasing another person can be disrespectful even if it doesn't cross the line of losing face.

NON-VERBAL
COMMUNICATION

Non-verbal communication includes most body language as well as personal space issues. Some of the information has been provided in previous sections and is repeated here along with some additional information.

Eye contact

Traditionally, eye contact between unrelated men and women was to be avoided as it violates the perception of modesty. Although some people, especially very traditional or very religious people may continue to look away when they are speaking to a member of the opposite sex, this is also changing.

In many business environments, direct but not overly steady eye contact can now be expected across the gender divide. The best advice for others is to match the behaviour of your Saudi counterpart. This behaviour can also be seen amongst people from elsewhere in the Middle East as well as people from much of the Indian subcontinent.

Very intense eye contact can also occur in Saudi Arabia, particularly amongst people of the same sex. This is not a sexual signal, nor is it meant to be aggressive or threatening, but rather it shows interest in the topic of conversation.

Personal space

Although many Saudis who become comfortable with another person can close the personal space gap to a very narrow distance, this will only happen between members of the same sex. People of the opposite sex should maintain a respectful distance between them, usually at least a full arm's length away.

Touch

Do not touch someone from the opposite sex in Saudi Arabia other than if a handshake is extended. Of course, it will become obvious that people of the same sex can be very tactile with one another beyond what is conventional in most of the West.

In the event of an emergency situation, such as helping someone of the opposite sex who has fallen or who has other mobility difficulties, it is conventional to offer a forearm rather than a hand in most situations.

Hand holding

It is commonplace to see two Saudi men or two women to hold hands openly in public. This is not seen as a sexual gesture but rather a high level of comfort between friends and sometimes business colleagues. Most Saudis are aware that this makes many Westerners uncomfortable, especially Western men, and are much less likely to try to engage you in this practice. But if they do, try not to flinch or reject the gesture.

Same sex but non-sexual hand holding is also common amongst many Asian communities and from parts of the African subcontinent as well.

Hand gestures

Although there are many hand gestures used in Saudi Arabia, some are much more common than others.

Do not point with your finger but use your open palm instead.

Beckoning can appear to be opposite of what many Westerners might expect. A raised hand motioning to the person is actually a gesture to pass through. A lowered hand with the palm turned down to the person motioning back and forth is actually a gesture to stop at that location. This is especially important to understand when passing through security check points.

Finally, there is the ubiquitous gesture where the four fingers and thumb of one hand are bunched together and raised, with the arm often moved up and down. This is not meant to be an insult but to indicate a need for more time or a warning to be patient.

The left hand

The left hand is considered dirty throughout the Middle East, as it is in most Asian cultures. The left hand has traditionally been used for unclean functions, including removing shoes and for the toilet. This will be an ongoing challenge for left-handed people no matter how long they work in Saudi Arabia.

The left hand should not be used when eating with the hands, such as when eating a sandwich. Never take food from a communal serving plate or bowl with your left hand, even when using cutlery. Approach buffets with the right hand only. Cutlery for individual use can be held in the left hand, as can pens and sporting equipment.

The left hand should never be used for passing items to another person. This includes food, an item in the office, business cards, money and bank cards, and gifts or other purchases. Items should be passed with the right hand, or with both hands when necessary.

The soles of your feet

The soles of the feet or shoes are considered dirty in Saudi Arabia and throughout the Middle East, most of Asia and much of Africa. They should never be seen by another person. Unlike the left hand issue, where a violation is looked upon as bad manners, exposing the soles of one's feet or shoes is actually offensive.

Western business professionals should not sit with their legs crossed at the knee, as the sole of your foot will inevitably be seen by someone else in the room. Westerners should also be prepared to sit on low cushions or even on the ground in a manner that does not show the bottoms of their feet. This is much trickier than it sounds, and may require quite a bit of dexterity. Bring a wrap or some other item to cover your feet if you cannot otherwise manage a suitable position.

SMALL TALK

As has been pointed out on several occasions, relationship building is important in Saudi Arabia. This includes the skill of small talk, which serves to facilitate relationship building, both with colleagues and often with service people as well.

Small talk is particularly critical in the 'getting to know you' phase of business as it helps your Saudi counterparts gauge expectations of your knowledge of the Kingdom as well as your possible behaviour. For example, a newly arrived Western expatriate may be forgiven for a small faux pas that a long term resident may not. Thus, Saudis who ask you how long you have been in the Kingdom and how do you like the Middle East are using small talk to facilitate gaining this knowledge.

Small talk is generally good form whenever you meet a business associate before getting down to business. Try not to abruptly start a business conversation without engaging in a bit of small talk. Ideally, let a Saudi transition the conversation to business.

Some people are naturally good at small talk; others may need to practice. The British characteristic of talking about the weather to strangers and new acquaintances (and indeed everyone else as well) becomes very useful in Saudi Arabia, even if the actual topic of the weather is mostly redundant.

For expatriates looking for good topics of conversation to develop their repertoire of small talk, here are some starting points:

- Anything positive you have experienced or are looking forward to in Saudi Arabia.
- Showing a positive interest in Saudi customs and traditions, including a genuine interest in learning more about Islam.

- General appreciation of family, but nothing familiar about women or older girls.
- Sport, especially football, F1, horse racing. Cricket can be good with people from the Indian subcontinent and much of the British Commonwealth.
- Food
- Technology, the latest consumer goods, gadgets, motor cars and similar
- Fashion – yes, really! – including luxury brands from Europe and the US.
- General economic trends such as stock market performance, interest rates, etc.

COMMUNICATION CHOICES

Most people make choices in how they communicate due to a number of factors. These include but are not limited to personal and national culture, corporate culture, line of business, language proficiency, practicalities such as time zone challenges, and convenience. They can also be driven by generational differences and comfort with the wide range of technology developed to make communicating even easier (some might also say more complicated as well).

Although there is no one best way for all Western expatriates to communicate in Saudi Arabia, there are cultural preferences in may impact your effectiveness. The following guide provides general information; your corporate culture or line of business may vary.

Face to face

In general, try to meet face to face where possible. Saudis and many other relationship cultures tend to prefer to get to know you by observing your behaviour in addition to what you say. This can work in your favour if you are personable, have a warm personality, and appear to be someone who can be liked and trusted. Of course, it can also be a problem if you come across as too impersonal, too much in a hurry, too business-only orientated, or simply too impatient.

Face to face relationships are especially appreciated if you have travelled in from abroad. It can accelerate relationship building even if you are working remote to Saudi Arabia and you are only able to meet your Saudi counterparts on a one-off trip.

The telephone

Naturally, it is not always possible to meet face to face. When this is the case, the next most effective way to communicate is generally by telephone, almost always by mobile phone as landlines are nearly obsolete in most lines of business outside government entities.

In general, most people working in Saudi Arabia are responsive to telephone calls, typically answering their mobiles no matter what else they might also be doing at the time. Although many Western cultures may consider being interrupted by someone answering their phone in the midst of their conversation to be rude, this is not the mind set in Saudi Arabia, perhaps other than in the presence of a VIP.

Western expatriates should strongly consider adapting to this practice whilst working in the Kingdom. Being available equates to being reliable and trustworthy. You can decide if the specific call should be taken then and there or if you should politely defer your conversation until a bit later; the important thing is to have picked up the call and responded to it. Some people have even gone as far as letting very important contacts know if they may be temporarily unavailable to answer their phone, such as on days where they might be visiting a venue where security needs preclude them from keeping their mobile phone switched on or if they are flying.

Emails

Although emails have their place in the Saudi business environment, they are not always used as robustly as they might be in many other Western cultures. This can be for a variety of reasons, from language proficiency to a fear of creating tangible evidence of commitment.

In general, when communicating for strategic reasons, try to avoid using email as a main form of communication. It is better to choose either a face to face meeting or to pick up the phone. An email can be sent summarising the conversation if Western business practices require a record of the conversation by providing key points in a bullet point fashion. Of course, complex exchanges of information, detailed reviews, providing explicit instructions etc continue to benefit through the use of email.

Other technology

It would seem likely that, in a culture where visuals and spoken language are favoured over written language, video conferencing would be popular in Saudi Arabia. However, this is not generally the case. Although the technology required to support video conferencing is readily available and is of an excellent standard, it is also perceived as being restrictive. Generally, Saudis don't like to be pinned down to being in a certain place at a certain time, and being in front of video conferencing equipment necessitates this behaviour.

Do not be surprised if you are working closely with a Saudi government entity that you may be required to use both very old as well as modern technology. For example, it is not unheard of to access rules, regulations and instructions on a local website, but to then send the formal, signed paperwork by fax! Or printed out and the originals sent by courier.

On the other hand, social media, from Facebook to WhatsApp to nearly any other popular app has been well received in Saudi Arabia. Social media is often used in business, often more robustly than in much of the West. It is not unusual for many Saudi businesses not to have their own dedicated website but to have an excellent Facebook page and to be able to communicate on multiple platforms with business partners, customers, and other interested parties. This is an especially important point for people in marketing and public relations roles to note.

COMMON COMMUNICATION
CONFLICT POINTS

When communicating across any combination of cultures, there is room for conflict and misunderstandings. Usually, there is no harm meant but an opportunity to see behaviour from a different perspective. However, communication style differences are not always immediately obvious, especially for the many Westerners whose communication style is blunt, objective, and task driven.

In addition to the common yes culture challenges and their cousins 'no' and silence, learning about body language and generally becoming more observant, additional situations can be encountered that can cause tensions and should be considered.

- Perceptions of politeness
    - Remember that courtesy words such as please and thank you are not always used in similar ways in different languages. People with a still-improving level of English may be translating from their own language and not make these distinctions until they become more proficient in English
- Showing respect
    - Using or expecting deferential language can be problematic if the other person uses more egalitarian language. It is generally good practice to be more deferential to Saudi nationals than your normal communication styles would be back home and to be respectful to everyone else.
- Delivering difficult messages
    - In general, the best way to deliver bad news or difficult messages to anyone from a face culture is to do so one-

on-one and privately. One of the most successful ways to do this is to deliver the 'message sandwich', where the two slices of bread are statements of praise and the filling in the middle is the difficult information, making it easier to swallow.

- Saying what is supposed to be said > literal truth
  - This is a manifestation of situationalism, which is explained in greater detail in the following chapter. Basically, there are times where form is more important than content. Most Westerners either miss this or become very frustrated and often suspicious of this way of communicating.
- Saying one thing…and doing nothing
  - This is not generally meant to be dishonest but can come across to many Westerners as such. From a Saudi perspective, it can simply happen because an authority figure reprioritised a task or never delegated authority for them to take action in the first place. For many people from most of Asia, doing nothing is another way to avoid confrontation rather than to say no directly.
- Do not force me to look at what I don't wish to see
  - There are many situations that can cause discomfort or are considered to be inappropriate by your Saudi counterparts, yet they have a positive relationship with whoever else is involved and don't want to compromise it. Westerners understand the concept of turning a blind eye. This is very similar behavior, although it may be applied more rigorously, and sometimes in different situations to what would occur in the West. Again, similar behavior can also be found in most Asian cultures as well.
- Not saying anything when angry or offended
  - Different cultures find different behaviours uncomfortable or offensive. Unfortunately, some of the same cultures, when offended, don't directly tell the offender, even when asked directly. Closely related to avoiding causing a loss of face, it's not unusual for Saudis who otherwise have or are developing a good relationship with Westerners *not* to

say when they are offended even if they are. In these situations, it's generally best to read body language to get an idea about what they really think.

- If it is written, it must be so
  - The written word has traditionally carried importance that can be even more significant than in most Western cultures. This often meant that, in the Arabic speaking world, commitments were only written down when they were considered to be very important and then only after a lot of consideration, checking and verifying, and only when given authority to do so once no changes were expected. A modern version of this mend-set can still be found in many Saudi business practices and can explain why so much business is done face to face or over the phone rather than via email.

- Being proactive < showing respect for authority
  - In nearly all status and hierarchy cultures, if a conflict is presented between task and respect for authority, it is almost certain that respect for authority will be prioritised. Thus, pressure to do something without a clear delegation of authority is most likely to result in inaction. 'If I have done nothing, I have done nothing wrong.'

- Fatalism and 'insh'allah'
  - Unfortunately, when things don't go to plan, Saudi business can take a very fatalistic approach, where the attitude is that it was or wasn't God's will. This can be further complicated from a Western perspective as this information is not always explicitly conveyed. Some Westerners may even take this frustration a step further and associate the term 'insh'allah' as an excuse. This has now become both religiously and culturally offensive to Saudis and other Muslims alike.
  - The best defence is open communication, status checks, and giving clear permission to report back any changes even if it appears to be bad news, and that bad news will not cause a reaction that leads to a loss of face.

SECTION 7

DOING BUSINESS
SUCCESSFULLY IN SAUDI ARABIA

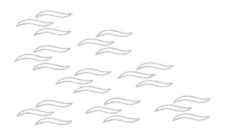

CORE CULTURAL VALUES IN THE BUSINESS ENVIRONMENT

Introduction

It is difficult to anticipate all of the considerations Westerners may have when working in Saudi Arabia. Areas of interest are dictated by your line of business, your corporate culture, how long it may have been trading in the Kingdom, your job title, expectations, experience and individual personality. It is not the intention of this book to provide a comprehensive set of instructions on how your specific business will become successful in Saudi Arabia. However, it does highlight the challenges and opportunities that most Western businesses and employees are likely to encounter, at least some of the time.

Overview

In the first chapter, the concept of culture was explored with Saudi core cultural values described in detail. These core cultural values are naturally important in a work environment as well.

A simple exercise comparing core values that have a direct impact in business between Saudis and Westerners is useful in highlighting these often very different perspectives. Additionally, other non-Western expatriates working in the Kingdom may also have a set of cultural values that may be distinct as compared to both Saudis and Westerners. Other non-Western expatriates may broadly share some Saudi values, especially if they also come from Islamic and/or relationship cultures.

Traditional Saudi Cultural Values at Work	Traditional Western Cultural Values at Work
Islam as a way of life	Religious freedom, including none
Islam as a moral code	Morals come from many sources
Family/group > individual	Individual > family/group
Hospitality	Politeness
Reputation	Achievement
Honour	Ability to take a joke
Relationships	Self sufficiency
Trust	Task orientation and ownership
Loyalty	Responsibility
Generosity	Qualifications
Respect	Experience

It is advised that Westerners working in Saudi Arabia keep these often very different cultural values in mind when conducting business and indeed in everyday life when interacting with Saudi nationals. Broadly speaking, these values also apply to varying degrees for people from elsewhere in the Middle East and much of Asia, the Islamic world and sub Saharan Africa.

Motivations at work

Some of the most important problems encountered in the Saudi work environment are the relative differences placed on the importance of relationship building and trust from the Saudi perspective. Most Westerners, on the other hand, often focus on tasks, ie getting things done. These often conflicting motivations are often a main source of culture clash, sometimes more often than Westerners are aware.

Saudi Motivations	Most Westerners' Motivations
Face	Credentials, experience
Relationships	Task
Trust	Relationships are a plus

Task	Trust backed by a contract
Fatalism	Control
Criticism is shameful	Criticism is an opportunity to learn
Criticism is personal	Criticism is not generally personal

As a group, it is clear that motivations between Saudis and Westerners are very different from each other. In fact, they can be polar opposites at times. How these very different values will impact your specific work environment will also be influenced by several factors. They can vary, but are usually determined by factors such as

- Age/generation
- Exposure to the West
- Education and/or work experience in the West
- English language skills
- Number and ratio of Saudi nationals in the work environment compared to expatriate nationalities

Perhaps most importantly, work motivations will be heavily influenced by the organisation's business culture.

Face

Face is a complicated concept for most Westerners to grasp. Although not unknown in the past, most Western cultures have lost the depth of face values in modern generations. Face is being treated with personal dignity and respect. On the surface, this doesn't sound very alien to most Westerners.

However, the concept is much more rigid and personal with Saudis and indeed most other Middle East and Asian cultures. For example, a joke at the expense of another person in the West is probably going to be tolerated. A joke at the expense of another person in Saudi Arabia is probably going to not only insult that person, but will be interpreted as insulting other members of that person's family or other group identity.

Criticism, pointing out mistakes, or accepting blame are all prob-lematic, again for the perception of losing face. They will probably be taken personally. In contrast, most Westerners are used to working in a business environment where constructive criticism is not only tolerated but expected as it is seen as a way to improve both the individual and the organisation.

Even acknowledging a mistake that Saudis or indeed other face culture people know they have made is also difficult. Unlike in the West, where most people would acknowledge that they have made a mistake, take responsibility to rectify it and move on, usually without fear or embarrassment, the typical reaction in face cultures is generally very different. Rather than stepping up and admitting their mistake, they are very likely to ignore it, dismiss it, deflect it, or deny it, even when the evidence is blatant and overwhelmingly concrete.

It is important to understand the basic difference between guilt and shame. Briefly, it can be said that guilt is when someone knows they have made a mistake. They may feel bad about it themselves, but would rarely externalise a mistake they have made, or consider it to be a negative reflection on anyone else. They own the mistake themselves and any guilt that comes with it. They will also probably be very action orientated to make appropriate amends, even if it is very public.

Shame is when someone makes a mistake and others find out about it. The bad feelings about the mistake are problematic for the person as well, but the problem is magnified, often with significant consequences for their family or group once it becomes public. There is no real Western equivalent. Thus, the main motivation for many people who come from face cultures is to hide their mistake. This is a stronger motivation even with the possibility that the mistake will be discovered anyway, often making the situation worse.

When working in Saudi Arabia, face issues are more important than anything else. Losing face will be avoided at all costs, as it is more important than winning business, progressing a project, meeting deadlines, or anything else related to getting things done. It will also have a significant impact on not always saying what is really meant, but instead saying what is 'correct' in order to avoid a face issue.

How you say something is generally more important than what you say. Be careful about being openly critical as this is a common reason why many Westerners cause a loss of face, even inadvertently, Criticism to a Saudi is a cause of embarrassment and shame and, for the reasons discussed, will be avoided or rejected. If criticism must be given, it should be done so one on one and privately. Deliver the message in between a lot of praise, ie the 'praise sandwich'.

Be careful not to be too abrupt, too direct, and especially too public when discussing sensitive topics. Be especially careful in the use of humour. What may be a light-hearted joke or gentle teasing to you might be an insult to the core of their identity to a Saudi or anyone else from a face culture.

Think of face as pride, but even stronger. Think of causing a loss of face as humiliation and you will be close.

The business of relationships

Once Saudi nationals are reasonably convinced you are unlikely to cause them to lose face, then relationship building begins in earnest. It is also important that they like you as a person. Your credentials, experience and ability are secondary.

Relationship building must be done on two levels: organisationally and personally. For some people about to work and possibly live in Saudi Arabia, the organisational relationship building may already be in process if they have predecessors who have already worked in the Kingdom.

If it is good, then they benefit already from being associated with that organisation. If it is not so good, then they may need to spend a lot of time repairing and rebuilding that relationship, often at the expense of accomplishing concrete tasks. On the other hand, an executive who inherits a poor organisational relationship and is able to turn it around can gain appreciation and loyalty to a higher level than usual as their Saudi counterparts will appreciate their efforts.

Organisations that are just beginning to work in Saudi Arabia can expect to build their organisational relationship alongside their personal relationships. It is advisable to spend time explaining the pedigree of your organisation, especially if it already has prestigious projects elsewhere in the Gulf or wider Middle East other than Israel. Family orientated businesses and Western organisations that are also very prestigious in their home countries should also play to this pedigree as these values are generally very important to Saudis.

Personal relationships must also be built in a professional capacity. Saudis want to work with people they know and trust. Once they start to trust their specific Western counterparts, they are likely to prioritise working with you more closely than with others who are still building their relationship or if their relationship is vague and unfocused.

They are also much more likely to open up new connections, introducing you to a wider range of trusted people that may not have happened if you didn't 'pass the test'.

Westerners working in Saudi Arabia should also take care in introducing their team members to their Saudi based counterparts. Personal relationships must also be built with team members, ideally starting with an introduction of who they are and what their roles are prior to their first visit.

Never randomly substitute one team member with another as this slows down the relationship building process and thus getting the tasks done. It could also possibly erode trust, especially if the substitution makes your Saudi counterpart feel that something or someone is more important than they are to you and your organisation. For example, explaining that Sarah was assigned to a project in India instead of making a trip to Riyadh or that Martin is filling in for Andrew, who is on holiday, but shows no other particular interest in the Kingdom can cause all sorts of damage.

When introducing subject matter experts, a new employee, or even explaining why an employee will no longer be working with Saudi Arabia, do take the time to describe the relationship in advance and how this will impact their business with you.

Relationship building remains important for the duration of your organisation's business in Saudi Arabia. It should never be taken for granted on either an organisational or personal level. On the other hand, a strong relationship with your Saudi counterparts will be rewarded by a significant degree of loyalty.

Trust

Westerners will always be outsiders in Saudi Arabia, no matter long we work or live in the Kingdom or how fluently we might speak Arabic. Even Arabs and Saudis from different tribes and regions may struggle to fully trust others. The good news for most Westerners working in Saudi Arabia is there is no expectation that we will ever become members of a trusted inner circle. That relieves us from some of the rigid structural behaviour expected from insiders. However, it also means we may never be fully trusted as we simply remain outsiders.

However, we can improve the perception of our trustworthiness in other ways. Trust is gained through the consistency of your behaviour. It is important to do what you say, even if it is seemingly insignificant.

'I'll give you a call next week' with the intention of providing updated information is a good example. In the West, many people would understand that the lack of a phone call next week is most likely due to the information has not yet come through, and that your counterpart will ring when it arrives. In Saudi Arabia, building trust means making that call anyway. They may not like that the information isn't available, but you have demonstrated your reliability and have been good to your word. You are trustworthy.

Fatalism

In most of the West, it is believed that time, task and in many ways, the future can be planned and controlled. Whilst Saudi nationals also plan, how they plan may be very different to their Western counterparts.

Most Westerners spend a lot of time planning. They will often consider all sorts of scenarios of what could happen and what the repercussions of these scenarios could be. Options and alternatives are all taken into account. A lot of time is spent analysing details as to what must be done when and by whom. Thus, project plans, budgets, agendas and the like are created after a lot of effort. The expectation is that once a plan is finalised and accepted, it will be methodically implemented, ideally without deviation to either task or time.

The Saudi working environment is very different, assuming the organisation functions in a traditional manner, Please note that genuinely multinational organisations and organisations run by Saudi nationals with a great deal of Western business experience may operate a blended approach to business or may even appear to be outwardly following Western business practices.

Traditionally run businesses in Saudi Arabia have different attitudes to controlling time and expectations of future activity can be very different. Although it would be foolish to even suggest that there is no planning in Saudi businesses, the approach and implementation of planning can be different. If something subsequently happens that was different to the plan, then the belief that it was God's will justifies the difference. That is, the future is not under a person's control but it is the will of Allah.

Individualism and situationalism

Most Westerners (and a few other cultures) behave in an individually driven manner. Their behaviour is determined by what they think is right for them; ie what is true to themselves. They tend to behave the same way no matter when, no matter who is around, no matter where they are.

Although individualists take others into account, they can also comfortably disagree with one another, often trying to persuade others to see their point of view. They are also able to agree to disagree if a difference of opinion is not resolved.

Most (but not all) other cultures are much more situational in their behaviour. Although they certainly have individual desires and preferences as regards their behaviour, they consider what is right for the group; ie what behaviour is correct for the group that will not damage the reputation of the group as a whole. They will then behave in the way that is most suitable for the situation, even if it means behaving in a way that is not their own personal preference.

Our first group, individualists, may regard situationalism as not always honest. They may consider it to be two-faced, misleading, dishonest or false, especially in a business environment.

Our second group, situationalists, may regard individualism as naïve and selfish, especially if their behaviour is perceived to harm the group. It can almost be perceived similar to the behaviour of a small child who has not yet learnt how to behave properly in public. Although situationalists certainly know where they stand with an individualist, they may never trust them.

Individualism, situationalism and culture clash can also be manifested in everyday business practices. For example,

Famously, many Saudis can be found in Bahrain, having driven over the Causeway from Saudi Arabia. Although many are there with their families, others may be enjoying activities not legal back home, including drinking alcohol or mixing more freely with the opposite sex. How they manage to justify this may be a good example of the difference between individualism/situationalism and pure hypocrisy.

Saudis who preach one set of morals and then practice another are undoubtedly hypocritical. However, Saudis who explain that they personally have little choice in their behaviour at home because it risks their entire family's livelihood such as access to a good education or an important job, but personally choose to behave differently when they are in an environment where nobody knows them is entirely different behaviour – it's situationalism.

HIERARCHY AND STATUS

Although Islam professes that all people are equal, this is far from evident in most traditional Saudi business environments. Instead, it is generally an environment where authority is strong and drawn along lines of hierarchy and status. Authority is often held at the very top echelons, with little latitude for Western concepts of direct challenge, pro-active behaviour or taking the initiative in the work environment. It can also mean that brainstorming, thinking outside the box, etc can be problematic, disrespectful or even threatening in some environments.

In reality, if workers are in conflict between respecting hierarchy and getting things done, hierarchy will be the priority, even if it means a deadline will be missed and even if they have previously had the authority, knowledge and ability to complete the task.

Many factors will impact where you will fit within the Saudi hierarchy. In general, the following criteria matter: nationality, job title, age, sometimes gender and religion, reputation – yours and your organisation's, and *wasta*.

Nationality

It can be argued that the single most factor that determines where an individual sits within the hierarchy and status of Saudi Arabia is their nationality.

As previously mentioned in chapter 2, Saudi Arabia has a total of approximately 10 million expatriates. All of these expatriates are either employed or are close dependent family members of an employee.

Saudi Arabia extends jobs to a large expatriate population for a number of reasons. These range from lack of expertise, especially for demanding and specialised technical skills, to physical, unskilled labour that Saudi nationals generally reject. As we will discuss in the following Saudisation/*nitaqat* section, the Kingdom is trying to reduce its reliance on expatriate labour, with mixed results at present.

The respected website American Bedu www.americanbedu.com reports the following labour demographic statistics, extrapolated from the Saudi Ministry of Planning: Of the 8.8 million workers estimated in 2009, about 6 million are Muslim, 1.5 million are Christians, and 1.3 million are Hindus and others. Some of the Muslims, ranging from 1 to 2 million, are illegal immigrants who have come into the country on Hajj or Umrah visas, and then stayed on. Some of the other illegals are runaways.

Of the 8.8 million expatriates, perhaps 6.5 million are bachelor status men, 500,000 married status men, 1 million working women (mostly bachelor status and some married wives), and 800,000 non-working wives and children.

Things change. For example, relatively skilled expatriates from Lebanon, Syria, and Yemen may currently find it very difficult to obtain a visa to visit, work or live in Saudi Arabia, especially if they come from a Shi'a background. This includes a number of loyal employees who have lived in the Kingdom, sometimes for decades. There are also periodic expulsions of foreign workers. For example, in 2013, an amnesty ended where many foreign workers had either overstayed their work visas or were working illegally, often after having changed jobs or employers.

Probable expectations at work

Who does what

Most Saudi employers consider certain nationalities and exclude others when making job offers. Your nationality will also determine your salary and additional perquisites, which may be different than your colleague doing the same job with the same experience, although in reality, many organisations avoid this by employing only one group of nationalities for specific positions.

The following is a very general guideline to how things generally work in the Saudi workplace. It assumes a multinational, private sector business. Your organisation's structure could be different, especially if it caters for a specialised market or limits the range of nationalities offered employment.

Decision makers are Saudi. A few other nationalities, usually Arab and some Westerners may be influencers, but the ultimate decisions will be from Saudi nationals.

Senior management are usually Arab nationals, usually from the Levant or Egypt, along with some other Saudis. Additionally, many positions are also held by Westerners, usually from Northern or Western Europe, North America, Australia or New Zealand. Other Westerners are less likely to hold the most senior management positions but may hold middle management positions.

Skilled workers following instructions can be the same nationalities but who are younger and less experienced, especially in public facing positions such as sales and marketing roles, as well as prestigious jobs such as engineering. However, they are much more likely to be well educated employees from the Indian subcontinent. IT and accountancy would be representative positions these nationalities are likely to hold.

Service roles are invariably held by less educated employees, nearly always from the Indian subcontinent or Southeast Asia. It is generally expected that these workers perform their work without question, often with few expectations or recognition of basic human rights. Domestic service roles such as maids and nannies can make these employees even more vulnerable to abuse from an irresponsible employer. Whilst horror stories that make the news are usually about Saudi households, other nationalities may not always be exemplary employers, either.

Other hierarchy and status factors

Although your nationality is often the most important factor in determining your status in Saudi Arabia, it is not the only one. Your job title, the reputation of your company and of course your own reputation matter a lot as well. Simply put, working in a senior position for a prestigious organisation, especially a Saudi or global Western organisation opens doors that remain shut for many others. Your gender and religion are less important than many Westerners may believe, although they should not be dismissed in some situations. Finally, your status will almost certainly grow with age – at least until you become too old to obtain a visa for the Kingdom. This is refreshing for many Westerners who may feel invisible in some work environments back home, where youth is often valued more than experience and wisdom.

Expectations and challenges

It should not be a surprise that working practices in a Saudi work environment can be very different to those in the West and can sometimes be very frustrating for achievement orientated Westerners.

Typically, there is a strong expectation that employees will show respect to authority, including people who may not always be competent in their job or may be unpredictable or unreliable. Most Westerners are likely to be self-starters and self-motivated, choosing to simply get on with the job at hand.

However, many Saudi managers would consider this approach to be disrespectful of their authority, as they would expect the employee to wait until they are given permission to complete the task – delegation of authority is received, not taken. Thus, common practices in the West such as being proactive or especially challenging authority can actually be risky in Saudi Arabia, especially in a traditional organisation.

Instead of an efficient work environment, this creates an environment of obedience and waiting. Both are an anathema to most Westerners, who are much more action and task orientated.

In a traditional Saudi organisation, once authority has been delegated, the default expectation is to do what you are told regardless of whether it is right or the best option available and to do so immediately. This can be especially frustrating for Westerners who are also expected to deal with situational decisions, especially if they negate previously agreed plans.

On the other hand, some Saudi organisations may seem to take a very long time to prioritise a project or make a decision. In these cases, the default is generally to do nothing, simply because if no action has been taken, then no mistakes have been made. 'If I haven't done anything, then I haven't done anything wrong.' This also serves to avoid a perception of directly disrespecting Saudi authority. If in conflict, most smart employees know that respecting hierarchy and authority is more important than measurable achievement in these situations.

Westerners who are used to taking the initiative and shouldering the blame if things go wrong may take time to learn this new behaviour. Other face cultures, especially those from the Indian Subcontinent and Asia in general already understand this expectation and are good at waiting, even if they are also inwardly frustrated. Westerners who are working with people from Asia in particular should not automatically assume that such a response is incompetent, uncooperative, or lacks initiative. Given the hierarchy, they are unlikely to be direct and open with Westerners, either.

Expatriates working in Saudi Arabia should understand that there are a number of powerful families who control much of Saudi business in the private sector as well as government owned entities. It should be noted that several royal family members are also prominent in business, both in Saudi Arabia and abroad.

How they approach business will depend on their exposure to the West, general attitude toward Westerners, how badly they need Westerners' expertise, and individual personality. However, there is no doubt that in all environments, the best advice is to recognise that Saudis have more status than any Westerners, regardless of how well they work.

ATTITUDES TO WESTERNERS

General attitudes to Westerners

Like many other cultural themes that have been explored, Saudis and indeed other non-Western expatriates have a wide range of attitudes toward Westerners. In the business environment, it is possible to highlight a few generalisations that can characterise many Westerners from a Saudi perspective. Some of these also apply to Westerners' everyday life. It is also important to keep in mind that they do not necessarily apply to everyone all the time.

The good

- Admire work ethic
- Admire innovation
- Admire punctuality and general time keeping
- Admire business planning and practices
- Admire business ethics
- Transparent and easy to understand
- Value economic achievements, eg technology, medical, finance, higher education, innovative business practices
- Admire experience

The not-so-good

- Inflexible due to too many rules that appear to hinder business
- Always in a hurry – don't stay long enough if on a business trip
- Simplistic approach to business – too task driven, no human touch

- Too informal, no manners, too casual, too direct
- Here to help as a condescending mind set
- Too detail orientated at too high a level
- Too money focused
- Confident but need to take care not to be too arrogant or too understated
- Too cautious/too risky depending on which culture
- Suspicious of Western political and social ethics, often emphasised in the media
- No real knowledge or appreciation of Middle East culture or history
- No recognition of regional cultural and social differences as if the Middle East is all the same

General attitudes to businesswomen

As a businesswoman, one of the most common questions heard by the author about Saudi Arabia is related to women and work. Many people still believe that women cannot work in the Kingdom at all, or if they can, it's in only in some traditional fields such as girls' education or nursing. Whilst it is true that there remain some specific challenges – think oil rigs, some military work, etc – women can and do work in Saudi Arabia in a wide range of roles, including foreign businesswomen. However, there are things we sometimes need to do differently.

The least of our worries as businesswomen should be whether a man will shake our hand or the fact that we cannot drive. The former is driven by religious or family values, the latter by Saudi convention. Neither are necessarily indications of their personal attitude toward the professional businesswoman.

It is also important to recognise that Saudi women themselves are making great strides in the world of work. Admittedly, they are collectively starting from a much lower place than most of their sisters from both the Gulf Countries and the wider Middle East. But they are a force to be reckoned with, and they are steadily increasing in numbers.

It should also be noted that many Saudi men are also advocates of women in the work force. They can hold a wide range of opinions on the topic, from the advocacy of segregated work environments to progressive attitudes of full equality not always achieved even in the West.

Advocated by the late King Abdullah, the *nitaqat* system is proving to be rather successful in getting more Saudi women into the work force in numbers never before seen. Progress is not only seen in the big cities, but is being established as the base business culture in places like KAEC, following the example of neighbouring KAUST, the educational city also practicing a strong level of social reform. Changes are even beginning to be made in rural areas where values are often significantly more conservative, although it is early days.

Examples of Prominent Saudi Businesswomen
It is worth noting some of the work done by prominent Saudi business-women in modern times. Many of these women started their career when it was much more difficult to do so; others are benefitting from the pioneering women who went before them.

Prominent Saudi businesswomen

A quick snapshot of businesswomen in trade and commerce, banking, education and medicine presents some formidably powerful female Saudi executives:

> Lubna Olayan - CEO, Olayan Financing Company
> Muna Abu Sulayman - Secretary General, Alwaleed Bin Talal Foundation
> Huda al Ghosan - Executive Director Saudi Aramco
> Somayya Jabarti - Editor in Chief, Saudi Gazette
> Dr Nahed Taher - CEO, Gulf Investment Bank
> Dr Samia Al Amoudi – ObGyn and raising breast cancer awareness amongst the population, CEO Sheikh Mohammed Hussien Al-Amoudi Center of Excellence in Breast Cancer, prof King Abdulaziz University
> Dr Prof Samira Islam, head of the medicine unit at King Fahd Centre of Medical Research at King Abdul Aziz University.
> In addition, women can now practice law in Saudi Arabia since licencing was permitted in 2013:

Bayan Mahmoud Al Zahran – amongst the first four women to be licenced as lawyers in Saudi Arabia and who has now opened her own female run law firm. Her female colleagues are Jihan Qurban, Sarra Al Omari and Ameera Quqani. Arwa al-Hujaili is the first trainee lawyer in the Kingdom

Even Royalty is represented, with two women particularly prominent.

Princess Adila bint Abdullah al Saud is a supporter of women's rights, legal and health issues, an advocate against domestic violence against women as well as businesswomen through a number of Saudi organisations. She had a semi public role on behalf of her father, the late King Abdullah, promoting these values.

Princess Ameera al-Taweel is a former wife of Prince Waleed bin Talal al Saud, one of the world's wealthiest businessmen. Princess Ameera is a businesswoman in her own right and continues the support of her ex-husband. She is currently Vice Chair of Al Waleed Philanthropies as well as Chair of Time Entertainment, both prominent Saudi organisations with a global reach.

Attitudes toward Western businesswomen

Most lasting changes that improve societies tend to be evolutionary rather than revolutionary. Thus, the author's philosophy is to push the boundaries sometimes but never to break them. As an outsider, the latter could easily have the opposite effect and cause difficulties both for Saudi women and could prevent Western women from working in the Kingdom in the future. Not known for her patience, it remains the author's opinion that patience is a virtue in the Kingdom and as an outsider, gentle pressure delivered patiently is probably more effective than other methods.

Setting a good example as a positive role model may well be more effective to improving business women's lives in the long run, including Saudi women.

As a strong advocate of women's rights, including the ability for a woman to work wherever and however she wants, these examples are provided to illustrate that women – even in Saudi Arabia – are indeed able to work. It is also important to understand that we sometimes need to do so in ways that are different to men.

Businesswomen must understand that our own behaviour is still scrutinised more closely than that of our male counter-parts, especially in public. This, it is extremely important that we get the little things and the surface stuff right, including the dress code and other social behaviour. On the other hand, most Saudis are likely to assume we are competent, especially women in high positions, by the simple fact that our own organisations are comfortable enough to send us to the Kingdom in the first place.

Businesswomen and limits in Saudi Arabia

Although the author is clearly a strong advocate for promoting businesswomen in Saudi Arabia, both Saudi nationals and expatriates, it is also realistic to acknowledge that there are some limits.

For example, on occasion, a businesswoman may find she is faced with a very traditional male business partner who may be reluctant or, on rare occasions, even refuse to work with women. In reality, Western businesswomen will find that many more men will be happy to show how progressive they are within their culture and welcome their female guest.

In the event that a man is unwilling to work with a businesswomen, that person will more often than not remove themselves from the difficult position of working across the gender barrier against their will by sending a colleague or proxy, or perhaps meet in a large mixed gender group in a more private venue.

Some exceptions to be prepared for:

- Some military organisations in certain settings
- Some remote locations within the Kingdom, especially if overnight accommodation is required but suitable accommodation for businesswomen is unavailable, such as some very rural communities or working on field camps, oil rigs, etc.
- Some events requiring gender segregation in public. In this situation, it is not necessarily impossible for men and women to work together, but they may need to manage limits of mixing, especially in a public setting such as a televised press conference.

- Additional requirements for businesswomen must be met for certain activities. For example, some publically held events where a woman is leading a group of men may require additional permission if conducted publically.

In conclusion, it is the author's strong opinion that Western businesses should never be responsible for limiting or barring women from working in Saudi Arabia. Nor should women themselves think it is not possible. Give it a chance – if it's not for you, make sure you come to that conclusion yourself for reasons that are true to your motivations and ethics, not someone else's.

GENERAL SAUDI BUSINESS STRUCTURE

Introduction

Western business professionals should be aware that there are significant differences between most Saudi office structures and the more casual and egalitarian environments found in modern offices in much of the West. This goes beyond work week, opening hours, and other differences described in greater detail in the Time section that follows.

Saudi sponsorship

All foreign organisations need to find a Saudi sponsor in order to do business in Saudi Arabia, including organisations planning to establish their business in special economic zones such as KAEC or Riyadh's developing financial district. The sponsor must be a Saudi national.

Finding a Saudi business partner

Finding the correct Saudi business partner for your organisation is obviously of paramount importance for Western businesses, whether they are simply seeking local representation for their goods or services, or if they are considering opening an office to establish a direct presence in the Kingdom.

Organisations that are thinking about setting up a presence in the Kingdom should take the follow key points into account. They should also consider any additional factors that are specific to their line of business or own corporate culture.

- Use your own *wasta* (network and connections).
  Recognise that business in Saudi Arabia is not run simply on cold calls, or on the stand alone merit of a business model. Business runs on relationships and often through references or other connections. Western organisations should start on a number of levels where possible, including within the Saudi community, through regional connections elsewhere in the Gulf or perhaps wider Middle East, and through Western connections and recommendations.

Other considerations:
- Can your prospective partner help to leverage all of the geographical markets your organisation is targeting? Many Saudis might claim they have national reach, but may actually have a positive track record only in certain regions. Others recognise the limits of their regional reach and partner with additional business partners from those other regions. Is your organisation prepared to manage this level of complexity?
- Can your prospective partner help you in your specific target markets? Many Saudi organisations may have connections that are stronger in public/government sectors; others have grown successful in the developing private sector. Many may have strength in niche markets, eg expatriate businesses, or as subcontractors. How well do you understand the intricacies of the interrelationship of the business you are considering to be a business partner? How high a priority would your business be for them, especially when under pressure?
- How deep are English language skills throughout the organisation? What about any additional important Western languages where necessary?
- How diverse is your prospective Saudi partner's organisation? Are they diverse enough to get things done if your business requires a broad reach? For example, if your business may appeal to non-Western expatriates, does your prospective business partner employ non-Western expatriates in key positions where they have the correct connections and level of influence? Or, if your own organisation brings a depth of expertise to the Kingdom, will its value be recognised and nurtured?

- Never underestimate the Sunni Shi'a divide in the Kingdom. For example, it would be very difficult for most Shi'a Saudis to have the desired influence in the Sunni government sector.

All potential business partners should be thoroughly vetted, which can also introduce sensitive issues, especially about financial and other claims. Try to explain this is not personal but a requirement that protects both parties and ultimately makes any future business partnership stronger and more trustworthy.

Never rush your decision. This advice applies to choice of business partners. It is much better to delay your business expanding into Saudi Arabia than it is to enter too early, where a failed venture (and most likely failed business relationships as well) are very difficult to recover from. Worse yet is when a Western organisation, belatedly recognising they are not yet ready to trade in Saudi Arabia, withdraws, leaving Saudi business partners in difficulty not to mention a loss of face.

Contracts and legal documents

It is beyond the scope of this book to provide legal advice. However, it is important to understand that professional legal advice should be given serious consideration for any contracts, agreements or other legal documents. In Saudi Arabia, only the Arabic language copy is considered valid. Legal decisions are based on Shari's law, not the law of the Western organisation's home country.

Do keep in mind that, although Saudis do sign contracts and other formal documents, they still prefer to rely on the strength of their business relationships to resolve most business disputes. If a business relationship has broken down, it is very difficult if not impossible to repair, at least in the short term, especially if it has also become public knowledge.

Some common differences between Saudi and Western offices

There are number of other common differences between many Saudi and many Western offices. Some of these are more general characteristics found throughout the Middle East; others are recognisably Saudi specific.

The prominence of prayer rooms, which are expected to be used by all Muslims during each prayer time that occurs during business hours. In some buildings that have experienced a rapid growth in employee numbers, prayers may be held in a more public area instead.

The existence of all male offices, including in lines of business that would be much more gender diverse in the West.

Gender segregated offices where both men and women are employed. In some offices, women work in a room or area separate from men. Communication may be restricted to intercoms or similar. In other offices, a screen or other less formal divide may be established. Communication is more relaxed, although personal space distance is respected. Some offices choose to ignore gender segregation conventions and function much more similar to those in the West. You may not always know, although Western women can have a distinct advantage in more traditional set-ups as we will almost certainly have access to both male and female work spaces.

Most Saudi offices are more status driven than Western offices, especially in English speaking countries. Outward signs include the design and use of office space, including bigger private offices, superior furniture, sometimes restricted access or use of rest room facilities, parking spaces, lifts, etc. Open plan offices are not generally popular.

There is often someone in the office who has the ability to get things done from a bureaucratic perspective. Once known as a fixer and now more of an office administrator and BPO liaison, they ensure that official transactions are taken care of. This can involve anything from getting goods cleared from Saudi customs to sorting out *iqama* problems. They often serve as an effective liaison between different offices in a large conglomerate or other complicated setup.

There is generally a much greater presence of support staff such as drivers, tea boys, general runners, etc

SAUDISATION - *NITAQAT*

Introduction

Saudi Arabia has long had a problem in its economy. Its young labour force is undereducated and underemployed. Due to population demographics, the number of young adults in need of an income continues to grow, with demands for more job opportunities increasing.

Unfortunately, many Saudis who do have an education, other than from elite families who have had the opportunity to study and live abroad, may also have a poor quality education that leaves the student ill equipped for the 21st century job market. Additionally, discriminatory practices have meant that young adults from families with few or no connections have had limited access to the job market. Women in the general population have traditionally had even fewer opportunities than men other than in exceptional circumstances.

The Saudi economy relies heavily on the oil and gas industry, which in turn relies on a labour force that requires specific skills. These skills are drawn mostly from hard sciences, mathematics, and especially engineering. Saudi children who are products of the basic Saudi education system are highly unlikely to be academically prepared to take up these positions as they are simply unqualified. The main reason is the Saudi education system's heavy focus on religious studies – generally at the expense of learning hard sciences (and other topics that would make the graduate employable as well). Although this is slowly changing, the impact on the labour force remains somewhere in the future.

King Abdullah and now King Salman have recognised that the heavy reliance on expatriate labour is a risk not only to the Saudi economy but also to the risk of the stability of the country. For example, young men in particular who are underemployed or unemployed have few marriage prospects in a society that demands it. Additionally, some idle young men may be tempted to become a social burden or even a menace at a time when the country is already on edge.

In 2011, the current *nitaqat* system was announced. The purpose is to reduce the reliance on expatriate labour and to empower Saudi nationals to fill these positions instead. This system supersedes previous failed attempts at Saudisation.

Employment demographics

There are approximately 8.8 million expatriate workers in Saudi Arabia; the remaining expatriate population are dependents of these workers. There are about 1.8 million Saudis in the workforce out of a Saudi national population of about 18 million people. About 40% of the Saudi population is under the age of 20. The unemployment figure amongst young adult Saudis in their early 20s exceeds 30%, and in reality is probably higher.

The *nitaqat* system is intended to encourage Saudi nationals to accept employment in the private sector and to encourage private sector employers to employ Saudi nationals as a priority over expatriate labour. How this is to be achieved depends on a number of factors, including the size of your organisation, the ratio of Saudi nationals already employed to expatriate employees, your line of business, and other specific factors.

The basics

It is important to keep in mind that labour laws can be very volatile in Saudi Arabia. Although this information is current at the time of publication, it is critical to check if it is still applicable to your organisation as you assess your own situation. For example, the Saudi Council of Ministers announced 38 amendments to Saudi Labour Law that impacts the *nitaqat* programme in 2015.

Promotion of Saudi nationals

Saudi labour law states that 75% of the total labour market must be comprised of Saudi nationals. As we can see from the employment figures above, there is a lot of change needed if this goal is to be achieved. As Saudi nationals are massively underrepresented in the private sector, the *nitaqat* system is geared toward making changes to these employers.

An increasing number of job titles are reserved for Saudi nationals only. At the time of publication, these jobs include a variety of human resources, clerical, security, and some retail positions. Of course, organisations looking to improve their *nitaqat* category status may unilaterally offer certain additional jobs only to Saudi nationals as well. Further details can be found on the qsaudi website referenced at the end of this section.

Additionally, the *nitaqat* system is designed to encourage employment in sectors of the Saudi population that have historically had limited opportunities, especially women, the disabled, students, and people who wish to work part time. For example, organisations employing a disabled Saudi national earn four credits instead of the usual one credit for a full time employee. However, the percentage of disabled employees is capped. Students can be counted but are required to be given training. A range of other conditions apply.

Saudi minimum wage

The *nitaqat* system has also formalised a Saudi minimum wage, currently SR3000 per month for full time Saudi national employees, both men and women. Although not typically affecting Western expatriates, it is important to note that many expatriates from developing countries may still be paid significantly less for doing the same job as a Saudi national (or another expat for that matter).

Hafiz unemployment benefits programme

In parallel with *nitaqat*, the Ministry of Labour has also implemented an unemployment benefits programme for Saudi nationals for the purpose of encouraging them into the job market. Known as the Hafiz, prospective beneficiaries must agree to participate in training programmes and to go on job interviews. The Hafiz programme is designed for both men and women and provides an equal monetary benefit for both genders.

Liqaat programme

The Liqaat programme supports job fairs for prospective Saudi national employees, matching them with suitable employers in attendance.

Nitaqat categories

Within the private sector, Saudi based businesses are categorised for the purposes of *nitaqat*. These categories are determined by a number of factors, including the line of business, total number of employees in an organisation, and the percentage of Saudi nationals employed. Short term employees that enter the Kingdom on a work visa but do not qualify for a residency visa are generally exempt.

At the time of publication, organisations are categorised into 45 different economic definitions and are additionally categorised by their size as defined by the number of employees as follows:

Number of employees:

Micro	0-9
Small	10-49
Medium	50-499
Large	500-2999
Giant	3000+

The number of Saudi national employees is then assessed on the organisation's line of business and size, which determines which *nitaqat* quota band they fall in.

Bands:

Platinum – organisations that have achieved or exceeded the quota of Saudi nationals specified for their size and line of business. Employees working for a platinum organisation can expect current employees' *iqamas* to be renewed and to be able to obtain new visas every two months. Employees' professions can be changed. They can also accept transfers of employees from organisations carrying a red or yellow categorisation. Employers are allowed to hire employees from anywhere in the world.

Green – organisations that perform in the upper 50% of their category are recognised by benefitting from similar conditions found for platinum organisations. Although expatriate new hires are permitted, policies and conditions might be somewhat more restrictive.

Yellow – organisations that perform in the lower 50% of their category have restrictions imposed on them, with the incentive to take more Saudi nationals on board. These organisations are not freely permitted to apply for new expatriate work visas, nor can they transfer visas or change employees' professions. Current employees have a cap on how long their visa can be extended – currently four years for most jobs. The organisation is permitted one new visa only after the departure of two expatriates. Nor do they have the right to ban an expatriate employee from transferring to an organisation with a green or platinum status. Yellow status organisations do have a nine month grace period to earn a higher colour status.

Red – organisations that perform in the lowest 20% of their category have additional restrictions imposed on them in addition to those restrictions imposed on yellow category organisations. They include a total ban on new expatriate visas. Nor do they have permission to renew an employee's work visa or *iqama*.

White – micro organisations currently exempt from a *nitaqat* system although a Saudi national sponsor is required.

If an organisation has not yet reached its quota of Saudi nationals, then a variety of remedial actions can be taken to improve their status. Organisations should also be aware that quotas for Saudi national employees will continue to increase over time.

The Saudi Ministry of Labour website provides a facility for employees to check their *iqama* status and their employer's *nitaqat* status. Although the website is only in Arabic, there are a number of helpful expatriate websites that will guide a non-Arabic reader to navigate the page and required fields to provide them with the relevant information.

Impact on Saudi based businesses

All businesses in Saudi Arabia must have a Saudi sponsor and at least one employee who is a Saudi national, no matter how small the organisation is.

Larger organisations must comply with *nitaqat* rules. Most organisations fear two major factors: increased labour costs and decreased efficiency. Both of these factors are realistic and should be planned for if your organisation intends to continue its presence in the Kingdom. The benevolent perspective is that your organisation is also participating in the transition to a Saudi economy that is becoming more diversified beyond its reliance on oil and is attempting to become more self sufficient.

Impact on expatriate residents

Long term secondees may wonder whether they have made a wise choice if they fear that the *nitaqat* system could prevent them from fulfilling their career goals whilst in Saudi Arabia.

Just getting there could be problematic if justifying an expatriate assignment becomes more difficult. Organisations should understand which job categories and titles will continue to be acceptable for expatriates to fill within their *nitaqat* category.

Additionally, expatriate residents may also be worried about the level of difficulty in getting their labour contract renewed once they have been living in the Kingdom for a period of time and wish to stay longer. Others may accept their employment with their current organisation might be coming to an end but worry about how difficult it might now be for them to transfer to another organisation depending on their original organisation's *nitaqat* category if they wish to stay and work longer in the Kingdom. Of course, both of these situations have a profound impact on the expatriate's and their family's residency status.

As time goes by, the *nitaqat* system means that expatriates will be working with an increased number and more diverse group of Saudi nationals. On a positive note, expatriate residents and frequent business travellers may also feel they have made a small difference in the progression of the Saudi economy by making a valuable contribution to the Saudi labour market. This is especially true if they feel they have empowered employees, whether through training or simply by giving them an opportunity that previously would not have been available to them.

The challenges

Although gainful employment for an increasing number of Saudi nationals is not only a worthy cause but a necessity to guarantee the

Kingdom's future, it also presents a number of concrete challenges, including to Western and multinational organisations.

Government vs private sector

According to a study published by Saudi Hollandi Bank in 2012, the Saudi labour force is recognised to be comprised of about 90% expatriate labour. Since this publication, it is believed that the number of Saudi nationals in the private sector has only risen by about 2%.

According to a Gallup poll published in 2015, only 17% of Saudis are considering the possibility of employment in the private sector. Most Saudis prefer employment in the government sector, for reasons ranging from stability to perceived higher salaries to feeling more welcome.

Furthermore, there is a perception that government sector jobs are generally higher status jobs and have more prestige. They also minimise challenges that many Saudis have about leadership issues, such as reporting to someone who is younger, less experienced, has less seniority, or is from the 'wrong' nationality. Their skill sets are also more likely to align with their peers. Finally, there is a perception that government employers are more sympathetic to family issues that might arise during the work day or otherwise have an impact on the job.

Salary expectations

The *nitaqat* system is designed for an expatriate worker to be replaced by a Saudi national. However, the salary system in Saudi Arabia, especially in the private sector, is inequitable, with employees paid to a large extent as determined by their nationality.

This means that Saudis who might be replacing an expatriate may also be expecting a salary that it significantly higher than what the employer has been paying. This difference can be as much as three times an expatriate's salary. Additionally, many Saudi nationals may consider a fair salary one that is determined simply by their nationality, ignoring the common business norms of pay influenced by skills and experience.

Absenteeism and commitment

It is not the intention of the author to criticise all Saudi employees as many workers, including many in the private sector, are qualified, reliable, dedicated employees who are making positive contributions to their employer and are building a robust career with a promising future.

However, there are some Saudis who place work lower down their priority list to what Western and multinational organisations would consider to be acceptable. This can include chronic absenteeism, short working hours with no evidence of 'working from home', or even blatantly conducting other business or dealing with personal matters whilst at work.

Organisations that are considering Saudi nationals during the hiring process should take their time and perform due diligence to minimise the chances of hiring an employee that does not perform to acceptable standards. It is very difficult to terminate employment of a Saudi national if you have chosen the wrong candidate.

Education

Education challenges have already been referenced above. Although the Kingdom has recognised the problem and has taken steps to reform its education system to make it more suitable for the 21st century, reforms are slow, uneven, and take time, not least waiting for enough time to pass for children who are benefitting from these changes to become adults and enter the labour force.

Even so, although the curricula is becoming more rounded, it still lacks sufficient numbers of students in the core subjects needed to become engineers, scientists, medical professionals and the like. Furthermore, the Saudi population continues to explode, with the Saudi Hollandi Bank noting that the under 20 population grew by 4.3% in five years in the lead-up to *nitaqat*, making educational reform difficult to keep up with and implement across the wider population.

Gender

As of 2015, 64% of university degrees in Saudi Arabia are earned by women. However, only 13% of Saudi women are in paid employment.

Many women who already have significant work experience in Saudi Arabia often come from elite families, are well educated, and may have spent time living, working and studying abroad. These women are often comfortable working in an environment that would not be unknown in the West.

However, as more women from ordinary backgrounds consider employment, they do so with the consensus of their family, who are likely to consider a wide range of social factors presented with a job offer before accepting employment. These include a range of issues, from household, spousal, and childcare responsibilities to structural issues at the workplace, ranging from gender segregation expectations to transport practicalities.

The common perception in Saudi Arabia is that the government sector is much more likely to understand, respect, and implement policies that align with women's expectations and those of her family, making a government job a 'safer' choice. Dignity, honour and reputation are much less likely to be compromised.

On the other hand, some women are looking at *nitaqat* as an empowerment tool that will provide them with an opportunity to put their education to work in a way that would not have been a choice for their mothers and aunts.

The *nitaqat* system appears to be a positive advancement for many women in the workforce. Women are given options to work from home where this is practical. Some of the social concerns are now being addressed in the private sector, giving them the possibility to accept gainful employment outside the home without fear of violating social norms, including unwanted gender mixing.

Juggling the expectations of potential female employees and their families should always be considered to maximise the possibilities of this often enthusiastic group of employees who are looking for a chance to put their skills and education to work.

Attitude

Not all jobs performed by expatriates are high paying, prestigious positions. The *nitaqat* system is designed for Saudis to accept a wide range of jobs, although some such as house maids and other domestic servant roles remain exempt.

This can present some difficulties as many Saudis consider themselves to be unsuitable for certain types of jobs, particularly unskilled or semi-skilled manual labour, including most service jobs, and may be reluctant to accept them. Many would refuse to even entertain the possibility and could consider it to be an insult to even suggest such employment, even if they are not qualified for more skilled positions.

Saudis are often motivated in the work force by their job title, visible perquisites, pay grade relative to others, seniority linked to promotion, and work/life balance issues. They will generally reject positions that they consider not to meet their minimum requirements, even if this does not match the view of their prospective employer.

Of course, this means that part of the *nitaqat* system will have serious difficulties in being implemented for all but the highest status positions. Organisations facing these employment challenges may wish to think creatively when recruiting Saudi nationals.

For example, publicising a well defined promotional scheme where clear path to a more prestigious job within a realistic time frame (and the consequences if the criteria are not met) might work. Some employers consider offering positions to Saudi nationals who have had limited opportunity for gainful employment in the past, including women, Shi'a Muslims, people with disabilities, and families who may not have had access to good education until recently.

Difficulty terminating employment

All Western and multinational organisations should recognise that, no matter how unfair it may be, it is very difficult to terminate a Saudi employee. This is not only due to the pressures of maintaining headcount numbers necessary to comply with *nitaqat* quotas. It is also unrealistic to expect to be in a position to win a potential dispute with a Saudi national no matter how well justified the grievance may be from a professional perspective. This is especially true if the dispute becomes public due to face and honour issues. It is also true that non-Saudi organisations are at a distinct disadvantage if they find themselves participating in the Saudi legal system over a dispute.

As a result, most organisations take their time to maximise the chances of hiring a Saudi national who will fit in with their organisation. If this doesn't happen, work must be distributed amongst other employees or, if the organisation is able to do so, hire another person to do the job not performed satisfactorily by the Saudi national.

Further information

Organisations impacted by *nitaqat* are strongly advised to seek legal council to understand the impact of employing expatriates and Saudi nationals has in the Kingdom under the *nitaqat* system. Do keep in mind that policies change, so ensure that you find up to date advice that meets your requirements. Here are some useful websites that explain the basics of *nitaqat* and Saudi labour law to get you started

http://www.lexology.com/library/detail.aspx?g=6ba28ace-2bcf-49a7-9cba-98b08a8ff5a6
http://www.shc.com.sa/en/PDF/RESEARCH/Labor%20and%20The%20Nitaqat%20Program.pdf
http://www.globalworkplaceinsider.com/2013/11/the-nitaqat-program-what-employers-in-saudi-arabia-need-to-know/
http://www.saudi-expatriates.com/2015/11/saudi-arabia-labor-law-2015-38.html
http://www.saudiexpatnews.com/2012/06/check-your-iqama-nitaqat-red-green.html
https://www.mol.gov.sa/services/inquiry/nonsaudiempinquiry.aspx
http://naderlaw.com.sa/books/laborlawenglish.pdf
http://qsaudi.com/list-professions-reserved-for-saudis/
http://www.gallup.com/businessjournal/184748/lure-government-jobs-saudis.aspx
http://www.arabnews.com/ministry-labor-launch-rating-system-saudis-under-nitaqat

TIME

The basics

Work week

Since mid-2013, the Saudi work week is Sunday through Thursday, with Friday and Saturday the weekend. Some small family owned businesses and niche businesses such as retailers may have a different work week.

Impact of the Islamic calendar

Many people are confused as to why religious dates and holidays are never stated until shortly before they actually occur. This is due to the fact that Islamic months are determined by a religious authority by ritual and thus are only declared when a new moon is successfully sighted at sunset. Islamic dates are calculated from this declaration. From a business perspective, this can wreak havoc on precise scheduling and other planning. It can also impact personal planning such as public holidays and time off.

Rhythm of business

Saudi Arabia works to different rhythms than the West and indeed even to many other countries in the region. Government offices tend to open early and close for the day in the early afternoon. Private sector businesses are more likely to open at conventional Western times. Some will work a 'straight day', ie with a 1 hour break for lunch, finishing at around 17.00 hours. Others will work a more traditional 'split day', where a break of about three hours is taken in the afternoon, with employees returning to work to complete their day into the evening hours. Many retail centres also operate to a split day although they remain open much later into the evening. Restaurants and some of the large hypermarkets are the main exceptions.

Saudi businesses must also accommodate all of the prayer times that come around during the business day.

Most Westerners quickly learn to adapt their day to these rhythms, with late morning typically the most productive hours for most businesses. Retail therapy blossoms once the sun goes down.

Additionally, the rhythm of the calendar year must be taken into account. Work slows down considerably during Ramadan, where official work hours are reduced to no more than six hours per day. Both Eids are public holidays, with Eid al Adha the longest break in the Saudi calendar for most employees. The Saudi national day is the only other public holiday celebrated, held on 23rd September.

Summers in Saudi Arabia are also times of reduced productivity, mostly because schools are out and many senior decision makers may be abroad, often for weeks at a time. Combined with the high temperatures, many Westerners choose to take their main holiday away from the Kingdom during the summer as well.

Western expatriates should note that holidays they are used to celebrating back home will not be celebrated in Saudi Arabia. This includes both Christmas and Easter, both of which would be technically illegal, as well as other national days such as North American Thanksgivings. Informal, discrete arrangements may be made with a tolerant employer, but this is not always possible.

General attitudes to time

In most of the West, time is regarded as finite and linear. There are only so many hours in a day. Time is money. The early bird gets the worm. We talk about spending time, saving time, borrowing time and wasting time. Our adages reinforce these beliefs.

In Saudi Arabia (and many other cultures), time is infinite and more holistic. It can be stretched, shrunk, reprioritised as required. There is always more of it if necessary. Now can also mean yesterday.

Westerners generally believe we can control time. Saudis and many others believe what happens over time is fatalistic, ie God's will. That's why the term *insh'allah* is typically used whenever referring to something in future. It might be their intention to do something, but ultimately it's down to God's will.

Managing time

How your Saudi counterparts manage time will depend on the level of traditional behaviour they favour as well as the practicalities of the business culture.

In general, Saudi business routinely mixes business with personal matters. It tends to run at hours most suitable to the senior Saudi's personality and working hour preferences; it is not unusual for some Westerners to hear from their Saudi management about a business issue very late into the evening or on a Sunday, even if you are back home.

Saudi business does incorporate planning practices familiar in the West, but these plans can easily be disrupted or even cancelled, often at short notice. This is usually because something more important has come up and the plan has now been reprioritised. This, from a Saudi perspective, is not considered to be rude but smart and flexible. Saudis are also generally adept at accommodating unexpected events that can work to the advantage of the Westerner, especially if their business is very important to their Saudi counterpart.

Saudis are not often known for their punctuality, especially as the day goes on. Again, this should not be taken personally, even if you have travelled a long way for your appointment.

Time etiquette

Many practices that would be considered rude in some Western cultures are the norm for Saudis and indeed for many other nationalities working in the Kingdom. They include multiple conversations, interruptions, and other routine multitasking that can unsettle many Westerners, although this is also changing in Western cultures amongst many young adults, especially with their use of technology.

Mobile phones are ubiquitous in Saudi Arabia. It would not be unusual for Saudis to carry multiple handsets for a variety of status and practical reasons. Answering a ringing mobile is generally expected regardless of whatever else you are doing from a business or personal perspective. This includes in meetings, training sessions, and pretty much any other normal business function. In fact, many people are uncomfortable with someone who does not answer their phone during the day and into the evening hours, as they are regarded as somewhat untrustworthy.

The main exceptions are at government ministries, military facilities, and secured sites, where mobile phones may be taken away for the duration of the visit. At the time of publication, Saudis are just about managing to not make calls during flights.

Final hints and tips:

- Do not ring Saudis or most other non-Westerners based in the Kingdom on a Friday at least until late afternoon and only then if necessary. It's the Muslim holy day and an important time to spend with family.
- Do ring ahead if you are unavoidably delayed for an appointment due to traffic delays, check points and any other security procedures.
- Finally, do keep in mind that time is a one way street in Saudi Arabia. Saudis may regard time as a guideline, but they do expect you to be on time, even if you are then kept waiting, especially when you are still establishing your relationship.

MEETINGS

Like business anywhere in the world, Saudi business involves meetings as well. However, a Saudi meeting may not be the same as a Western meeting. This can include a meeting's purpose, structure, behaviour, rhythm, and follow up expectations.

Purpose

Most Westerners plan meetings with the intention of advancing or completing a tangible, measurable task. Saudi meetings, especially in the early stages of a business partnership, are much more relationship orientated. In fact, the entire purpose of the meeting may be little more than getting to know the attendees better. In this instance, the entire conversation may be polite small talk that may even include personal questions as well as your level of comfort of your stay in Saudi Arabia. Westerners who do not recognise this important ritual or show impatience in wanting to quickly get to 'real business' miss the point of Saudi priorities.

Structure

Of course, your line of business has a big impact on how meetings are structured. So does the type of meeting. For example, a strategic planning meeting will naturally work differently to a detailed review of a sales forecast. The following general information may apply more to strategic meetings than to detail orientated meetings.

Appointments
Appointments and scheduling can be much more flexible than in many Western business environments, especially if your meeting is relatively

important to your Saudi counterparts. Appointments can often be obtained at short notice. In fact, it may be well planned appointments booked well in advance that have a higher probability of being changed or postponed.

In general, scheduling an appointment mid to late morning is most effective. Some organisations remain traditional and may simply invite you to come by the office 'in the morning' or 'on Wednesday'. Be prepared to wait.

Agendas

Most Western organisations like to plan. This is reflected in agendas in planning meetings. Similar to appointments, whilst many Saudi organisations appreciate a high level agenda, they don't always like too much detail or rigidity in an agenda. This gives more room for flexibility, especially if they are not yet willing or able to address some details. On the other hand, it is bad form to ask for a meeting with no agenda at all. This can lead to a feeling of too much uncertainty and runs the risk of having a low priority placed on your meeting or sending someone else to attend that has no real authority other than to politely host you and to report what was said.

Don't be surprised if you don't strictly follow the agenda. Meetings are rarely linear in either content or behaviour. Of course, this also happens in the West, but usually due to poor planning. Saudis often deviate from an agenda for many reasons, including the belief that an unexpected opportunity may have been presented. It is generally best to follow any redirection of the meeting in these situations.

Behaviour

Meeting and greeting

In a traditional Saudi meeting, the process of meeting and greeting can seem long and drawn out, especially between Saudis, other Gulf nationals, and other people from the Middle East. For Westerners, the expectation is simply to give others sufficient time to complete their greeting rituals.

Westerners can expect a handshake, with the occasional exception across the gender barrier, where a verbal greeting, sometimes accompanied with a hand over heart gesture, is given instead.

Business cards

Business cards are almost always given immediately after handshakes if this is a first meeting. Western business people should always ensure they are carrying many more business cards than they anticipate needing for the day or, if visiting, for your entire trip.

Business cards should contain all of your credentials, including job title, educational degrees and honours, and any achievements recognised in your profession such as Engineer, Doctor, or Professor. They should be printed in English on one side and Arabic on the other, taking care that logos are placed in a logical position, taking into account the right to left Arabic script. You should have a local Saudi telephone number if you are a frequent visitor and of course if you are an expatriate resident.

Business cards should be given to the most important person first and then as closely as possible in descending order of importance. Business cards are given with the right hand, with the appropriate language face up and with the writing facing the recipient. Cards you receive should be looked at and studied more than is usual in the West.

Business cards should be handled with care and can be laid out on the table if you have met more than one person for the first time. Take care to collect business cards carefully and put them away in a clean place, ideally a business card holder, once the meeting is over.

How Saudi names work

Saudi names work broadly in the same sequence as they do in the English speaking world. The first or given name follows any title used. The second name is generally a combination of bin/bint (son of/daughter of) followed by the person's father's given name. The final name is the surname, which may be preceded by 'al'.

The correct etiquette to address a Saudi national is to use the title and given name, ie Engineer Mohammed, Dr Fatima, or Mr Abdullah. Never shorten a name that is 'double barrelled', typically Abdul Latif, Abdul Rahman, Abdul Aziz or similar – these are descriptions of a person's relationship with Allah and shortening them changes their meaning.

It is beyond the scope of this book to define name structures of other expatriates. It is generally ok to ask someone what they prefer to be called, especially from the Indian subcontinent as naming conventions change from region to region.

Seating plan

Seating plans vary in a meeting depending on how formal the organisation is, the purpose of the meeting, and who is in attendance. In some meetings, seating may seem nearly as informal as in much of the West.

However, in formal meetings, the host will sit in a prime position, usually at the head of a table and usually facing a door, depending on the design of the room. Guests are expected to be seated to the host's right in descending order of importance. The host's own staff will sit in broadly equal positions to the host's left.

Rhythm

The welcome

Unless it's Ramadan, guests will almost always be offered something to drink and perhaps a small item to nibble. Traditional offerings include Saudi coffee, often flavoured with cardamom seeds and substantial amounts of sugar. Nibbles typically include dates or biscuits. More modern offices may have picked up items from the local Costa Coffee or Lebanese pastry shop.

As a guest, it is important – effectively our obligation - to accept all of these gestures of hospitality. It is less about what you like or don't like and more about acknowledging the courtesy. If you don't like what's on offer, taking a sip and a small bite is acceptable. If you do like what's on offer, then enjoy, but don't be too greedy beyond a refill of your coffee cup.

Importance of small talk

As mentioned in the communication section of this book, small talk is a very important part of Saudi culture. This includes in business meetings, where small talk is seen as polite and as a way to develop and nurture a good business relationship. Don't be surprised if you are asked about your stay in the Kingdom. You may also be asked personal questions, which are not meant to be intrusive but as an aid to relationship building. It is a good idea to engage in small talk in a relaxed, pleasant and positive manner, even if it continues for several minutes.

The main event

It is typically better to let your Saudi counterpart transition the conversation from small talk to business.

If your meeting is conducted in the traditional style, then the host tends to conduct the meeting. The host may also delegate to his or her second in command. Other attendees speak with other equals, and then generally only when invited to do so; otherwise, they remain silent. This should not be a sign of disinterest or incompetency, but is a reflection of respecting hierarchy and status. Western organisations should generally mirror this behaviour and should never openly challenge anyone.

In an informal meeting do not be surprised if some attendees are multitasking such as answering their mobile, having a side conversation, etc. In many meetings, regardless of level of formality, there may also be a number of routine interruptions. These should not be considered rude but simply another example of multitasking.

Note taking

In traditional strategic meetings, few notes are taken by Saudis. Most Westerners may struggle to remember the same level of detail as their Saudi counterparts, which unfortunately can appear as a weakness. For those organisations that feel the need to take notes (most of us) in spite of this perception challenge, it is generally best to have a junior member of your team to take the notes and to do so in a bullet point form rather than appearing to record the entire meeting.

Ending a meeting

Finally, it is a good idea to avoid being too focused on timekeeping during a meeting. Saudis are much more likely to control the start time, end time and duration of your meeting. It is especially important not to show impatience for a meeting to end, nor should you mention that you will be late for another meeting scheduled if your meeting runs over the expected time. You have effectively just told your Saudi host that they are not as important as your next meeting. Keep in mind that time is flexible.

Follow-up expectations

Many Westerners, especially those new to working in Saudi Arabia, often walk away from a meeting with very positive feelings that their business prospects are very good. Whilst this may be the case, it is more often a reaction to the excellent hospitality and vague comments about what could happen. Do keep in mind that Saudis reprioritise their business in stream and whilst your meeting may have seemed very encouraging at the time, it may also be pushed back behind the next meeting that has just become more important, at least for the moment.

The best advice is to discuss follow up strategies, including a broad timescale. Then follow up as discussed. Be persistent, as part of the process is to keep placing your organisation's business in the forefront of their mind. Regular contact is fine and is not seen as an intrusion unless it becomes aggressive or feels desperate. Try to continue have as many additional face to face meetings as is practical. Be patient.

PRESENTATIONS

In most lines of business, there will be times when presentations are necessary. This is true for most Westerners doing business in Saudi Arabia as well. As with any audience, it is important to consider what type of presentation will be effective.

It is a good idea to keep several things in mind when preparing and giving a presentation to a Saudi audience, as they may respond to your presentation differently than a Western audience. This information is more useful for strategic presentations. Very detail orientated presentations, such as a technical presentation, have their own styles that rely heavily on the skills and expectations of their specialised audience.

Purpose

Purpose – is it the same? You may be trying to lead your audience to a specific point of view or conclusion. However, your audience may simply be absorbing your information and reporting it back to their own management.

Style and content

Expectations of the presenter

In general, presenters are expected to be expert, eloquent, speak without an overreliance of notes, and to speak in a confident but not arrogant manner. Humour does have its place in Saudi business culture, but keep in mind that jokes and word play can easily backfire if not culturally appropriate.

Saudi audiences are generally less interested in the financial particulars of your organisation than they are in what your product or service can do for them. Thus, the presenter should focus on this context.

The presentation itself should generally be much more visual, with generous inclusion of graphs, charts, illustrations, photos, etc. For presentations that would normally be very text heavy, the presenter may wish to consider producing separate, well produced handout material that provides this level of detail. Presentations should generally be shorter, both in content and duration, than in many Western environments.

Expectations of the audience

Many Saudi audiences expect that their participation is to listen respectfully, especially most other non-Western expatriates and anyone other than the senior most members of the audience.

Singling out someone in the audience is often received badly as it introduces any number of opportunities to lose face. Presenters should generally avoid asking questions all together during the presentation. This means that any audience questions are more likely to occur once the formal presentation is over. The presenter should take this into account and provide extra time at the end of the session to be approached by audience members who are now ready to ask their questions more informally and privately.

Other behaviour expectations

Do not be surprised if presentations do not start on time or run to time. Be mindful of prayer times and try to schedule presentations at other times. Mid to late morning is generally best.

Don't be surprised about many other interruptions that are not uncommon during presentations in Saudi Arabia. They include audience members arriving later than others, leaving early, and coming and going in general. Mobile phones will invariably ring and will almost always be answered. Some people will leave the presentation to speak on the phone; others may stay in the room and speak quietly. There are also generally in room side conversations as well. Try to look at this behaviour as typical multi-tasking as it is not meant to be offensive.

Always thank your audience once the presentation is over.

TRAINING

Training sessions in Saudi Arabia must also take local cultural and practical considerations into account.

Purpose

Training programmes where business partners, suppliers, clients, customers and other external attendees are invited will generally require an explicit description of the purpose of the training. The training session is also more likely to be successful if it considered to be a prestigious training programme.

Planning

Scheduling training during Ramadan or close to Hajj and Eid al Adha is generally a bad idea and should be avoided. At all other times of the year, training programmes should be well catered with snacks, drinks and lunch all in plentiful supply.

In general, training sessions should not start too early in the morning, although this may not always apply in some government or military settings.

Prayer times must be accommodated whenever a public training programme is planned. In general, training sessions held in a more private venue should also accommodate prayer times as well unless your host indicates that this is not necessary.

Any gender issues should also be managed well in advance of the training and made clear to the attendees. Some Western organisations are successful training mixed gender groups, especially in a private setting where it is not generally an issue if endorsed by your Saudi counterpart. Other Western organisations choose to conduct gender segregated training sessions, especially when held in a very public venue such as a hotel or conference centre. Gender segregated sessions can take many forms, from placing a physical divider in the room to holding simultaneous trainings in separate locations. Be aware of any gender matching requirements of the trainer in some public venues.

In a situation where a Western organisation is training only other Westerners, most of these rules will be relaxed, including in most upscale hotels. However, the session should be discrete, especially during breaks when public facilities might be accessed.

Finally, it is a good idea for the training coordinator to contact the list of attendees about 24 hours before the training session to reconfirm attendance and remind them of the value of the training programme.

Style and content

Most training programmes will be delivered in the English language. This includes nearly all programmes where Westerners and other expatriates are involved. The trainer should be cognisant of using easy to understand, global English that avoids slang, cultural references that do not travel, and be careful of their own dialect and accent. Whether delivered in British, American or other English, the trainer should be consistent in their use of spelling, grammar and syntax.

For any long training sessions, scheduling several short breaks after approximately one hour is generally a good idea. This will accommodate smokers as well as those who want a break to chat with friends and enjoy a refreshment. It also gives people thinking time, especially if their mother tongue is not English.

Training sessions that run for a full day should have a full lunch break of at least one hour scheduled, with a catered buffet or similar.

Learning styles

It is important to recognise that different cultures have different learning styles. Much of this depends on the learning style they have been exposed to as a child. For example, most Westerners have been taught to think critically and to challenge any ideas or information they might not agree with or think might be wrong. They are not generally shy in directly challenging others, including the trainer or teacher as well as other students. This is not considered disrespectful but a good exercise in their intellectual abilities.

Westerners tend to learn through inductive and/or inductive reasoning. Thus they may apply a principle to a specific situation, or draw a conclusion or generalisation from observing and studying detailed evidence. They are generally objective, applying a variety of logical practices in their learning styles.

Many other cultures, especially non-Western cultures, have emphasised rote learning, usually in combination with showing unquestioning respect for authority, ie the teacher or trainer. For these students, the ability to memorise and retain large swathes of facts, statistics and other detail is considered to be a sign of a good student. Challenging ideas or information they might agree with or think might be wrong would not be questioned. They are much more likely to keep these parallel truths to themselves as any direct challenge would be disrespectful, especially to the trainer or teacher.

Most other non-Western cultures tend to learn through copying, repetition, and practice. Knowledge transfer through inference is less effective than through the literal delivery of concrete information. This approach is also generally more successful than expecting a student to publically voice their own ideas, even when directly asked to do so. This means techniques that encourage thinking outside the box, brainstorming, etc can be counterproductive.

Trainers should be very careful not to question an individual in front of the class as this can not only be an unexpected training style but may also present the possibility of losing face. Eliciting information, creative thinking and similar is generally much more effective by placing students in to well-defined groups. In this environment, any rejected responses are not personalised, avoiding an individual loss of face. It also increases the students' ability to apply a principle more creatively.

Recognising achievement

Ensuring that attendees receive a certificate of completion can be a very good idea. Photographing the recipients receiving their certificates is also generally appreciated, although any photographic sensitivities, especially across the gender barrier should be kept in mind.

NEGOTIATING

Negotiating – bartering and haggling – has been an integral part of most Saudis' lives for generations. Although Saudi Arabia may be moving to a fixed price shopping environment, this is still new and practiced mostly in upscale urban areas. The rest of the country still shops traditionally and people have long collective memories. This means there is every possibility that the average Saudi may be better at negotiating than the average Westerner, especially those from northern and western Europe or North America.

In business environments, there are as many ways to negotiate as there are people doing the negotiating. However, there are a few characteristics to bear in mind that can assist most Westerners. They broadly apply in situations found in business and in everyday life.

Style

If your business relationship is good, then negotiating with your Saudi counterpart can be a positive process that, although serious and often protracted, can reinforce the strength of the relationship. You may need to negotiate with vigour with your Saudi counterparts, but a strong result will be respected.

No matter how difficult the negotiation process may seem, try to protect the integrity of your business relationship as this is generally much more valuable in the long run than saving a bit more money. This is also the time to ensure that the personal relationships of all of your negotiating team are good with your Saudi counterparts. Negotiation teams with poor relationships or no relationship at all will not generally be very successful. It is generally not a good idea to bring in negotiators who are unknown at this point in the process.

Never make anyone feel embarrassed or otherwise lose face during the negotiation process as it is rarely possible to recover the relationship, even if you have agreed the final details of the deal.

Remember that your word is your honour in Saudi Arabia. Be prepared to commit to anything you say if it is clear you are making an offer or counteroffer. Try to use language that is precise. Avoid conversations that appear to be thinking out loud as they could be taken as commitments you never had any intention of making.

Don't be surprised if your Saudi counterparts reference something you have discussed early in the process, sometimes even years ago in a long sales cycle. Do your homework and review the content of previous meetings in detail before you step up to the negotiating table.

Try to ensure that no concessions are made unless you receive something of broadly equivalent value in return at the same time. The main motivation in a strong business relationship is for both parties to show strength but also for both parties to gain, ie a win:win scenario.

Cautions

In general, Westerners are in more of a hurry to complete a negotiation than their Saudi counterparts. Saudis assume this and can use it to their advantage, especially if Westerners show impatience or public feeling of dissatisfaction.

Finally, ensure that the agreement you have negotiated is fixed and final until either the agreement expires, or it is violated and reparations cannot be made. Although not as likely as in the past, some Saudi businesses may wish to renegotiate if the circumstances or conditions have changed, usually to their disadvantage, since the agreement has been reached.

CONFLICT RESOLUTION

Working across cultures can put people in a position of conflict. How conflict is managed and resolved depends on who is involved, what is considered to be reasonable and fair, and of course the personalities of the individuals involved.

Style

Human nature leads people to behave in a number of often disparate ways when in conflict. Studies show that they tend to vary in levels of cooperation and assertiveness. For example, many strong hierarchy cultures that also value harmony may try to avoid confrontation all together and, if it does happen, withdraw from the situation.

Other cultures, especially those that are inward looking and outwardly confident may try to push, compete and force their point of view and their way forward as the best way or only way. This latter style is found in some but not all Western cultures. Other Western cultures may focus on and deal with conflict by looking at the issue in a detached, forensic manner that can come across as cold and impersonal to others, especially strong relationship cultures.

Many Saudis have the ability to be both tough yet protective of the broader relationship between parties, generally without being directly confrontational or competitive.

Conflicts are resolved through compromise, keeping in mind that, like during any negotiation process, give and take happens at the same time and is seen as fair. If this is achieved, most Saudis would see this as a strength.

Cautions

Although most Westerners do not regard conflict in a professional environment as personal, many Saudis might not agree. Protect the long term business relationship if you wish to continue doing business in the Kingdom. The adage about winning a battle and losing the war holds true. Never make anyone feel as though they have lost face.

DECISION MAKING

Decision making styles can also be driven by cultural influences. These can include nationality, personality, hierarchy and line of business, to name a few. As with so many other working practices, the decision making processes Westerners can expect to encounter will depend on their specific work environment.

In general, the following information reflects some of the more common practices on the ground in Saudi Arabia.

Understanding motivations

Most Westerners are likely to make business decisions driven by what's best for their organisation financially. Some emphasise short term gain; others take a longer view. Profitability is a top priority, often beginning with the first deal, and often the only priority that matters to corporations when the decision making process takes place.

Clear processes, timescales and other objective, task orientated practices are also considered.

Saudi businesses may take some of these factors into account during the decision making process. However, they are unlikely to prioritise them in the same way that most Westerners would.

Furthermore, Saudi decision making is not always about the best price or sometimes not even the fastest delivery but what makes them and their organisation look good. Quality, prestige, limited edition, limited supply, bespoke, or first to market can all have a positive influence on the decision maker.

Identifying the real decision maker

Since most authority is held at the very top of most Saudi organisations, Westerners may have limited opportunity to meet the real decision maker other then perhaps during critical negotiations. However, they are probably well aware of the important steps taken to reach the critical decision making point as they will have been briefed along the way by their trusted management team.

Of course, in Western organisations, there are a wide range of decision makers, from relatively junior positions in the US to a collaborative decision making process in many Nordic countries. It is probably worth taking some time to explain your organisation's decision making process to your Saudi counterparts to facilitate setting expectations and also to avoid inaccurate assumptions. For example, many Saudis may not be comfortable negotiating with someone they perceive to be significantly junior to them, at least until they realise they have the same level of authority in the decision making process.

Before and after the decision

Most Westerners tend to invest a lot of time planning, a reasonable time to make a decision, followed by measured implementation of the decision.

Most Saudis tend to invest a lot of time building relationships, lots of time prioritising and reprioritising that makes decision making appear to take a long time, followed by the expectation of a speedy implementation of the decision.

All of these steps are fraught with the possibility of misunderstanding and frustration. Good communication and understanding the process on both sides will help reduce these difficulties.

Don't forget the Saudi calendar and work rhythm as well. For example, in the lead up to Ramadan, it may be possible to see Saudi organisations accelerate decisions if they are close to being ready. Otherwise, a delay through Ramadan and Eid al Fitr is probable.

HOSTING EVENTS

Hosting events can be an excellent way to enhance business relationships and to create good publicity for your organisation in Saudi Arabia.

Ideas

Typical events that are well received include celebrations such as formally acknowledging a new business partnership or opening a new office. They can also be acknowledging an achievement through an awards ceremony. Hosting an *iftar* during Ramadan is also a good idea.

Style

The most important aspect of hosting an event is to be a good host. Showing generosity is a must, and includes choosing a prestigious venue such as a restaurant in a top end hotel, offering a buffet or multi course menu. Giving a small gift or memento of the occasion to each person in attendance is generally good form.

Considerations

Holding your event in a top end hotel or similar means that the facility will almost certainly have someone your own organising team can work with to ensure issues that Westerners may not have considered are taken care of.

Do keep prayer times in mind when scheduling an event.

Check to make sure that anything you plan to use or present during the session does not violate Saudi rules. This can include items that are innocuous elsewhere in the region, such as pop up banner stands containing banned images (sometimes even including faces). Moving images can also sometimes present problems.

Be aware that many events held in very public settings must adhere to gender segregation rules if it is a mixed gender event. This includes separate seating arrangements, usually achieved with a room divider.

Permissions may be required if a woman is scheduled to speak to a mixed gender audience. Check with your sponsor, who can help with the requirements if this becomes necessary, especially if the media are present.

It is generally a good idea to call around to those invited 24 hours before the event to remind them, improving the chance of good attendance.

Return on investment

The return on investment for hosting elaborate events may not be immediately measurable in financial terms. However, there are many things that can be done to leverage the experience and ensure it adds value to your organisation.

Get the most out of the event from a PR perspective. If you have a prestigious speaker at your event, ensure this is publicised, as VIP guests still attract a lot of attention in Saudi Arabia. Prestigious speakers in Saudi Arabia should not necessarily be limited to your own organisation and its expertise, but can often include representatives from your country's trade organisations. Diplomatic representation may be possible on some occasions. Of course, your Saudi sponsor should have a prominent role that enhances his or her status as well.

Most events hosted by Western organisations are possibly also newsworthy from a Saudi media perspective. Ensure that your event is covered in Saudi media, especially in the newspapers' business sections as well as in special interest trade publications. Try to arrange regional media coverage where relevant. For example, many media organisations covering the region are based in Dubai. Inviting someone along from Dubai may help you reach a wider audience to facilitate good regional coverage.

Don't forget to publicise the event in your home market and on your own website.

Finally, consider prestigious sponsors that get a mention in return for supporting your event. If the event is big enough, the Saudi market can respond well to a sponsorship tier system such as platinum, gold, silver, bronze sponsors.

SALES AND MARKETING CONSIDERATIONS

Sales strategies and marketing campaigns are not only driven by the quality of your goods and services in a global economy; they are also culturally driven. This is particularly true in Saudi Arabia, where practices that are successful elsewhere, often including other countries in the region, will not work or may not even be legal in Saudi Arabia.

The following hints and tips are intended to be a simple starting point. Your organisation may have many more considerations that are specific to your line of business or corporate culture.

Sales hints and tips

A generation ago, Western organisations were often expected to offer exclusivity agreements to protect the market from other Saudi business partners from also representing outside products and services. Whilst this might have worked well in a few excellent Saudi/Western business partnerships, it was also a formula for disaster if your Saudi counterpart was less interested in your organisation than it was with other, often unrelated business priorities. It also presented major problems if a Western organisation fell out with their Saudi business partner as the exclusivity agreement often also prevented termination of the agreement without severe penalties, often including the ability to negotiate a new partnership agreement with another Saudi organisation.

Exclusivity agreements should be considered a thing of the past. Western organisations should not agree to any significant restrictions to accessing the Saudi market. Things can change quickly.

Many Saudis are good at hyping sales opportunities with your organisation, especially early in the sales cycle. It is strongly recommended that Western organisations do not take these opportunities at face value. It is probably better to consider this as an 'if all goes well, this could potentially happen' attitude rather than a specific intent to oversell or, worse, trick your organisation.

New business development management should be aware that Saudis can also overstate their connections within the region and even within the Kingdom. Although there are indeed many Saudi business people with excellent contacts, others may be hoping that an opportunity that does present itself outside of their core markets can be followed up with a satisfactory level of success. It's also a major reason why there may be additional layers of business partners and other complicated agreements.

All of these realities can have an impact on anything from motivations to the level of reliability of forecast figures and timescales.

Western organisations must also keep in mind that the different rhythm of the Saudi year means that it may not always align with your own corporate calendar. It is particularly important to keep this in mind when managing events as routine as sales promotions, allocation of product, impact of fiscal year timings, etc.

It is also important to keep in mind the impact of any sales awards. These can range from 100% achievement clubs to gifts given in acknowledgement of achieving or exceeding a sales target. For example, inviting a Saudi achiever to a beach resort orientated event may not be suitable (at least publically) and may preclude their family from attending. Gift baskets, especially those including food and alcohol are also inappropriate.

Marketing hints and tips

Marketing your product or service in Saudi Arabia can be particularly challenging, especially if you are targeting a public audience.

Do keep in mind that product content must comply with social morals and may be subject to government approval to be sold in the Kingdom, from consumer goods to books. This includes product packaging, where many of the challenges are particularly difficult for products in some lines of business, for example those aimed at the beauty market. For example, clothing retailers must not show mannequins with their heads attached and generally must pixilate or refrain from showing a model's face. On the other hand, bling often sells very well.

Product promotions should also take market conditions into account. Marketing cautions include bans on raffles/games of chance, 'sex & sizzle', music, and most live events that could be interpreted as a performance. Promotions for Ramadan and both Eids can work well. Christmas and many other promotions seen elsewhere in the GCC and regionally are banned in Saudi Arabia, especially if they have any religious overtones.

Other challenges

Although Saudi Arabia is a wealthy country, the wealth is not evenly distributed amongst the general population. Pricing pressures can be surprisingly strong in some lines of business.

Never underestimate the importance of protecting your organisation's intellectual property and copyright assets. These challenges come from both a sharing culture as well as different attitudes to how intangibles can be owned and used.

Business ethics and values can be regarded very differently and can run into difficulties with anti-bribery legislation found in most of the West. Take special care with commissions, marketing funds and any other financial incentives.

Learn how to accurately trust your business partner's information. Whilst the author does not wish to suggest dishonesty in most business partnerships between Saudis and Westerners, there can be a conflict of motivations and priorities.

Finally, the best piece of general advice the author can give is to assume that there are no secrets in Saudi Arabia.

MANAGING EXPECTATIONS

Managing expectations when working in Saudi Arabia can make all the difference between success and failure. Westerners who travel to the Kingdom thinking they can conduct themselves the same way they do back home because they are working for the same organisation will be in for an unpleasant surprise.

Others who unilaterally think they are on assignment to fix all that is wrong with Saudi Arabia will inevitably end up in a situation of culture clash, probably sooner rather than later, and will most likely never gain the trust necessary to become effective in doing their job.

Those who come to the Kingdom with a well-intended attitude of 'helping' can find their attitude misguided if it comes across as condescending, assuming Saudis are somehow incapable of doing things their own way.

There are also a number of Westerners who come to Saudi Arabia solely for the financial advantages that may not always be possible back home. Although the author makes no judgement about the motivations for making and probably saving a lot of money, it would be sad if they also didn't take time to experience and learn more about Saudi culture, get to know Saudis and indeed the tremendous opportunity to get to know other cultures as well though the rich diversity of the vast, global expatriate community.

In Saudi Arabia

Throughout this book, major areas of potential conflict between Western cultures and the realities of working in Saudi Arabia have been highlighted. In summary,

- Things can take time
- Things can change
- Things may seem to be driven by emotion
- Things are not always rational
- Things may not always seem fair
- Things may not always be as they seem to be

Back home

Most people who become successful working in Saudi Arabia do so because they adapt their style to working conditions on the ground but without giving up their own core values. This is achieved by not only managing their own expectations but also by changing their behaviour to fit in better without losing their own identity.

Expatriates and frequent business visitors who discover this formula for success often report that, once they become proficient working in the Kingdom, any remaining frustrations are often related to unrealistic expectations set from their own corporate offices. This can be particularly exasperating if their hard-won expertise doing business in Saudi Arabia is ignored or dismissed.

Paradoxically, these expatriates may find that testing their flexibility and patience becomes more applicable with other Westerners back home than they to do the diverse workforce found in Saudi Arabia. How you manage this challenge will be dependent on your wider corporate culture, keeping in mind how important your organisation considers the Saudi market as well as your personal commitment to your expatriate assignment.

BUSINESS AND SOCIALISING

Gift giving

Gift giving is a strong tradition in Saudi Arabia and indeed throughout most of the Middle East. This has included gift giving in a business environment.

Times are changing. Saudi businesses are well aware of strict laws imposed in the West that are in place to discourage anything that hints of bribery or corruption, including the acceptance of many gifts. Many Saudi organisations have stopped giving gifts, at least those that were blatantly elaborate and often very expensive.

However, some Westerners may still find themselves in an awkward situation where they are offered a gift that, although toned down from the past, is still clearly in violation of their organisation's HR policy and very possibly the laws of their country.

What is a gift?
The definition of a gift is something given in appreciation after a transaction has been completed. It is not considered a bribe when given with sincerity. Gifts are also often given when a VIP visits, or when a major milestone has been reached, such as opening an office, or during elaborate ceremonial events as a thank you for attending.

Cash is _not_ a gift. Nor is giving or receiving something to facilitate a sale/business before or during a transaction.

What to do when offered a genuine gift
From a strictly cultural point of view, genuine gifts should be accepted graciously and should not be refused. Saudis tend to give a great deal of

thought to gifts they choose and rejecting this gesture of courtesy and hospitality can seriously damage a working relationship, often irreparably.

Many organisations have a clear compliance policy in place to address ways to receive a gift without violating laws that apply to you such as the UK Bribery Act. They generally include reporting the gift to your manager, HR, or compliance officer as soon as possible upon receiving it. This also avoids the problem of offending your Saudi hosts by refusing a genuine gesture of thanks.

Gift etiquette, ideas and cautions

Gifts are received with a simple thank you (right hand or both hands only) and are opened in private. If you are giving a gift, try to give something thoughtful from your home country.

From a cultural point of view:

Good gift ideas can include:

- Sweets, nuts, dates, fruit, sometimes gifts for small children
- Branded luxury items including the shopping bag and logo wrapping
- Something bespoke or limited edition
- Something from Harrods or your country's nearest equivalent

Gifts to avoid:

- Pork
- Alcohol and products containing alcohol
- Immodest depictions especially of women
- Gold, silk and diamonds for religious men
- Anything that appears to be of poor quality
- Anything that looks like it is from a bulk purchase and feels like a bargain
- Anything that does not seem to have any relevance to the person receiving the gift
- Anything poorly wrapped

Business dinners

Business dinners remain a common form of entertainment in Saudi Arabia. They are often held in an elaborate restaurant, often Lebanese, either in an upscale hotel or a well-regarded free standing facility, especially if there are a lot of people in attendance. Smaller business dinners may be held in trendy restaurants that cater to the taste of the host or sometimes the guest. Although still held in an upscale restaurant, the cuisine could vary from a Brazilian churrascaria to the latest popular sushi bar.

Westerners who receive an invitation for a Saudi business dinner should regard it as another business appointment and should accept the invitation. It is much more important than routinely checking in with the office, catching up on emails, or simply putting your feet up after a long day. Remember, Saudis generally mix business and socialising, often well into the late hours of the evening.

Dining etiquette depends on how formal the venue is and to an extent, the style of cuisine. Buffets are popular as they display generosity. Multicourse meals display the same thing.

The following information applies to most formal business dinners. Casual dining or simply 'refuelling' at a fast food restaurant or canteen is an entirely different matter.

- Be aware that there may be a seating plan and wait to be seated. Hierarchy rules generally apply similar to how they apply in business meetings.
- Of course, pork and alcohol will not be present in any Saudi restaurant.
- Don't be surprised if smoking is allowed in some venues, especially outdoors or in some private dining arrangements
- European table manners are the norm in Saudi Arabia at restaurants where Western cutlery is used.
- Don't use your left hand to pass food or to eat anything directly from your hand. Both hands are fine where necessary.
- It's good manners to leave 'one bite' at the end of each course to show satisfaction
- Do not stay after coffee is served. This is a polite signal that the meal is over and it's time to leave.

- The host pays the bill. It is very bad form for a guest to even attempt to pay the bill as it insults the host's generosity. Most often, the host avoids this dilemma by arranging to pay the bill without having it presented at the table in the first place. You will have ample time to show your generosity if you are in a position to host a meal yourself at a later date.

An invitation to someone's home in Saudi Arabia

If you are fortunate enough to receive an invitation to a Saudi's home, you should feel honoured. Meals will follow many of the same rules, including seating arrangements, table manners, and generous portions served during each course.

Do not be surprised if alcohol appears in some Saudi homes. Of course, this presents another dilemma. However, it is the author's opinion that if a Saudi has offered alcohol in their own home, it is best to accept it, regardless of its legal status unless you have driven.

Some Saudi homes are run similar to those in the West, where you might meet several family members. Women will almost certainly be invited to remove their *abayas* in this situation. Make sure you are wearing appropriate business attire underneath.

Other homes will practice strict gender segregation, where male guests are hosted by men in the main *diwan* and female guests are hosted by women in their own reception room. Western business-women who are invited to a Saudi home will almost always be regarded as an honorary man and thus invited to dine and socialise with the men. Women may also be invited to meet the women of the family, which would be highly unlikely for their Western male counterparts.

Don't be surprised if you are served food and drink either on a low table or on a cloth laid out on the floor in a traditionally run Saudi home. Women of the family will not be present, even if Western women may be.

Hosting a meal

It will be very difficult for visitors to host a meal in Saudi Arabia unless arranged and agreed to in advance as hosting duties are taken very seriously in the Kingdom. However, for expatriates living in the Kingdom, it becomes more acceptable. The same rules apply as described above.

Hosting Saudis abroad in your home country

It is not unusual for Saudis to travel to your home country for a business meeting. They may also be combining their travel to incorporate a family visit or simply to enjoy a holiday as well.

It is good form to offer to host Saudis during their visit. Popular choices include dining out and shopping recommendations. They may also include activities that are not available back home. The latter may include shopping opportunities, but they may also involve activities such as visits to pubs, bars, casinos, sex clubs, and similar. It is beyond the scope of this book to suggest or limit which activities are acceptable for you and your organisation. It is also important to recognise that some Saudis may also appreciate your hosting these activities as well. If you agree, you will probably be expected to pick up the bill.

SUMMARY OF DO'S
AND DON'TS

Do's and don'ts have been highlighted throughout this book along with other cultural and social etiquette. This is a handy summary of the most important topics to keep in mind that could cause offence, make your Saudi counterparts feel uncomfortable, or both. Do keep in mind that when you are working alongside other cultures, they have their own set of do's and don'ts as well. So do Westerners.

Saudi religious and political issues

- Questioning Islam
    - Validity, beliefs, social and political impact to begin with. Questions that are a sincere attempt to learn more about Islam are generally welcome.
- Atheism and agnosticism
    - Associated with no morals and is generally not accepted by Saudis.
- Personal enquiries about local women
    - Enquiring after the well-being of a Saudi's family is generally very well-received; enquiring after mothers, sisters, wives, daughters, and nieces is too personal for most Saudis and can cause offence.
- Sunni/Shi'a divide issues
    - Religiously, politically and socially contentious, particularly amongst many of Saudi Arabia's large Salafist Sunni community, who may regard followers of Shi'a sects as not truly Muslim

- General references to terrorism associated with Saudi Arabia and/or Islam
  - This can include anything from referencing the events of Sept 11 to Saudi financial support of mosques abroad that are subsequently found to create cultural conflict or worse in their host countries.
- Criticising the Saudi ruling family
  - Unlike in most Western countries with royalty, there is no tolerance in Saudi Arabia against any comments that are perceived as negative toward a royal family member. If detected, this can attract imprisonment or deportation.
- Criticising ruling families in the region
  - Criticising the ruling families of the other GCC member nations, Jordan or even Morocco would also be a serious breach of protocol at a minimum. Most Saudis also consider any negative comments about a Westerner's own royalty as inappropriate and disrespectful, even if it would not be regarded as such back home.
- Sensitive GCC political issues
  - These would typically be topics of conversation such as democracy, human rights, free speech, and a host of social behaviour that is controlled by each country's government.
- Muslim Brotherhood issues
  - Following the immediate aftermath of the Egyptian Revolution, that country's Muslim Brotherhood movement gained significant if temporary support. This support is seen as a direct threat to the Saudi ruling family.
  - Saudi Arabia recalled its ambassador to Egypt during the short-lived Morsi era. Diplomatic relations with the current military backed el Sisi government have been restored to a good condition.
  - It was also the reason why many countries withdrew their ambassadors from Qatar, including Saudi Arabia, when the Qatari Emir was perceived as being too close in his support of the organisation.

- IS/ISIS/ISIL/Daesh issues
  - Saudi Arabia has expanded its geographical and philo-sophical concerns in the region. Currently, they include the obvious threat of the group known variously as IS/ISIS/ISIL/Daesh, who have specifically named both Mecca and Medina as targets to be taken over to the consterna-tion of the Kingdom (and others).
- All Yemen issues
  - The recent military activity in Yemen, where the Saudi campaign is backing the ousted Hadi government against the Houthi rebels. Many believe this is a proxy conflict between neighbouring Sunni (Hadi) and Shi'a (Houthi) factions.
- All Iran issues
  - Saudi Arabia and Iran have been seen as major regional and religious rivalries throughout much of the history of both modern countries. This was accelerated first during the Iranian Revolution in 1979 and more recently in the aftermath of neighbouring Arab revolutions of the early 2010's and especially the ongoing fragmented conflict in Syria.
  - Iran is seen as supporting the current Syrian government, with their Alawite background and associated with Shi'a Islam. Saudi Arabia is seen as supporting many Sunni based rebel groups fighting the Syrian government and ISIS. Many people also believe the Syria (and sometimes Lebanese unrest as well) is a proxy conflict between Saudi Arabia and Iran.
- All Israel/Palestine Issues
  - Saudi Arabia declared war on the State of Israel the day after the latter's independence. This declaration has never been rescinded. Support for an independent Palestinian state remains; some but not all Saudis also support the elimination of the Israeli state. The entire topic of conver-sation is best avoided. Even a mention of Israel in an in-nocuous context such as showing a map that labels Israel in a presentation can cause serious offence.

- You must _not_ have any evidence of travelling to Israel with you or in your passport
  - Travellers to Saudi Arabia are not eligible to enter the Kingdom if any evidence of past travel or future intention to travel to Israel is discovered. This condition applies even if the visitor was successful in gaining a valid visa. Their visa would be immediately voided, they would be denied entry to Saudi Arabia at the border, and would be immediately placed on the next available flight back to their country from which they arrived to the Kingdom. Evidence includes but is not restricted to Israeli entry stamps, possession of currency, business documents, or even items such as a guide book with notes.

Saudi social and everyday issues

- Pork and pork products are illegal.
- Alcohol and alcohol products are illegal.
- It is better not to use your left hand when touching food or passing an item.
- The soles of your feet or shoes should never be exposed to another person.
- Pornography is forbidden. This includes all nudity and even innocent exposure of too much skin such as a beauty advert in a magazine. It can also include exposing any tattoos that could be considered as too risqué.
- No public displays of affection between a man and a woman, including a married couple.
- Avoid situations compromising woman's honour such as close physical proximity or personal questions about women.
- Although many gender segregation challenges are slowly being eroded, it is important to keep in mind that they apply to all Westerners whenever and wherever they are being enforced. This includes venues such as family sections in restaurants, entrance to shopping malls, use of hotel swimming pools and

health club facilities, and any expectations in offices where you may be working or visiting.

- Although women travelling alone or in same sex groups is generally no longer problematic in the major cities where the vast majority of Western expatriates are likely to frequent, women should remember that they could be asked where their *mahram* (male guardian) is when out in public. Finding your driver is generally sufficient to satisfy this situation.
- Similarly, although it remains technically taboo for unrelated mixed gender groups to travel together, in practice, simply take care and perhaps be more discrete during Ramadan or when in a very conservative area.
- Remember that all Westerners are expected to be modestly dressed other than in a very limited number of venues such as a Western orientated compound. This applies to all men and women who have reached puberty. Nor should small children ever be nude or semi-nude in public.
- Homosexuality and any other sexual behaviour outside a heterosexual marriage are all illegal and can attract severe punishment, from lashes to death in certain circumstances.
- Dogs are considered unclean. Most Saudis and many other expatriates may be frightened in the presence of dogs. Expatriates considering a move to the Kingdom whose family includes their pet dog should ensure they move to an expatriate compound that is dog friendly.
- Gambling and lotteries are illegal, as are games of chance. Prudent travellers and expatriates avoid importing playing cards and board games into the Kingdom.
- Illegal drugs (including over the counter drugs that are legal in your home country), especially anything including codeine or other opiates can attract severe punishment including the death penalty if accused of drug trafficking.
- Gold, silk and often diamonds are considered to be forbidden for Muslim men to wear. Non-Muslim men can continue to wear their normal attire.
- Ignoring the restrictions imposed during prayer times is not only disrespectful but can also attract the religious police in some public environments.

- Visiting all mosques is forbidden unless you are Muslim.
- Proselytising another faith is illegal throughout Saudi Arabia and can also attract severe punishment. Do keep in mind that in Saudi Arabia, it is also a capital crime to renounce the Islamic faith for all Muslims.
- Importing or even wearing non-Islamic religious artefacts and symbols is illegal. This includes crosses, bibles, Christmas items, Sikh turbans, Hindu sacred threads and statues of gods, etc. It can also impact items that most Westerners may not have given much thought to such as your souvenir Buddha bells from Asia or even St Valentine's Day greeting cards. Exposed tattoos with any religious reference or even tattoos containing Arabic script can be problematic.
- Attempting to travel to Mecca and the centre of Medina is strictly forbidden for all non-Muslims.

THREE MAGIC WORDS

1. Flexibility

   Can you see more than one way to achieve something?

2. Tolerance

   Can you see the world through more than just your own cultural lens?

3. Patience

   Can you manage to stay calm even when things become frustrating or simply don't go your own way?

If you have these characteristics and demonstrate them, at least most of the time, then you have a good chance of succeeding in Saudi Arabia.

Enjoy your opportunity.

ADDITIONAL INFORMATION AND REFERENCES

Recommended reading for Saudi Arabia

Current publications:
Recommended for everyone:

- Lacey, Robert (2009) *Inside the Kingdom*
- Marsh, Donna (2015) *Doing Business in the Middle East: A Cultural and Practical Guide for All Business Professionals*
- UKTI (2016) *Doing Business in Saudi Arabia: Saudi Arabia Trade and Export Guide* – updated annually
- *The Saudi British Trade Directory(2016)* – Mead Management Services - updated annually

May appeal to some readers:

- Kathy Cuddihy (2012) *Anywhere but Saudi Arabia! Experiences of a Once Reluctant Expat*
- Karen Elliott House (2012) *On Saudi Arabia*
- John Paul Jones (2007) *If Olaya Street Could Talk*
- Rajaa al Sanea (2008) *Girls of Riyadh*

Publications that might appeal but are probably available only in Saudi Arabia/GCC:

- Entertainer Riyadh/Jeddah
- Destination Riyadh/Jeddah
- Riyadh Today/Jeddah Today/Eastern Province Today (updated annually)

English language newspapers on line or in print in Saudi Arabia:

- Arab News: http://www.arabnews.com/saudiarabia
- Saudi Gazette: http://saudigazette.com.sa/

Trade:

- Saudi Vision 2030: http://vision2030.gov.sa/en
- King Abdullah Economic City (KAEC): http://www.kaec.net/about/
- UKTI: https://www.gov.uk/government/world/organisations/uk-trade-investment-saudi-arabia

Major Western embassies and consulates:

- Australia http://saudiarabia.embassy.gov.au/
- Canada http://www.canadainternational.gc.ca/
- France http://www.ambafrance.org.sa
  http://www.consulfrance-djeddah.org
- Germany http://www.saudiarabien.diplo.de/Vertretung/saudiarabien/en/Startseite.html
- Ireland https://www.dfa.ie/irish-embassy/saudi-arabia/
- New Zealand https://www.mfat.govt.nz/en/countries-and-regions/middle-east/saudi-arabia/new-zealand-embassy/
- South Africa www.southafrica.com.sa
- Spain http://www.exteriores.gob.es/embajadas/riad/es/Paginas/inicio.aspx
- United Kingdom https://www.gov.uk/government/world/organisations/british-embassy-riyadh
- United States https://sa.usembassy.gov/

Mobile phone and STC websites:

- Mobily - http://www.mobily.com.sa/
- STC – http://www.stc.com.sa/
- Zain – www.zain.com

Other websites:

Many websites are incomplete, out of date, out of touch, or are unfairly negative. Readers should conduct their own searches and determine what sites are most suitable for them. A good start to avoid some of these undesirable sources are these recommended websites:

Informational:

- http://www.simbacom.com/riyadh-ksa/souqs/batha.html
- http://www.fitfortravel.nhs.uk/destinations/middle-east/saudi-arabia/saudi-arabia-malaria-map.aspx
- http://www.movers.com/international_movers/customs-regulations/saudi-arabia.html
- http://kfca.com.sa/en/
- http://www.expatarrivals.com/saudi-arabia/
- www.get2knowsaudiarabia.com
- www.internations.org/saudi-arabia-expats
- http://saudiarabia.angloinfo.com/

Good quality expatriate websites and blogs:

- American Bedu www.americanbedu.com
- Blue Abaya http://www.blueabaya.com/
- Susie of Arabia http://susiesbigadventure.blogspot.co.uk/2014/04/souvenirs-from-saudi-arabia.html
- Kiwi in Saudi http://www.nzpounamu.com/

INDEX

Council, Shoura 20
country code 41
courtesy 7
CPR Bahrain 134
criticism 247-249
Crown Prince Mohammed bin Nayef 18
crime 62, 18188, 319
cuisines 167, 311
cultural values 3-9
culture 1
Custodian of the Two Holy Mosques 16, 55

D
Dammam 27, 31, 41, 89, 98, 105, 106, 108, 133, 134, 138, 147, 148, 152, 164-166, 176
dallah 177
data protection 189
dates, Islamic 67-68
death penalty 24, 62, 186, 188, 318, 319
debt 20, 119, 120, 157
decision making 66, 89, 256, 281, 299, 300
dehydration 150, 190
dentists 153
Deputy Crown Prince Mohammed bin Salman 15, 18, 19, 23, 31, 187
desert 8, 25, 39, 79, 180, 182, 198
devices, electronic 79, 83-86, 189
Dhahran 27, 31, 41, 108, 133, 134, 137, 138, 148, 152, 166, 176
dialling codes 41-43
difficult messages 240, 241, 249
dignity 247, 277
dining etiquette 167-170, 311
dining out 211, 212, 313
Diplomatic Quarter 26, 129, 201, 208, 210

Diriyah 13, 53, 182
disability 74
disagreement 252
diversity 24, 71-74
diving, scuba 179
diwan 213, 214, 312
diyya 63
do's and don'ts 314-319
doctors 149
dogs 59, 60, 115, 318
dress, business 199, 206, 208
dress code, children 194, 203, 318
dress code, men 17, 20, 54, 107, 108, 203-208, 211
dress code, Ramadan 65, 208
dress code, women 17, 20, 54, 72, 107, 108, 194-202, 211, 214, 263
dressing rooms 171
driving 43, 104, 105, 159-162, 180, 191, 211
driving licences 38, 160-161
drugs, illegal 95, 146, 318
drugs, prescription 153, 154, 192

E
Eastern Province 18, 26-28, 32, 40, 79, 108, 124, 133, 134, 138, 147, 152, 173, 175-181, 185, 199, 207, 213, 321
Economic Cities 32, 33, 132, 147, 265, 322
Education 16, 17, 23, 32, 33, 48, 76, 143, 148, 188, 210, 247, 253, 259-261, 269, 276-278, 286
Egypt 22, 25, 35, 87, 149, 153, 256
Eid al Adha 68, 281, 292
Eid al Fitr 68, 300
electrical goods 128, 137, 139, 158
electricity 40, 136

vehicles, insurance 105, 162
vehicles, lease 161-162
vehicles, ownership 161, 162
video games 140, 142
VIP card 135
visa, commercial 92-97
visa, business 17, 72, 85, 92-97, 112, 135, 202
visa, exit/re-entry 115, 118, 119, 134, 181
visa, family 75, 120-122
visa, family visit 76, 97, 122
visa, final exit 118-120
visa, pilgrimage 90, 96, 97, 113, 255
visa process 73, 89, 91, 94-97
visa, resident 72, 75-77, 112-119, 121, 124, 126, 156, 272
visa, Saudi 87, 93-95, 114, 181
visa, types 91
visa, visitor 92, 93, 96, 97
visa, work 92, 96, 111, 117, 118, 124, 149, 156, 159, 202, 255, 278
visitors, first time visa 89, 96, 98, 101, 102
visitors, re-entry visa 115, 118, 119, 234
VPNs 139, 140
voting rights 17

W
wadi 182
waiting 101, 102, 123, 163, 193, 257, 258, 283
waiting lists 33, 128, 129, 145
Wahhabi 3, 13, 14, 19, 52-54
war 14, 15, 22, 186, 316
wasta 254, 266
water, drinking 42, 50, 81, 136, 169, 190

water, sports 28, 108, 179, 181
weather 39, 79, 89, 150, 199, 207, 235
women, business 17, 72, 75, 99, 107, 163, 199, 202, 210, 260-264, 301-306
women, expatriate 17, 43, 72-81, 93, 94, 99-104, 108, 115, 125, 163, 164, 178, 179, 192, 193, 194-202, 260, 318
women, Saudi 2, 4-6, 17, 20, 32, 34, 43, 48, 50, 59, 143, 165, 171, 172, 177, 194, 196, 202, 260-262, 271, 276-278, 314, 317
women, Western 6, 43, 59, 72, 99-104, 113, 165, 172, 180, 195-202, 210-214, 262-264, 268, 312
work week 38, 39, 265, 280
working hours 39, 66, 121, 172, 265, 276, 280-283, 311

X

Y
Yanbu 29, 41, 132, 147, 152, 165, 175, 179
Yemen 19, 23-25, 30, 35, 62, 78, 112, 150, 185, 186, 221, 255, 316
yes and no 230, 240

Z

AUTHOR INFORMATION:

Grace Edwards is a pseudonym for the author, who has been working throughout the Middle East for decades, including Saudi Arabia as a Western business woman in her own right. She has worked for multinational corporations in a number of key roles. The author is currently a business and cultural consultant working in Saudi Arabia, the wider Middle East, and in the West, working with a number of prestigious Western, Middle East and multinational organisations.